Promoting Community Resilience in Disasters
The Role for Schools, Youth, and Families

Kevin R. Ronan
Massey University
Palmerston North, New Zealand

and

David M. Johnston
Institute of Geological and Nuclear Sciences
Lower Hutt, New Zealand

 Springer

Library of Congress Cataloging-in-Publication Data

Ronan, Kevin. R.
    Promoting community resilience in disasters: the role for schools, youth, and families /
Kevin R. Ronan and David M. Johnston.
        p.   cm.
    Includes bibliographical references and index.

    1. Emergency management—Citizen participation.   2. Disaster relief—Citizen participation.
3. Disasters—Social aspects.   4. Community power.   5. Community and school.   6. Resilience
(Personality trait)   I. Johnston, David Moore, 1966-   II. Title.

HV551.2.R66 2005
363.34'58—dc22

                                                                                2004063223

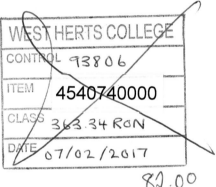

A C.I.P. Catalogue record for this book is available
from the Library of Congress.

ISBN 13: 978-1-4419-3665-3

e-ISBN 13: 978-0-387-23821-0   e-ISBN 0-387-23821-2   Printed on acid-free paper.

© 2010 Springer Science+Business Media Inc

Printed in the United States of America.

9 8 7 6 5 4 3 2 1   (TB/IBT)

springeronline.com

To my wife Isabel and our girls Emily and Kaitlin
KRR

To Carol and Joshua
DMJ

Acknowledgments

There are a number of people to thank for their assistance in preparing this book. First, we would like to thank all of the schools, children, and families that have participated in our programs and our research. We would also like to thank a number of colleagues for their ideas, assistance, hosting (on sabbatical), troubleshooting, and general support: Jerry Jacobs, Gil Reyes, Randy Quevillon, and Jon Elhai at the Disaster Mental Health Institute; Dennis Mileti, now of Palm Springs; Douglas Paton at the University of Tasmania; Ralph Swisher at the Federal Emergency Management Agency. We would also like to acknowledge the contributions of Kirsten Finnis to various chapters, particularly Chapters 5 and 6. Finally, we would like to thank Melanie Robertson at Massey University for her tireless dedication and support in the preparation of this manuscript.

Contents

Chapter 1

Introduction to a Community Resilience Framework

H azards and disasters worldwide are a major, and growing, problem (Peek & Mileti, 2002; Tierney, Lindell, & Perry, 2001). While terrorism and technological disasters have been on the increase and produce a clear threat for traumatic events, people in many areas are far more vulnerable to natural hazards. In fact, in the early 1990s, Norris (1992) reported that approximately one seventh of the population were at risk for a natural hazard. However, that number has increased since that time. For example, more people are moving to areas at higher risk including areas prone to coastal (e.g., Johnston et al., 2005), seismic (Mitchell & Thomas, 2001), volcanic (Ronan & Johnston, 1999; Ronan, Finnis, & Johnston, 2005), and other hazards including floods. Here, currently one sixth of the world's population, approximately one billion people, are vulnerable to a "worst-case flood." However, by 2050, the United Nations (UN) University predicts that number will double to 2 billion people (United Nations News, 2004).

The UN cites a number of reasons including deforestation, sea levels on the rise, and population growth in vulnerable areas. The vulnerability around population growth is linked to a number of inter-linked factors that includes the build up of urban areas in hazard-prone areas and efforts at flood mitigation concentrating on those urban areas. As an example, some recent major flooding in our own local area was mitigated through what was seen to be at the time useful advanced planning: the building of major flood control efforts (diversion, stopbanks) was designed to

1

protect the town from 100 year events. However, while the town itself was protected from a recent 100 year event, it meant that the water had to go somewhere.
Where it did go downstream affected the livelihoods of many in rural areas,
including farmers and others. In addition, while the town itself was protected,
there is no guarantee that continuing build-up in the urban area won't find itself
vulnerable to a later flood. In fact, more generally, what is seen as a protective
measure at one point in time can later be assessed to have been poor planning
(Tierney et al., 2001).

Adding to this complexity is the fact that disasters represent not only a physical event but also the social influences that are interwoven with that event. How
people prepare for, respond to, and cope with natural, technological, or mass violence is linked to how well a community can "bounce back" after a major disaster. The focus of this book is on helping to increase that bounce back, or resilience,
factor within local communities. Given the links between preparedness, response,
and recovery from a disaster, and between physical response and psychosocial
forces, our focus is on helping people to prepare more effectively so that they can
respond and recover more quickly. However, we know that most local communities are simply not prepared for a major hazardous event. Given that problem, we
know further that low levels of preparedness are obstacles to effective responding
and then have a further flow on effect to delaying overall recovery (Peek & Mileti,
2002).

Better means are therefore needed to help communities prepare for and cope
with disasters. One main segment in a community involves the links between
schools, youth, and families. Schools are a centrally located part in any community
that links the adults of tomorrow with the majority of the adults, and households,
of today. Despite early calls for linking schools with hazard and risk awareness and
education in communities (e.g., Slovic et al., 1981), little systematic work has
been done in this area until more recently. While a primary focus is on helping
schools, youth, and families prepare for and cope with a disaster, we are also
mindful of Slovic's call for communities tapping into this potential resource. We
are also advocates for more recent concensus-based, expert recommendations on
the need for establishing more links between different community 'systems' in the
interest of what is referred to as "hazards sustainability." Schools, youth, and families represent major segments in any community that have multiple links with
others (Epstein, Sanders, Simon, Salinas, Jansorn, & Van Voorhis, 2002).

At the same time, as we discuss at length in this book, youth and families
represent two groups identified as more vulnerable to the effects of a disaster. In
fact, in terms of severity of reactions to a disaster, youth have been identified as
one of the most vulnerable groups. Thus, our purpose is twofold: (1) how to help
communities be better prepared through capitalizing on an as yet untapped
resource and (2) how to help a group that is at higher risk for problems prepare
for, respond, and cope with a large scale natural, technological, or mass violence
event. We feel that efforts to achieve these goals can be maximized in a number of

ways starting with linking our practice directly with the available science. As we expand on starting in the next section, we also advocate for increasing accountability for practice through the use of science to inform and measure the effectiveness of our efforts.

HAZARDS EDUCATION AS A SCIENCE AND A PRACTICE

The most prominent models of community resilience to hazards currently promote the idea of "local hazards sustainability:"

> Sustainability means that a locality can tolerate—and overcome—damage, diminished productivity, and reduced quality of life from an extreme event without significant outside assistance (Mileti, 1999, p. 4).

The essence of this idea centers on incorporating an ethos of long-term prevention and resilience starting with the building of networks within a community. By contrast, current practice in hazards management often includes professionals like scientists, hazard specialists, emergency and community planners, school and clinical psychologists working on their own in relative isolation. This model has been shown to be inadequate as a defence against a growth in risk for disasters in many communities in the world. For example, as we describe in more detail later, findings have demonstrated low levels of individual, household, and organizational preparedness almost universally for a hazard even for those communities in high hazard zones (Ronan & Johnston, 2001, 2003; Tierney et al., 2001). When a disaster does strike, inadequate, uncoordinated efforts at providing assistance are often the norm (e.g., Perry & Lindell, 2003). As a proposed answer to such inadequacies, the sustainability model is based on the notion of local concensus building and collaborative problem-solving between networks. Without question, the youth-family-school system represents a major "network" in any community (Ronan, Johnston, & Finnis, 2004). In addition, educating the youth and families of today portends increased awareness and support for such a model both currently and for the future.

More urgently, as introduced earlier, youths are a high risk group. This high risk status was perhaps highlighted in the media following the 9/11 attack. Much social science accumulated over the past two decades and longer supports such anecdotal reports. For example, more recently, based on a large scale review of disaster studies carried out over 20 years from 1981-2001 (Norris et al., 2002), Watson et al. (2003) reported that 62% of youth in those studies met criteria for "severe" impairment whereas only 39% of adult survivors (and 7% of rescue/recovery workers) met severity criteria. In addition, the research has identified that a risk factor for adults' distress is the presence of a child in the household and, not surprisingly, perhaps the most prominent risk factor for a child's distress is a parent's distress. Consequently, it is quite clear from this sort of evidence that youth and families need special attention.

To help provide that attention, this book combines research and theory with practice-based needs to help those who work day-to-day with schools, youth, and families as well as those who engage in research. To underscore these aims, we provide throughout the book strategies for assisting youth, families, and schools prepare for and cope effectively with hazardous and traumatic events. These strategies will keep with our commitment to a 'scientist-practitioner' approach. We feel strongly that the best way forward in the area of increasing *community resilience* is by basing practice on a foundation of common sense and empirical evidence. In fact, our own research program has been explicitly geared to converting research evidence to assist those who are active in the emergency management, hazards education, disaster recovery, and scientific communities. In line with this approach, and compatible with the idea of hazards sustainability, our own practice model is intended to reflect the science-practice duality and is defined by principles about how best to help youth, families, and schools prepare and cope with a hazard as well as link in with other community networks. Referred to as the *Strengthening Systems 4R (Risk Reduction, Readiness, Response, Recovery) Prevention Model*, it promotes a number of features that are introduced in the next section.

EMERGENCY MANAGEMENT AND COMMUNITY RESILIENCE: STRENGTHENING MULTIPLE SYSTEMS

The days are gone where emergency management activity is carried out by a select group of "civil defence" officers directing advice and prescribing response-based activities towards a mainly passive public. Active participation by all community members has now become the moving force. That participation retains a focus on what to do from the time a disaster occurs. However, it now concentrates much more on prevention. This book agrees with the prominence of prevention as the setting the stage for most effective disaster response. Accordingly, we emphasize all of the 4 R's of hazard education and emergency management: readiness, risk reduction, response, and recovery. We also favor an "all hazards" approach (Ronan, Paton, Johnston, & Houghton, 2000). In other words, the research community has identified a set of core principles and activities that are applicable across both natural and human-caused hazards (see Table 1) that inform our SS4R model. However, we will also highlight information applicable in specific circumstances to supplement an all hazards approach. For example, the risk for severe psychosocial impairment increases following a mass violence event versus a natural disaster. However, it is also the case that specific natural disasters are far more likely than mass casualty events in many localities. We review and summarize the research to date in the area of readiness through recovery in Chapter 2. This research then provides one foundation for our SS4R model of assessment and intervention.

TABLE 1. Hazards and Disasters Covered by the SS4R Model
of Community Resilience

Natural Hazards*
  Floods
  Storms with High Winds
    Hurricanes
    Cyclones
    Tornadoes
  Thunderstorms/Lightning Strikes
  Extremes in Temperature
    Cold
    Heat
  Earthquakes
  Volcanoes
  Tsunamis
  Landslides, Avalanches, and Mudslides (Debris Flow)
  Fires
Technological and Man-Made Hazards
  Hazardous Materials
    Chemical Spills
    Household Chemical Emergencies
  Nuclear Accidents
    National Security Emergencies
    Terrorism and Mass Violence
    Chemical and Biological Incidents
    Nuclear and Radiological Incidents

---

* These hazards are categorized according to traditional categorization used (e.g., FEMA, 2002). However, it is noted that the categorization here is oversimplified for reader convenience. That is, some hazards depicted as natural have at times human-made origins (e.g., fires, landslides, floods).

The Role for Schools, Youth, and Families and the 4 Rs

Within a community resilience model, there has been an increased focus on the potential for schools and the family to be main conduits for 4R material to be disseminated (e.g., Ronan & Johnston, 2003). As mentioned at the outset, youth and families comprise risk groups for increased problems following a hazardous event. In addition, a focus on educating youth, the adults of tomorrow, has considerable promise. However, in terms of more current concerns, youth also link into the family setting who, in turn, link into multiple community settings and groups. A consideration of the current and future potential for school- and community-based programs that have youth and families as a centerpiece comprises the basis for Chapter 3. In that chapter, we review available research as well present our SS4R prevention model.

Most of the models of disaster prevention and response are now geared towards incorporating the idea of resilience. In other words, the idea is assisting communities to have the necessary pieces in place to rebound as quickly as possible after a hazardous event. In recent years, the idea of resilience has had the effect of reframing preparation and recovery efforts within a more strengths-based model. In other words, rather than just simple recovery from loss, the emphasis now is increasingly on prevention, reduction, and restoration of the strengths of the system. Similarly, in sustainability models, building on the strengths of the community as one means to prepare for and bounce back from a hazard is an explicit focus (Mileti, 1999). Our approach incorporates such a philosophy.

Linked to the 4R model, the movement in both the research and the practice has been towards increasing collaborations between: (a) practitioners (e.g., emergency managers, hazards educators, psychologists) and the research community, (b) various professional groups, and (c) multiple community-based governmental and non-governmental organizations, and community groups and individuals. For example, there has been the emergence in recent years of 4R multidisciplinary collaborations between physical scientists, social scientists, school personnel, community organizations, emergency managers, and a variety of professional and citizen groups (e.g., Bailey & Woodcock, 2003; Ronan et al., 2000). The value of such collaborations and community partnerships is discussed in Chapter 4.

Given a primary focus on prevention in the SS4R model, Chapter 5 focuses on primary prevention aimed at both readiness and risk reduction. While it considers the overall area of disaster-focused community prevention, it emphasizes the role of schools and families as optimal settings in which to promote prevention and as useful links to other community initiatives. Similarly, Chapters 6 and 7 focus on response and recovery efforts, respectively.

Across these chapters, the focus will necessarily be on the hazards- and disaster-based, 4R literature. However, research done in areas other than hazards- or disaster-focused areas is also at times highlighted. These areas reviewed include research that might supplement hazards research and perhaps better inform current hazards education and emergency management practice. Important to efforts at prevention, and as a brief example, active participation by youth and adults in helping efforts has been shown to predict their recovery from a range of social problems (e.g., Chu & Kendall, 2004; Clarkin & Levy, 2004; Kazdin, 2004). In addition, various efforts at motivating people, including youth and families, to become more actively involved in helping efforts have focused on a variety of strategies that include "strengths as levers for change" (e.g., Hengeller et al., 1998), increasing hope and motivation through provision of information and "evidence-based" encouragement (Ronan, Johnston, & Finnis, 2005), and the use of motivational techniques (Miller & Rollnick, 2002). That is, as preparing for a hazard is often a low priority in almost all communities (Peek & Mileti, 2002), a first need in educating and helping communities prepare for a hazard is to provide them with some motivation for preparing. Thus, while the hazards research literature offers up some clues on how better to motivate community preparedness and response (see Chapters 2-6), so too does some other research that we will describe in those upcoming chapters. In the area of recovery, little research has assessed child and family focused interventions following a disaster. However, much more research has accrued on how to help children and families where anxiety problems, including traumatic reactions, are apparent (e.g., Ronan & Deane, 1998; Ronan, Finnis, & Johnston, 2005). In Chapter 7, we describe and consider the promise of these approaches.

A main theme of our SS4R model is on the role of *motivation* and its kindred cousin, engagement. The idea of motivation is as opposed to necessary knowledge and skills. The evidence tells us that both motivation and knowledge/skills areas are a necessary focus in assisting people to solve problems including preparing for and responding to a hazardous event. In terms of knowledge and skills, people may or may not know what to do and how to do it. In terms of motivation, despite the fact that people may be aware of both risk as well as strategies that can mitigate that risk, it does not follow directly that they will take the necessary action. In fact, the link between risk awareness and action is a notoriously weak relationship, even taking into account people having knowledge and skills about what might mitigate risk. Thus, it is clear from our view that the chain of events that leads from readiness to response to recovery necessarily begins at motivation. In fact, we see motivation as the *sine qua non* of educational and intervention efforts across a community planning for hazards readiness through recovery. Motivation is the psychological factor that fuels interest, concern, and action. We consider those factors related to motivation starting in Chapter 3. To anticipate that and later discussions, it is our contention that schools, youth, and families represent an untapped reservoir of community-level motivation and action.

PUTTING THE EVIDENCE TOGETHER: COHERENT STRATEGIES FOR HELPING

The culmination of the book in Chapters 8 and 9 brings together the available evidence and presents first a coherent "how to" model designed to be useful for those who are working in this area. The summary guidelines are aimed at (a) all hazards and (b) relevant disciplines including school personnel, emergency and community planners, psychologists, and others who practice and engage in research on the role of schools, youth, and families play in promoting local hazards sustainability. Incorporated with the basic "how to" principles and strategies are links to more specific information in earlier chapters that can provide additional guidance. In Chapter 9, we discuss research and comment on training in this area. Included here, as at other points in the book, is an emphasis on research designed specifically as an integral part of local help provision.

SUMMARY

A myriad of models are available to guide practice before, during, and following disasters. As emphasized in this book, we value the role of research in informing our assessment, education, and intervention efforts in this area. Keeping an eye on those elements that have research backing certainly assists with quality control generally. However, more specifically, we also stress the idea that there is evidence to support a role for hope and positive expectations in the motivation and engagement process. In addition, the more that people, including youth and adults, actively participate in efforts designed to help, the more benefits they tend to receive. The role of research in providing that initial hope and inspiring more active engagement with internal and external resources before, during, and after a disaster is part of the foundation of our practice in this area. In fact, in the clinical psychology training program directed by the senior author, the idea that we attempt to inculcate with our trainees is the idea of "hope and engagement on an evidence-based foundation."

Consequently, we do advocate for models of practice that have identified "active ingredients" that are included: those particularly identified through controlled evaluation research. However, it is also the case that a number of risk and protective factors identified through a number of studies (e.g., see Chapter 2) have as yet to be systematically included. Additionally, a number of features that do have an evidence basis (e.g., educational and psychological intervention components) have neither been included as yet in hazard education and intervention programs but most definitely carry with them promise for the future.

How best then to ensure that educational programs and interventions are "evidence based?" While this issue is considered more fully throughout the book, the initial answer is a two-part answer. The first part of the answer is to use information and elements that have been directly tested and validated, or those that have evidence-based promise. Those factors that have most promise include (i) directly validated elements, (ii) those factors included that have been identified in the hazards and disaster literatures as risk or protective factors, and (iii) those that appear to have promise based on research in related areas or (iv) based on theory.

The second part of the answer is to assess systematically the effectiveness of one's own programs. No matter the nature of the education program or intervention carried out, we strongly advocate for the idea of the "practitioner as local scientist," ensuring that one's own practice has empirical backing, that the practitioner is willing to be accountable for outcomes, and that practitioners and communities are able to use such information for a number of purposes. These include informing ongoing service delivery and generating additional momentum within a school and community. We consider more fully in this book the practical benefits of this philosophy to (a) communities, schools, youth, and families and (b) the practitioner and researcher.

Chapter 2

Community Resilience to Disasters
Introduction to Theory and Review of Research

M ost policy and research in the area of hazards and disaster readiness have until more recently emphasized a "loss reduction" model. However, a shift to a more comprehensive model of community resilience and local hazards sustainability includes ideas that are based on sustainability, systems, and community problem-solving approaches. In other words, rather than simply preventing loss, resilience assumes the idea of factors that promote healthy communities that are able to sustain and rebound from the effects of a hazardous event. Within healthy communities, various factors will serve to increase, or protect, strengths. Other factors will increase community vulnerability. Within the Strengthening Systems 4R (SS4R) approach, and in line with current emergency management philosophy (e.g., Haddow & Bullock, 2003), resilience assumes cooperation and communication across multiple organizations, professionals, and community groups. The focus of this book is on the school and family systems before, during, and after a disaster. However, to understand the role of schools, youth, and families, it is important first to understand where this network fits into the bigger picture within a local community. Consequently, this and the first part of the next chapter is aimed at providing a foundation for our practice model by describing the idea of

9

community resilience and through reviewing background research in the overall area of hazards and disaster management. Against the backdrop of these findings, we then begin to articulate a role for schools and families within a community first through a review of available research and then through a description of the SS4R model in Chapter 3. First considered is the idea of community resilience to disasters.

COMMUNITY RESILIENCE TO DISASTERS

The basic idea of community resilience and local hazards sustainability derives from the idea of "bouncing back" following negative life events (Mileti & Peek, 2002; Paton, Violanti, & Smith, 2003). As early as the middle of the last century, the idea began to germinate that natural and other hazards included the intersection of not only physical, but also social influences. It was also seen that these effects could be mitigated similarly through the interaction of physical and social means (or "adjustments"; White & Haas, 1975). Other early conceptions of hazards (e.g., Prince, 1920) included the idea of hazards leading to "social disorganization." However, this idea of panic and disorganization gave way after it was observed that hazards not only tend not to produce social chaos, they have actually been seen in a number of instances to strengthen communities (e.g., Drabek & Key, 1984).

Given the growing focus on strengths and health in a variety of areas including emergency management (Paton et al., 2003), mental health (e.g., Seligman, 2003), school- and family-focused areas (Curtis, Ronan, & Borduin, 2004), there is an increasing focus not only on coping with adversity but, in some cases, allowing for that adversity to promote positive change. Kumpfer (1999) links the ideas of resilience to change by delineating between different levels of outcome following adverse events: (a) resilient reintegration (i.e., coping adaptively and making additional positive change), (b) homeostatic reintegration (i.e., coping adaptively but not necessarily making added positive change), (c) maladaptive and dysfunctional reintegration (i.e., not coping adaptively; continuing or added problems). Of course, the focus in this book is on promoting the first two forms and preventing the third. The main point to be taken here is that in the first priority of promoting communities bouncing back after a hazardous event, that we can also allow for those events to be an impetus for transformation within a community.

A growing body of literature is beginning to focus more on this idea of drawing strength from adversity (e.g., McCrae, 1984), transformational coping (Aldwin, 1994) and posttraumatic growth (Tedeschi & Calhoun, 2003). However, the hazards literature to date, and current policy and practice, has focused mainly on loss reduction and the more basic notion of coping with stress and adversity, returning to prior levels of functioning (i.e., reducing distress and other problems in living), and returning to a sense of routine and normalcy. The main goal currently is to help local communities prepare for an event in such a way that response is effective: lives are saved, property damage is minimized, and the community can recover both physically as well as psychosocially. In summarizing the overall research on preparedness and response, Peek and Mileti (2002) state:

> ... effective preparedness and response activities help save lives, reduce injuries, limit property damage, and minimize all sorts of disruptions that disasters cause, and research into preparedness and response has done much to effectively inform how we plan for and respond to disasters (p. 520).

We would add that additional research into recovery has also accumulated to the extent that findings are now increasingly being used routinely by some to help communities recover (Norris et al., 2002; Ronan et al., 2005). By contrast, but perhaps more importantly, this overall database has not as yet fully been put to use to help people prepare for and respond to a hazardous event (Ronan et al., 2005).

HAZARDS READINESS THROUGH RECOVERY RESEARCH

The Big Picture

The preparation of a community for hazards has become an increasing focus in recent years. Preparation itself involves a variety of activities: training both the public as well as responders with specific strategies (e.g., evacuation; search and rescue; "duck, cover, and hold"), and educating the public in a community— individuals, households, organizations—about hazards and encouraging them to prepare. Preparation efforts include creating and practicing emergency plans, making adjustments in households and organizations to reduce risk (building modifications; insurance purchase) and increasing response capacity (e.g., storing food and water, practicing family and organizational emergency plans). Interestingly, the major preparation that appears to have most merit is making structural adjustments to buildings: most people killed in hazards are hurt or killed by poor construction (Cuny, 1983). However, as pointed out by Lindell and Whitney (2000), many other adjustments, including both physical and psychosocial preparation, have undoubted and research-supported utility in helping a community better respond and recover from a disaster (see also Peek & Mileti, 2002; Tierney et al., 2001).

Despite a fairly substantial increase in funding for public preparedness, community-level readiness for a disaster has not followed. Levels of preparation are almost universally low, including in risk prone areas. In fact, in trying to combat low levels of preparedness, providing information about risk and other aspects of hazards to a community may in fact not translate directly to large scale community preparedness activities. Further, communications to the public have also been shown to reduce concern about hazards (Paton & Johnston, 2001). For example, Ballantyne et al. (2000) found that over one-fourth of recipients of a hazard risk communication program actually felt less concerned about hazards after receiving information. Apparently, these participants felt that local government agencies—who disseminated the information—would take the responsibility for increasing safety as well as mitigation and response (Paton & Johnston, 2001). Such a view would quite obviously reduce the amount of responsibility one would feel for taking direct readiness actions. Reflecting the trend of a lack of motivation and engagement, during the response and recovery phases of a hazard, and as reviewed later, it has been found that many people who may benefit from direct forms of help in the wake of a disaster may also be less likely to seek such help (Ronan et al. 2005).

On the other hand, in terms of preparing for a disaster, while direct efforts have fallen short of expectations (Mileti, 1999; Tierney et al., 2001), it is also the case that readiness overall in certain areas has increased over time. As seen shortly in our review of the readiness research, household preparation for earthquakes has increased in California on a number of mitigation indices from the 1970s up to the current time (Lindell & Perry, 2000). Further, a number of factors have been found to predict readiness. As for response and recovery efforts, there is also cause for optimism: the database that has accrued to date has seen an increasing sophistication in both understanding and help provision, including means to identify those who may need help, those at lower risk, and the forms of assistance that have more or less potential. For this and other reasons, emergency management capabilities appear to have improved significantly in the United States with more effort being expended on advance planning and preparations (Peek & Mileti, 2002).

While the areas of readiness, response, and recovery are reviewed in more detail, this cause for optimism is highlighted by the role of education efforts during the readiness and risk reduction phases. Educating the public in various ways has been found to help. Multiple education efforts, provision of specific information and guidance, and increased interactions between those educated (e.g., youth, schools, government agencies) and other intended recipients (e.g., parents, households, community and other organizations) predicts increased readiness and response to a hazard (e.g., Mileti & Darlington, 1997; Ronan & Johnston, 2001, 2003). Related to increased readiness and response, as indicated earlier, it has been found that after a disaster those who do better are better equipped both physically and psychosocially (Ronan et al., 2005). In addition, as detailed in later chapters, there is some real cause for additional optimism in communities beginning to consider an increased role for linking with schools, youth, and families in preparation, response, and recovery efforts. For example, we know that families are willing to undertake a significant number of readiness activities when encouraged to do so as simply as a result of a child bringing home some quite basic educational material (see Chapter 3). As another brief example, a school-based prevention campaign can be a catalyst to community level initiatives (e.g., see Chapters 4 and 5).

Consequently, a foundation for our model of increasing community protective factors and reducing vulnerability is to identify those factors that research has identified to (a) predict readiness, response, and recovery and (b) predict increased vulnerability in each of these areas. In other words, addressed directly in the SS4R model is an education and intervention focus on evidence-based protective and risk factors, respectively.

The many disciplines that focus on readiness and recovery from disasters have often disseminated research without extensive cross-reference to other disciplines in the area. Historically, different lines of research emerged across physical and social sciences. In the social sciences, independent lines of inquiry emerged from the sociology and geography disciplines focusing on emergency preparedness and response compared with research on psychosocial aspects of recovery, which were more often in the domain of the psychological sciences. Initial efforts at integration across many disciplines including the physical sciences, social sciences, public planning, policy, and emergency management was reported as early as the 1970s (e.g., White & Haas, 1975). However, most of the science, engineering, social, educational, business, and emergency management research in this area tended to be disseminated through discipline-specific journals. For example, in the area of recovery, much of the research and theory on mental health effects and recovery from trauma, including hazards and disasters, were almost exclusively published in psychology journals as well as psychiatric and other mental health discipline outlets.

That situation appears to see more recent improvements in links being made across disciplines. For example, in a recent authoritative text on volcanology, a number of chapters are focused on social factors, including community-based risk education and intervention (Johnston & Ronan, 2000). That area too has seen an increased multidisciplinary focus in professional meetings. For example, a series of conferences reflecting the role of urbanization as a major hazards risk factor, "Cities on Volcanoes", have been held in three international locales from 1998–2003 (Rome/Naples, Auckland, and Hilo, Hawaii). Represented at these conferences have been those from the traditional geological sciences, social sciences, insurance industry, business, law enforcement, voluntary and citizens' organizations, planning and emergency management (national, state/provincial, local), educational and school settings, and citizens' groups. As another example, recent APEC-sponsored hazard mitigation workshops have been held in Taiwan in 1999 and again in 2001 with a similar range of groups represented. At each of these series of conferences, there was a clear focus on both readiness and recovery and calls for more multidisciplinary collaborations.

Such developments coupled with the fact that there has been an increase in multidisciplinary journals (e.g., *Natural Hazards Review, Disaster Prevention and Research, Risk Analysis,* see Table 2.1) certainly represent an improvement from the past.

TABLE 2.1. Journals with a Hazards and Disasters Focus

American Society of Professional Emergency Planners
Australasian Journal of Disaster and Trauma Studies
Australian Journal of Emergency Management
Contemporary Disaster Review
Contingency Planning & Management
Disasters
Disaster Prevention and Management
Disaster Recovery Journal
Disaster Resource
Environmental Hazards
Hazards Literature Database
Natural Hazards Research/Applied Information Center, Univ of CO, Boulder
International Journal of Mass Emergencies and Disasters
Journal of Civil Defense
Journal of Contingency and Crisis Management
Journal of Environmental Management
Journal of Homeland Security
Natural Hazards
Natural Hazards Review
Sustainable Communities Review
The Electronic Journal of Emergency Management

Given what is clearly increasing cooperation across disciplines, a more fundamental problem has to do with how to translate research into day-to-day practice in a local community. In the next sections, we first review research that comes from different areas with an eye to those factors that can be used in community-based practice.

READINESS AND RISK REDUCTION

Communities vulnerable to a hazard's occurrence are at risk for a variety of consequences of that hazard. These consequences include physical risk to persons and property as well as social and economic risks. Measures taken to reduce vulnerability have been referred to by various terms including *hazard adjustment, hazard mitigation or risk reduction, emergency preparedness or readiness.* For the purposes of this book, we will follow others (e.g., Lindell & Whitney, 2000; Mileti, 1999) and at various times refer to all of these terms. However, we would like here to orient the reader by emphasizing the idea of readiness in the form of *hazard adjustments* (Burton, Kates, & White, 1978; Moore, 1964). These actions are those that reduce risk or increase preparedness for a future hazard. Consequently, the forms of adjustment most often referred to are those that are more specifically focused on both *hazard mitigation (risk reduction)* and *emergency preparedness (readiness)* (Lindell & Perry, 2000). Hazard mitigation refers to reducing risk to a particular area of vulnerability (e.g., property) during the time of the hazard's occurrence (e.g., securing the foundation of a home prior to an earthquake prevents house damage). This type of activity, carried out prior to a hazard's occurrence, affords what has been termed "passive protection at impact" (Lindell & Perry, 2000). While *insurance purchase* might be classified as a form of mitigation or risk reduction, it has also been identified recently as a category on its own. We will include it as part of the larger class of risk reduction activities. Emergency preparedness refers to actions taken to support activities during and following impact (e.g., knowledge and practice around protective activities at impact; knowing how to put out fires, how to administer first aid, having fire extinguishers, first aid kits). Table 2.2 lists some representative household based adjustments.

TABLE 2.2. Some Representative Adjustments That Can Be Carried Out at Homes and Other Places

1. Have a flashlight
2. Rearrange breakable household items
3. Put strong latches on cabinet doors
4. Store hazardous materials safely
5. Add lips to shelves to keep things from sliding off
6. Secure water heater
7. Install flexible piping to gas appliances
8. Secure house walls
9. Bolt house to foundation
10. Arrange bracing for foundation
11. Stockpile water and food for three days
12. Have a transistor radio and spare batteries
13. Have a fire extinguisher
14. Have a smoke detector
15. Have a first aid kit
16. Store emergency equipment (for example, flashlights and batteries, fire extinguisher, first-aid kit)
17. Put wrench by gas turn-off valve
18. Pick an emergency contact person outside area
19. Someone in family has learned how to put out fires
20. Buy additional insurance (e.g., home)
21. Learn to provide first aid
22. Find out kinds of natural or technological hazards possible in local area (including house fires)
23. Have home inspected for earthquake resistance
24. Have a family emergency plan
25. Have a house plan showing exits, assembly areas, where to turn off water, electricity, gas
26. Know who is responsible for collecting children from school
27. Know school emergency plan
28. Know where child would meet family or leave a message if everyone can't be at home
29. Attend an education program about hazards and preparation
30. Would like additional information about hazards readiness including factors that help when a hazard does occur (e.g., research information on responding and recovering; factors that promote response and recovery)

Sources: Items adapted based on measures used in Mileti and Darlington (1997) and Ronan and Johnston (2001, 2003). Reprinted with permission from Dennis Mileti.

While an increasing number of emergency management practitioners and researchers focus on an all hazards approach currently, much research previously has focused on singular hazards and disasters. The area that has had the most attention has been readiness and risk reduction related to earthquakes (Lindell & Perry, 2000). For a number of reasons, reviewed first are the main research findings from that area. One reason for starting here is that this area of research has demonstrated that continuing efforts at educating the public to prepare for a hazard is worthwhile. In addition, this research has been useful in identifying predictors of readiness – those factors we need to keep in mind when designing education efforts. Following this review, a summary of some additional research across other hazards that add to the knowledge base is provided. We then summarize the overall research in this area highlighting those findings that might most inform community- and school-based education programs.

WHAT PREDICTS READINESS?

Earthquake Hazard Adjustment Research

Rates of Household Seismic Adjustments over Time

One problem in this and other areas of hazards research is that statistical aggregation of findings across studies (e.g., meta-analysis) is not yet possible. The reason for this is that studies to date in the earthquake hazard area do not have available or report enough statistics to make aggregation possible. Given this state of affairs, a recent qualitative review has identified 23 studies that assessed factors related to household adjustments to seismic risk (see review by Lindell and Perry, 2000). The main finding of this review, and of findings since that review (e.g., Lindell & Prater, 2000; Lindell & Whitney, 2000; McClure, Allen, & Walkey, 2001; Rustelmi & Daranci, 1999), are that *household adjustment rates* have increased over time. For example, studies in the late 1970s and early 1980s reported the percent of residents in seismic risk area, who had engaged in at least one adjustment to be less than 33% (Endo & Nielsen, 1979; Jackson, 1977, 1981). However, more recently, Lindell and Whitney (2000) reported that approximately 75% of their sample had reported more than two seismic adjustments. In addition, the mean number of seismic adjustments in their sample was over four per household (X = 4.76; SD = 3.0). While this mean figure certainly represents improvement, the standard deviation indicates that there continues to be a good amount of variability in adjustment activity across households. In addition, while the rate of improvement overall has been encouraging, most people continue to engage in selective adjustment activities. Lindell and Whitney (2000) also reported that 75% of their sample reported adopting half or fewer of 12 seismic adjustments.

Not surprisingly, it does appear that knowledge-based adjustments (e.g., knowing location of nearby emergency room; knowing how to shut off utilities) are generally more prevalent than those that require some form of behavioral activity or expenditure of resources including effort, time, money, or skill (e.g., attending preparedness meetings; strapping, latching, and lipping; purchasing insurance; structural modifications to the home). Additionally, in terms of the relative prevalence of those that do require effort, some are more popular than others. Here again, while there are likely to be exceptions, it appears those that require less effort (e.g., storing emergency equipment including first aid kits; stockpiling food and water) tend to be more prevalent than actions that require increased effort (e.g., installing cabinet latches; purchasing insurance; attending preparedness meetings) (e.g., Lindell & Prater, 2000; Lindell & Whitney, 2000; Mileti & Darlington, 1997). However, it may also be the case that adjustment activities that require more effort, cost and so forth may also be increased over time. As a salient example, rates of earthquake insurance purchase have been seen to rise markedly in California over the past quarter century: from 5-8% in the early 1970s to 26-45% by the early 1990s (Lindell and Perry, 2000). To provide clues about how best to capitalize on this progress and motivate the public to prepare more thoroughly, research has identified a range of factors that have been seen to predict increased adjustment activity.

Factors Related to Household Adjustments

Demographic Factors and Past Experience. Most studies have found small, but statistically significant, correlations between various demographic factors and adjustment adoption (Lindell & Perry, 2000). The demographic factors that have been found to relate to adjustment adoption include income, presence of children in the home, ethnicity (Caucasion), gender (female), age, and a composite measure referred to as *community bondedness*. This variable refers to embeddedness within a community as indicated by community organization involvement, *neighborhood tenure* including identification of the neighborhood as home, and the nearby presence of friends and relatives (Lindell & Perry, 2000).

Findings regarding location, fault proximity, and past earthquake experience overall are mixed. In addition, these variables are often difficult to interpret. For example, past earthquake experience (e.g., number of earthquakes experienced, Russell et al., 1995) does not take into account various physical factors (e.g., property damage, injury) nor social factors (e.g., distress, community upheaval). Even when items are specific such as "knowing someone who was injured", there is obviously a large range of injuries that could presumably impact future risk perceptions, adjustment adoptions and so forth. Location and fault proximity also have similar problems in interpretation (Lindell & Whitney, 2000).

Given these ambiguities, some studies have found location (Palm et al., 1990), fault proximity (Farley et al., 1993) and various forms of past experience including number of earthquakes experienced (Russell et al., 1995), losses to self or others (Turner et al., 1986), amount of losses (Jackson, 1981), and exposure-related fear (Dooley et al., 1992) to relate to adjustment adoption. However, particularly with regard to previous experience, others (Mileti & Darlington, 1997; Palm & Hodgson, 1992) have not.

Perceptions, Beliefs, and Feelings: Cognitive and Emotional Factors

Risk Perceptions. Most studies over time have found a prevalence of perceptions of risk for future earthquakes commensurate with the level of actual hazard. For example, even in early studies, risk perceptions for earthquakes in areas near faults were high (e.g., Sullivan, Mustart, & Galehouse, 1977). In addition, risk perceptions in high versus moderate seismic hazard areas have been found to be significantly different. Residents in southern California reported higher levels of risk perceptions than those in an area of moderate hazard (western Washington) (Lindell & Prater, 2000). However, while effect sizes were not able to be calculated owing to the fact that standard deviations were not reported in this study, visual inspection indicated that the magnitude of differences in these risk perceptions was not all that great (modal difference of .3 on various items using a 5 point scale). Nonetheless, risk perceptions appear to be a factor that a number of studies have shown to be relatively accurate (e.g., Lindell & Whitney, 2000).

In terms of the role of risk perceptions in preparedness activity, with a few exceptions, most studies have found correlations between various types of risk perceptions and various adjustments. These perceptions of risk are as follows (Lindell & Perry, 2000):

- perceived earthquake likelihood/anticipation of death, injury, damage (De Man & Simpson-Housley, 1987; Farley et al., 1993; Kunreuther et al., 1978; Lindell & Prater, 2000; Palm et al., 1990; Showalter, 1993);
- perception of aftershock likelihood (Mileti & O'Brien, 1992);
- general concern about seismic activity (i.e., *earthquake concern*, Dooley, Catalano, Mishra, & Serxner, 1992);
- perception of seismic hazard as a disadvantage of living in a particular location (i.e., *hazard salience*, Jackson, 1977, 1981);
- awareness and personalization of risk (Turner et al., 1986).

On the other hand, some studies have not found significant relationships between adjustments and (a) forms of earthquake risk perceptions (i.e., perception of likelihood of earthquake occurring in next couple of years causing injury or damage, Mileti & Darlington, 1997; composite of four risk perception items addressing the likelihood of earthquake occurring in next 5 years causing injury or damage, Lindell & Whitney, 2000; expectations of future earthquake-related losses, Jackson, 1977, 1981) and (b) earthquake concern (i.e., perception of earthquakes as hazard of most concern, Mileti & Darlington, 1997; frequent thoughts about earthquakes, Russell et al., 1995).

Even in a number of cases where various risk perceptions are significantly correlated with adjustments (e.g., Lindell & Prater, 2000), the correlations are often small in magnitude (e.g., average r = .07 in that study). In addition, findings in some of the most recent research (Lindell & Prater, 2000; Lindell & Whitney, 2000; Mileti & Darlington, 1997; see also Turner et al., 1986) have converged and suggest that factors other than generalized risk perceptions are better predictors of seismic adjustments. One such factor is personalized risk – a factor identified as distinct from hazard (risk) awareness (i.e., knowledge of the potential for a hazard). In other words, when people perceive and personalize a risk, it is common sense that they are then more likely to be in a position to do something to mitigate that risk compared to those who perceive no risk at all.

Who Is Responsible and Do Adjustments Work: Responsibility, Efficacy, and Effort Beliefs

Perceived Protection Responsibility. Perceived personal protection beliefs have been found to relate to households' adoption of adjustments (Mulilis & DuVal, 1995). Given that finding, it is encouraging that people's beliefs about perceived personal responsibility appear to have risen markedly in California over the course of 10-15 years. Research published in the late 1970s and early 1980s indicated low levels of household responsibility beliefs (10%) and higher levels of government responsibility (federal, 54%; local, 23%; state, 19%) (Jackson, 1977, 1981). By contrast, Garcia (1989) found that almost all (98%) of the participants in that study indicated readiness activities to be a personal responsibility. Given that finding, it is not surprising that Garcia's study also found much greater adjustment activity than did Jackson's. Similarly, Lindell and Whitney (2000) also found that respondents in their study in Southern California also reported themselves to report feeling significantly higher levels of personal responsibility for seismic protection compared to others including government sources at all levels.

Awareness of adjustments, perceived efficacy, and effort: "Do adjustments work and are they worth it" beliefs. Various attributes of activities related to adjustments have been examined including (a) simple awareness of the adjustment, (b) perceived advantages including (i) effectiveness for mitigation and preparedness as well as (ii) effectiveness for other purposes, and (c) perceived requirements including effort, cost, time, specialized knowledge and skills, and needing cooperation from others.

In terms of awareness of seismic adjustments, it does appear that people have become more informed. One early study showed that almost half of respondents (45%) had a total lack of awareness of adjustments (Jackson & Mukerjee, 1974). However, awareness by the mid to late 1980s was seen to be much more prevalent (Davis, 1989). Of course, as pointed out by Lindell & Perry (2000), awareness alone does not imply accurate knowledge of advantages or requirements (e.g., Kunreuther et al., 1978).

Unlike some other areas of research (e.g., role of risk perceptions in adjustment activity), the area of perceived advantages of adjustments requires more research. However, findings to date appear to support the initial conclusion that effectiveness variables correlate with both future intentions for adoption and adjustment adoption itself. While requirement or effort variables have also been found to predict adjustment adoption, they don't appear to have as strong a relationship with adoption as do effectiveness factors. A recent study provided a direct comparison of the role of effectiveness versus requirement variables in adjustment adoption (Lindell & Whitney, 2000). That study clearly demonstrated the precedence of beliefs about effectiveness over beliefs about requirements. All effectiveness factors—beliefs about adjustments (a) protecting persons, (b) protecting property, (c) useful for another purpose—were significantly correlated with both adjustment adoption (r's = .20-.32) and adjustment intention (r's = .42-.49). By contrast, all requirement variables measured—cost, skill, time, effort, need for cooperation from others—were not related to either adoption or intention.

An interesting finding from Lindell and Whitney's study and another study (Russell et al., 1995) was that there are indications that a person's perceptions of an adjustment's effectiveness for a function other than hazard preparedness may be an important consideration when deciding on whether to carry out a particular adjustment activity. The strongest magnitude correlations seen in Lindell and Whitney involving effectiveness were between "effectiveness for other use" and both adoption and intention. In Russell et al. (1995), this same perception was seen to help move adoption of basic survival tools from 7% to 26%. Thus, at least for adjustments emphasizing basic survival needs, there are clear suggestions from these two studies that a supplemental focus on an adjustment's utility for purposes other than simply hazard mitigation and preparedness may lead to increased public action.

Emotional and Attributional Factors: The Role of Earthquake Worries, General Fears, and Fatalism

One factor that has been understudied is the relationship between emotions and readiness activities. A well-known finding in the psychology and mental health literatures is that moderate levels of anxiety are correlated with maximal performance on various tasks and with healthy functioning (Yerkes-Dodson law; Yerkes & Dodson, 1908). By contrast, too little anxiety as well as too much anxiety has been found to relate to problematic functioning (e.g., Ronan & Deane, 1998). For example, too little anxiety has been related to a lack of regulation of important social functions and a lack of concern for consequences. Too much anxiety has been found to relate to inhibited functioning and outright avoidance, a tendency not to engage in behavior that would assist in coping with various demands of living.

No seismic studies included in the Lindell and Perry (2000) review looked comprehensively at the role of emotional factors in preparation for earthquakes. Some suggestive research in that review as well as some more in depth research done since does indicate a potential role for emotional factors. As reviewed in sections earlier, "earthquake concern" (Dooley et al., 1992) has been found to correlate with increased preparedness activities (Dooley et al., 1992). However, Mileti and Darlington (1997) found that the concern factor was not significantly correlated with seismic readiness actions. However, these two studies operationalized the constructs quite differently. Dooley et al. (1992) asked in their phone survey "how much do you worry" (presumably in relation to earthquakes but not specified in the Method section of the research report) on a four point likert scale. By contrast, Mileti & Darlington (1997) asked in their mail-out survey for respondents to indicate which hazard from a list caused the "most concern." Earthquake concern was then coded based on respondent choice on a dichotomous scale (earthquake = 1; non-earthquake = 0).

Thus, in terms of an emotional construct, the Dooley et al. item is preferable to the Mileti and Darlington item, both in terms of content and criterion-related validity and potential for increased variability (necessary to produce correlations). In terms of predictors of earthquake-related concern or worry, exposure to an "earthquake that scared you" was found to be the strongest predictor in Dooley et al. (1992). As seen later in the review of the literature having to do with response and recovery, a factor inhibiting post-impact recovery is excessive fear and threat perception including being exposed to a hazard and having the fear of being hurt or killed.

Indeed, in an interesting study carried out 16 months after a major earthquake in Turkey, Rustelmi & Karanci (1999) found that lower levels of perceived control over the future, low social support, perceptions of lower home strength, and a higher expectation of another earthquake all were significantly correlated with a generalized form of anxiety and fear (i.e., 13 anxiety and fear items based on the past two weeks). In turn, this factor (increased anxiety) was the strongest predictor of earthquake preparedness behavior (a weighted index of actual and intentional behaviors) in regression analyses. The only other predictor of adjustment activity was perceived control over the future: perceptions of increased, not reduced, control predicted preparedness levels. Thus, taking the findings of this section together to this point, it may be that some form of personalized risk and concern or worry about the future combined with a sense of efficacy about being able to alter the future can motivate people to consider or do something to reduce future risk.

However, given a large body of literature that some forms of anxiety, and other emotions, are known to produce avoidance behavior (e.g., Ronan & Deane, 1998), the type, form and intensity of the emotional arousal may be quite important. For example, while not specifically measuring emotional levels directly, the attribute "fatalism" suggests a state of resignation, or perhaps lack of control, about the future. Such negative attributions have been related to emotions such as depression and anxiety (Peterson, Maier, & Seligman, 1993). Fatalism itself has been assessed in terms of its relation to preparedness for earthquakes and has been found to relate to decreased readiness activities (e.g., Turner et al., 1986). Conversely, lower fatalism has been found to relate to increased adjustment adoption prior to, but not following, an earthquake prediction (Farley et al., 1993). There has been the suggestion that fatalism may actually represent less a sense of helplessness about the future per se than a lack of information, or awareness, about adjustment measures that actually might be effective (Lindell & Perry, 2000). From our view, these positions are not mutually exclusive.

In terms of countering various fatalistic attitudes (e.g., Turner et al., 1986), a recent series of studies have looked into this problem (McClure, Allen, & Walkey, 2001). These studies assumed the view that fatalism involves attributions for events emphasizing a lack of control. Specifically, the view assumed by McClure and associates is that if people attribute damage from earthquakes to causes that are uncontrollable, this attitude will lead people to prepare less often for a future earthquake. By contrast, if people see aspects of earthquake damage as *controllable*, they will be more likely to be in a position to be persuaded to prepare. As reviewed earlier, this view is reasonable in light of the fact that perceived efficacy of household adjustments has been found to relate to increased adjustment intention and adoption (Lindell & Whitney, 2000; Russell, 1995).

In their study, McClure et al. (2001) wanted to ascertain whether varying accounts of earthquakes and damage to buildings would affect peoples' attributions and subsequent judgements about whether damage could be prevented. This research was done in the context of findings that media accounts of earthquakes typically tend to emphasize areas not where damage has been prevented but instead where it has been most severe (e.g., Gaddy & Tanjong, 1987; Hiroi, Mikami, & Miyata, 1985). A series of four studies carried out by McClure et al. (2001) looked at damage distinctiveness (i.e., one but not other buildings affected in an earthquake) and damage consensus and consistency (i.e., the extent to which earthquakes produce the same damage over time). Overall, this research found a clear effect of varying these types of information on participants' attributions. In terms of the effect of this information on people's views of preventability, findings indicated a stronger effect for consensus and to a lesser extent, distinctiveness, information. McClure et al. (2001) concluded that while informing the general public about both distinctiveness and consistency/consensus information may be useful, it may be more worthwhile to highlight consistency information:

> The consistent performance of buildings across a number of occasions is likely to be a more reliable indicator of the role of building design in the outcome than a building's performance in a single earthquake (p. 119).

That is, emphasizing the consistent performance of most buildings, while also including distinctiveness information, may prove to be useful indicators to the general public of damage preventability. Given that many public education programs often portray generalized rather than more differentiated accounts of damage not only to buildings but also to other areas including household items, property, and animal and human life, this is an area that has potential in hazards education programs. For example, some education programs portray scenes of generalized damage, and perhaps devastation, to motivate the public to prepare (Gaddy & Tanjong, 1987; Lopes, 1992). Such findings call into question such an approach. In fact, such an approach might have an effect opposite to that intended (e.g., increased fatalism or helplessness). As McClure et al. (2001) suggest, a preferable strategy would be to include scenes where damage is not apparent or slight—emphasizing consistency across other hazardous occasions—with the accompanying message that preparation efforts are worthwhile.

Of course, helping people to accept the idea that adjustment adoption can be effective for protecting property and lives is not the same as assisting them to take direct action. In other words:

> [the current pattern of findings] suggests that agencies can present information in ways that focus people's attention on the controllable factors contributing to earthquake damage . . . However, the judgment that earthquake damage is preventable may be a prerequisite to voluntary action that mitigates damage; in other words, this judgment may be a necessary cause for voluntary action even if it is not a sufficient one (McClure et al., 2001, p. 120).

In fact, in a large scale study, Lopes (1992) demonstrated that scenes of mass damage did indeed lead to significantly less preparedness for earthquakes and other hazards. We review that study more fully in the next main section looking at research in other hazardous areas. This idea of emotional arousal and attributional judgements and their role in readiness and risk reduction motivational efforts will be returned to in more detail later in this review.

Do (or At Least Intend to Do) Something: Behavioral Factors

A well-known maxim in the social sciences is that initial behavior is often the best predictor of future behavior (e.g., Wortman, Loftus, & Weaver, 1999). This idea has found its way into preparation for earthquakes (and other hazards). Three different lines of investigation have thus far looked at the role of behavioral factors as predictors of adjustment adoption.

The Effects of Information Searching. Information searching refers to the active process of seeking information about risk and preparatory actions from various sources (e.g., informal discussion of earthquakes, attending meetings related to earthquakes, seeking information from government and NGO agencies). Mileti and colleagues have found information searching to relate strongly to readiness actions. For example, Mileti and Darlington (1997) found that this factor—measured in this study as seeking information from government and NGOs—correlated strongly with adjustment adoption (r = .47). In addition, it was the strongest predictor by far in multiple regression analyses (by over a factor of three compared to the next strongest predictor, response/adjustment guidance). Other studies have also found a significant relationship between information searching and readiness actions (Mileti & Fitzpatrick, 1992; Ronan, Johnston, & Hull, 1998; Ronan, Johnston, & Paton, 2001; Turner et al., 1986).

Past Adoption. Past adjustment adoption has been found to predict current adoption in a few studies (e.g., Mileti & Darlington, 1997; Mileti & O'Brien, 1992). However, the predictive power of this factor has varied with one reason perhaps being context factors (Lindell & Perry, 2000). For example, Mileti and O'Brien found significant correlations between pre-mainshock adjustment activities and aftershock warning response (r = .18-.26) following the 1989 Loma Prieta earthquake. By contrast, Mileti and Darlington (1997) found a significant, but smaller, correlation (r = .11) between past and current readiness activities in the Bay Area following a public education campaign carried out 11 months following Loma Prieta (see later section for more information on this campaign). In addition, Mileti & O'Brien (1992) found nonsignificant correlations between these factors in the Parkfield earthquake prediction experiment.

Intention to Adopt. Intention to adopt has been found to predict adoption. However, only a couple of studies (Farley et al., 1993; Lindell & Whitney,

2000) have addressed this issue. Lindell and Whitney found a strong correlation between intention to adopt (i.e., "something I am likely to do") and actual adoption (r = .65). However, as the correlation suggests, even though strong in magnitude, the relationship between intention and adoption is less than a 1:1 relationship. Further, Farley et al. (1993) demonstrated that intentions in fact appear to overestimate later readiness activities, and perhaps by a large factor (see also Farley, 1998). For example, 6 percent reported intending to leave the New Madrid Missouri area (Farley, 1998) in advance of a predicted earthquake (i.e., Browning's pseudoscientific earthquake prediction, Gori, 1993). However, follow-up data indicated that only 1% had actually left the area for that specific reason. Nevertheless, the idea of behavioral intention clearly has a relationship to actual behavior. In fact, we see it as a vital issue to consider for education programs and as an intrinsic link in motivational efforts (see Chapter 3).

Educational and Social Influences: Direct Provision of Information and Modelling Influences

The Effects of Public Education and Predictions. Studies in this area have focused primarily on information provided through mass media and more informal influences (Lindell & Perry, 2000). In terms of media campaigns, evidence has accrued that campaigns designed to raise awareness as well as motivate adoption adjustment do have an effect. In fact, as pointed out by Peek and Mileti (2002), those who watch the news media are also those more likely to prepare for a hazard. In terms of the effectiveness of media campaigns themselves, Mileti and Darlington (1997) studied the effects of a mass media campaign in the Bay Area California. The campaign centered on a newspaper insert distributed to Bay Area residents 11 months after the 1989 Loma Prieta earthquake that included long-term prediction and adjustment information. The campaign also included pre- and post-insert press conferences designed to increase the impact of the insert. They found that even in an area where many households had already adopted a relatively large number of adjustments following a major earthquake, more were seen to be taken on following the insert. For example, storing hazardous materials safely rose by about 50% (from 29% to 44%); storing emergency equipment, 60% (from 50% to 81%); and stockpiling food and water, 70% (from 44% to 75%). Short-term warnings also have been found to increase preparedness activity (e.g., Borque, 1997; Farley et al., 1993; Kunreuther, 1993; Showalter, 1993; Turner et al., 1986) and response behavior (see also Chapter 6).

However, some data are suggestive that as the salience of media campaigns decreases, so too do perceptions of earthquake probability (Mulilis & Lippa, 1990) and adjustment activities (Borque et al., 1997). Additional findings that support this "educational half life" idea come from Mileti and colleagues on predictors of preparedness in such campaigns. Factors in public education campaigns that have been found to predict increased preparedness activities include (e.g., Mileti, 1999; Mileti & Darlington, 1995, 1997; Mileti & Fitzpatrick, 1992; Mileti & O'Brien, 1992):

- frequency of information and number of warnings;
- specific response guidance consistent across multiple sources or channels;
- source certainty.

Consequently, as discussed more in upcoming chapters, the idea of education campaigns having a half-life needs to be taken into account in long-term educational and intervention planning in school and community settings. As pointed out by Lindell and Perry (2000), the salience of even a highly successful warning or readiness-based media campaign is likely with time to give way to other current concerns involved in households and families coping with the demands of day-to-day living.

Thus, education campaigns need to be planned and carried out over time and be coordinated across multiple, trusted sources. The messages being put out also need to be consistent and not just raise awareness but provide specific guidance to a variety of community recipients. We review and explore the role for school- and family-based education programs in Chapter 3.

Modelling Influences. Mileti and associates and our own research have found that seeing other people (friends, family, neighbors, workplace, government agencies, businesses, others; Mileti & Darlington, 1997; see also Mileti & Fitzpatrick, 1992; Ronan, Johnston, & Hull, 1998; Ronan, Johnston, & Paton, 2001) prepare is significantly correlated with household preparedness activities. However, while simple correlations were significant in Mileti and Darlington and Ronan et al., these studies found that this variable (i.e., seeing others prepare) became non-significant when considered together with other factors (i.e., in multiple regression analyses). In these studies, the strongest predictor of readiness actions was information searching. However, in Mileti and Darlington, seeing others prepare was found to be the strongest predictor of information searching in regression analyses followed by multiple sources of received information, level of objective risk (i.e., living closer to an area designated as hazardous), and adjustment guidance. In our study, seeing others prepare was significantly, but not strongly, correlated with both readiness activities ($r = .15$) and search ($r = .19$) but was not significant in multiple regression analyses. Taking these findings together, this factor does appear to have at least some role in education efforts, perhaps in terms of motivating people to consider taking some initial action.

ADJUSTMENT ADOPTION RESEARCH ACROSS OTHER HAZARDS: HIGHLIGHTED FINDINGS

This section reviews some other representative research in the risk reduction and readiness area, including some initial research that has looked at youth. We then summarize the overall hazards readiness and risk reduction research.

Perceptions about Who Is Responsible for Readiness and Response: Perceived Protection Responsibility

As seen in the seismic preparedness literature, increased perceptions of personal responsibility have been found to relate to increased activities aimed at preparing the household for a future earthquake. Further, perceptions of personal responsibility have risen in California over the past 30 years. When looking at a range of risks that include natural, technological, biological, and man-made hazards, personal responsibility for action may be higher for some hazards (e.g., tornadoes, lightning, fires in the home) than for others (e.g., floods, earthquakes, hurricanes, nuclear radiation, chemical-related, war- or terrorist-related). In fact, there are indications that even if people perceive some personal efficacy (i.e., that they can reduce a risk), that belief can be attenuated by a feeling that if the government can also do something, then government should take the responsibility (Baron et al., 2000).

Similarly, as introduced earlier, Ballantyne et al. (2000) found that 28 percent of respondents actually felt less concerned about hazards after receiving information about those hazards from local government. Respondents appeared to infer that local government—the source of the information—would take the responsibility for safety and hazard management (Paton & Johnston, 2001). Such a state of affairs would obviously not be conducive to people attending to future education and risk communication campaigns. What appears obvious from this line of research is that the nature of the message delivered from government agencies—such as that seen in some earthquake prone areas on California—needs to highlight the role of personal responsibility.

Emotional Factors

Worry, Upset, Emotional Coping Ability

As seen in the area of seismic preparedness, the role for emotional factors in readiness and risk reduction is as yet unclear. Similarly, in other related research on risk awareness and reduction, findings have been mixed. For example, some studies have found that worry or preoccupation about various risks increases both risk reduction activities (Myers, Henderson-King, & Henderson-King, 1997; Weinstein, Lyon, Rothman, & Cuite, 2000) and increased priority for risk reduction activities (Baron, Hershey, & Kunreuther, 2000). In turn, worry about future risk itself appears to be mediated by judgements about the future likelihood of that risk as well as other factors (e.g., belief in experts; perceived "badness" of the risk; personal experience; lack of knowledge) (Baron et al., 2000). On the other hand, in Baron et al., reasons that were cited in face-to-face interviews as leading significantly more often to reduced worry included: (a) increased personal control and (b) perceptions of reduced risk probability for the person.

Our own findings related to hazard-related upset (i.e, becoming scared or upset when discussing or thinking about hazards) have been mixed (Ronan & Johnston, 1997; Ronan, Johnston, Daly, & Fairley, 2001). In line with previous research, "hazard upset" children have been found in a correlational study (Ronan et al., 2001) to report slightly higher percentages of physical preparedness indicators (e.g., having a family emergency plan, having a flashlight and transistor radio) compared to children not upset about hazards. By contrast, knowledge-based indicators of preparedness (i.e., knowing what to do to protect oneself) across a range of hazards was uniformly lower, and much lower in some instances, for this upset group (Ronan et al., 2001). In addition, more recent quasi-experimental research found no relationships between hazard-related upset and preparedness indicators either before or after a school-based hazards education program (Ronan & Johnston, 2003).

However, similar to Baron et al. (2001) and other findings (e.g., Myers et al., 1997), negative affect (hazard-related upset) in Ronan et al. (2001) was related to probability estimates. In our case, upset was related to unrealistic perceptions of future likelihood. Those youth who perceived low frequency events as higher in likelihood were also seen to be those higher in hazard-related upset as well as slightly lower in the perception of the ability to cope emotionally with a future hazard (Ronan et al., 2001).

If emotional arousal is related to preparedness, while a question clearly not answered adequately as yet, one issue worth considering in the event that it does play a role is what exactly is the influence at work here? That is, does concern, worry, distress or other factors influence risk perceptions and readiness activities in some cases but not others? Are some emotions better than others for influencing intentionality, knowledge, and action? Can the same form of emotional arousal (e.g., distress/preoccupation/fear) affect one area positively (e.g., adjustment activity) and another negatively (e.g., knowledge of protective behaviors)?

While more research is needed, the relationship between affect and behavior has been studied in a number of areas of psychology. As introduced earlier, moderate levels of anxiety have been found to relate to optimal performance whereas extreme forms of anxiety (both high and low) have more often been associated with problematic conditions (e.g., anxiety and mood disorders; some forms of antisocial behavioral problems, respectively). Following such a finding, might it be that moderate amounts of anxiety are a better predictor when compared to high or low levels? Thus, while worry, concern and other related factors have shown some ability to predict readiness activity, most studies to date have not differentiated constructs in such a way so as to be able to address this or other possibilities.

An exception here is a 14-month prospective study done by Weinstein and colleagues (Weinstein, Lyon, Rothman, & Cuite, 2000). Here, they looked at the relationship between different forms of affective arousal, cognitive activity, and other factors in predicting protective actions following a tornado. Like previous research discussed earlier (e.g., Baron et al., 2001; Ronan et al., 2001), it was found that, by itself, worry related to tornadoes predicted increased protective actions. However, they also found differentiation between the preoccupation component of worry (intrusive thoughts, vigilance, frequency of thoughts) and the intensity dimensions (i.e., current anxiety levels; fear levels at the time of the tornado). That is, current anxiety on its own predicted to a small extent preparedness; however, with other variables controlled, higher levels of anxiety intensity tended to get in the way (i.e., intensity related to reduced preparedness). Additionally, high fear levels experienced at the time of the tornado predicted preparedness soon after the tornado but only in the event of low levels of preoccupation. By contrast, high levels of fear and high levels of preoccupation together uniformly led to low activity levels (Weinstein et al., 2000, p. 358).

Related to the idea of moderate anxiety as useful, in an earlier study, Faupel and Styles (1992) found that those who had prepared for a future hazard (hurricane) reported increased stress levels. However, given the small magnitude of the correlations (around r = .15), and in line with the authors' argument and the Yerkes-Dodson law referred to earlier, we might conjecture that some stress or anxiety or worry or hazard-related concern is adaptive in this area. In line with the adaptive function of anxiety, such concern might function to help to orient and mobilize a person's resources to begin to attend to, rather than avoid, the possibility of such a future event. With anxiety too low or high, avoidance of stimuli tends to follow (i.e., owing to lack of concern and being overwhelmed, respectively). On the other hand, some increase in anxiety or *hazard concern* can then help a person tap into other factors that appear useful for preparation efforts including a sense of personal responsibility and control (i.e., personal or self-efficacy) and a sense that preparation efforts might actually help (i.e., adjustment efficacy). Consequently, our view is that some concern is a necessary but clearly not sufficient factor. Concern is likely necessary in the first instance to fuel increased attention to the hazard. However, as reviewed in the next major section, a number of decision-making factors, or biases, can also reduce concern or motivation to prepare.

Public Education

Far less research has looked into educating the public to prepare for hazards other than earthquakes. However, a notable study mentioned earlier was carried out by

Lopes (1992). Lopes assessed levels of preparedness of over 4,000 people who attended disaster education programs across the U.S in areas prone to various hazards (floods, tornadoes, earthquakes). The most notable, and robust finding, was that those people who attended programs and were shown disaster images prepared significantly less across a range of adjustments compared to people who were shown images of "the right thing to do" (i.e., specific adjustment activities). Those who were shown damage images did recall the presentation more readily 6 months later; however, in terms of motivating people to take action, the effects of these images were negligible. On the other hand, showing people what to do had a significant effect on preparation efforts. For example, when asked about having emergency supplies on hand, there was an average increase of just over 45% (45.8%) for the group shown what to do. By contrast, those shown disaster images demonstrated an average increase of only 5%. Similarly, in terms of practicing a disaster plan, there was a sixfold difference between groups indicating, again, that demonstrating what to do is better than showing disaster images. A confound of this study was that some aspects of what to do were actually demonstrated if there was no slide available. Thus, the "how to do it" intervention actually consisted of showing specific "how to" images as well as demonstrations. Nonetheless, this study does provide evidence that showing people what to do has merit; showing them disastrous images may not, unless perhaps they are shown in such a way so as to reflect preventable damage as reviewed in a previous section (McClure et al., 2001). However, while this possibility appears tenable, research is needed to confirm its tenability.

WHAT ARE OBSTACLES TO PREPAREDNESS?

The first place to start here is by addressing those factors reviewed to this point. That is, in most cases, the absence, or lower levels, of a number of factors appear to prevent readiness. These include:

- *preparedness or warning messages* that do not provide specific guidance, are not consistent and repeated over time, do not emphasize controllable and preventable aspects of the hazard, and do not emanate from multiple sources that can be trusted;
- *personal factors* including low levels of personal responsibility, concern, self-efficacy and personal control, low levels of belief in adjustment efficacy, low levels of community bondedness.

Some other factors have also been found to have an influence on preparing for a disaster. These include decision-making processes and larger scale influences.

Decision-Making Influences

Decision-making at individual and organizational levels that can reduce the effects of message or personal variables include various biases such as a normalization bias, optimistic bias, availability bias, adjustment and anchoring bias, selective attention to information, social conformity, and others (Paton & Johnston, 2001).

When making judgements about planning for a hazard, estimates of risk are based on objective analyses of the likelihood of hazard activity and its consequences within a specific area. However, it is common to find considerable disparity between objective considerations and the manner in which they are acted on (Adams, 1995), even when people are presented with accurate scientific information. Such disparities have significant implications on the extent to which readiness plans are implemented. Consequently, effective planning for disasters requires an understanding of the way risk perceptions shape risk decision-making.

Risk perception has received considerable attention over the last few decades (Sjoberg, 2000). Social scientists are aware that people's understanding of risk and response to risk are determined not only by scientific information or direct physical consequences, but also by the interaction of psychological, social, cultural, institutional and political processes (Burns et al., 1993). Factors affecting risk perception are usually not independent and have also been found to vary between different hazard types.

A process with some relevance for emergency planning is "risk compensation" (e.g., Adams, 1995). This describes how people make judgements based on the relative balance between risk and safety. Thus, if an external action is perceived to increase safety, people's behavior may then actually become 'riskier' as a result. This phenomenon has also been referred to as 'levee syndrome': it was found that installing levees in flood prone areas quickly led to increased human habitation of these areas on the incorrect assumption that the risk had been eliminated. Of course, as discussed in Chapter 1, the risk in such circumstances is rarely eliminated entirely and is instead only better contained within certain limits of hazard activity. Under these circumstances, people may then perceive they are safe and not feel it necessary to adopt other adjustments. Until a hazard activity then exceeds expected levels (e.g., as an interaction between flood intensity and increased habitation or downstream effects), little effort may be undertaken in a given community.

Beliefs about risk, and risk reduction behaviour, are also influenced by attributional processes. As introduced earlier, processes relevant here include unrealistic optimism and normalization bias (Paton et al., 2003). In the former, people underestimate the risk to themselves and overestimate the risk to others. Thus, while people may readily acknowledge objective risk in their community, they are more likely to attribute its negative implications to others rather than themselves.

Normalization bias results when people extrapolate from a minor but rarely occurring hazard experience that they have more of a capability to deal with more serious consequences than they actually possess. For example, organizations experiencing only light ash fall during a series of volcanic eruptions perceived the need to prepare for future events less than those that had had greater impacts (Paton, et al. 1999, Johnston, et al. 2000). Both unrealistic optimism and normalization bias result in people underestimating risk relative to scientific and objective planning estimates. This can then lead to reduced hazard concern and acting in ways that, from a more objective perspective, might be counterintuitive and in fact unwise.

Another bias relates to the communication of risk information. This phenomena has been termed "the social amplification of risk" (Kasperson et al., 1988). The amplification process can translate a risk into extreme concern or alternatively, lead to an increased sense of fatalism. This phenomenon can then also lead to those risks which are more significant being underestimated by communities and organizations. Accusations of "irresponsible media" leading to "public hysteria" have been common (Rip, 1988). As reviewed earlier, problems can arise when sources, such as the media (McClure et al., 2001) or education programs (Lopes, 1992), overemphasize adverse or catastrophic aspects of a hazard and fail to provide a balanced view. This can then lead potentially to an increased sense of fatalism and increased sense that preparation may not be worth it.

A final issue to consider is that as introduced earlier in this chapter, changing risk perceptions alone is normally insufficient in bringing about actual behavior change and increased preparedness activity in relation to a particular risk (Lindell & Prater, 2000). Rather, motivating people to change behavior is in part a function of emotional and cognitive processes that govern the relationship between perceived risk and risk reduction actions. People may not be motivated to prepare if they do not perceive or accept their risk status or perceive hazards as salient to their own lives (i.e., have what we are referring to as personalized risk in the form of hazard concern). Irrespective of the level of risk, action will also be constrained if people perceive hazard effects as not preventable, lack belief in the usefulness of an adjustment, transfer responsibility for safety to others, lack trust in information sources, or because of a lack of urgency related to the timing of hazard's occurrence (Paton, Smith, Johnston, Johnson, & Ronan, 2003). We take these issues up in Chapter 3 in the context of motivating communities to prepare for a future hazard.

Larger Scale Influences

Social, cultural, economic, organizational, legal and political influences affect community preparedness (Prater & Lindell, 2001; Peek & Mileti, 2002). For example, statutorily requiring or encouraging the public, organizations, and government agencies to do something in terms of preparedness (and response and recovery) is a pathway that has obvious merit and, by definition, leads to increased preparedness and response capability. However, as research has demonstrated, politicians have been shown generally to be resistant to legal inducements (Burby & French, 1980; Mader et al., 1980). Other more salient influences related to land use and other factors might hold more sway. In other words, politicians tend to have a focus on more pressing short-term issues and be influenced by interests not particularly focused on hazards mitigation. In addition, voluntary organizational preparedness for a disaster is low (Tierney et al., 2001). We discuss school readiness and response planning more fully in later chapters and its links to child and family preparedness and other community initiatives.

With respect to these larger scale influences, these are considered more fully when discussing how to implement education and intervention programs. As a preface, our model of education and intervention delivery takes into account not only the necessary factors for the program itself, its delivery, and the characteristics of the targeted population, but also those larger scale factors (e.g., organizational, cultural, political) that might impede, or facilitate, the delivery of programs. Also focused on later is not only child, family and household preparedness, but also school response capability linking in with such efforts. The little research done in the area of organizational preparedness indicates that settings that deal with children may, like other organizations, have low levels of preparedness. More research is required on school planning and response capacity.

SUMMARY OF RISK REDUCTION AND READINESS RESEARCH

A main finding across hazards mitigation and readiness research is that, unless some particular features are in place in terms of the (a) hazards preparation message and (b) the intended recipient of the message, hazards preparation by and large is low across people and hazards. However, we must be encouraged by the fact that some increases in some areas of preparation have been noted across time as is reflected more generally after public and, as seen in Chapter 3, school education campaigns.

Significantly, one area that has seen an increase is the notion of personal responsibility for looking after oneself and one's family for at least a minimum period following a hazardous event. Given that earlier research found very low levels and later research very high levels of personalized responsibility, this alone provides encouragement. In other words, efforts at assisting communities to become more resilient is worthwhile. However, it must also be said that a new model of education and its delivery needs to be considered. Such a model would clearly include more systemic intervention efforts that are based on empirically identified components and that are researched using experimental, or quasi-experimental, methodologies (e.g., Ronan & Johnston, 2003). A second main issue discussed in Chapter 3, and a theme of this book, is one of embedding a hazards awareness and readiness culture within schools and communities through sustained and coordinated educational and preparedness-based efforts.

Relative Importance of Factors Reviewed: What Does the Research Tell Us Thus Far?

The Active Ingredients

Readiness programs will likely benefit from considering these factors:

- providing specific guidance;
- guidance that is consistent across multiple channels;
- guidance by multiple, linked sources that can be trusted;
- guidance that emphasizes controllable, differentiated effects of a hazard, preventable damage;
- guidance that is repeated over time.

This form of communication is best received by an audience targeting the following, non-fixed characteristics:

- moderate level of concern/worry/anxiety and a sense of personalized risk (I am concerned about the future in relation to this hazard);
- sense of personal responsibility (readiness for a hazard is my responsibility);
- sense of personal control/self-efficacy (what I do can make a difference);
- belief in adjustment efficacy (i.e., this thing called an adjustment is actually going to work to protect myself, my loved ones, and our property; by the way, doing this just might be useful for other purposes as well);
- community bondedness (I feel connected to where I live and work and that connection is worth making an effort to preserve it);
- motivation and intention to seek information from formal and informal sources and to engage in doing something (I intend to do something about my concern and feel confident my action will prove useful).

The Research in the Future

Research in the future needs to use more sophisticated correlation-based strategies included hierarchical linear modeling and structural equation modeling. However, in our estimation, the more important arbiter of the soundness of any education effort rests in what many in this type of research consider to be the gold standard, randomized, controlled experimental or quasi-experimental trials (e.g., Kazantzis, Ronan, & Deane, 2001; Ronan & Johnston, 2003). In addition, the movement ahead of any applied area of a field often rests on the quality of the research that underpins that area. In other words, a focus on improving methodologies will clearly have practical advantage over both the short- and long-term. In addition, increased efforts at evaluation of a more pragmatic nature will also assist greatly. We expand more on these themes beginning in Chapter 3.

Concluding Comments: Prefacing the Role for Readiness and Risk Reduction in School and Family Settings

Given the findings to date from the hazards readiness literature, how might we consider the role of schools and families? To preface our more comprehensive discussion in Chapter 3, there is justifiable cause for optimism for an increased role for schools and families in promoting community resilience. This optimism is borne out of additional and more specific research on this topic that is reviewed in that chapter. However, and importantly, the research reviewed to this point gives us specific avenues to pursue, and not to pursue, as we anticipate a model of evidence-based practice that promotes community resilience and local hazards sustainability.

RESPONSE AND RECOVERY: A REVIEW OF FINDINGS

Two sources of data are implicated here. The first set of findings addresses the question of "what are the effects of warnings to hazards and the hazards themselves on larger groups?" and the second looks more at "what are the effects at a more individual and family-based level?" The next section looks at response to warnings and patterns of community responding.

Responding to Hazards in Communities

Response to Warnings Including Evacuation

A fairly significant body of knowledge on organizational and individual response to warnings has been developed. Response to warnings by individuals has been found to relate to i) individual risk perception (understanding, belief, and personalization); ii) the nature of the warning information (specificity, consistency, certainty, accuracy, clarity, media, frequency); and iii) the personal characteristics of the recipient (demographics, knowledge, experience of the hazard, social network and so on) (Mileti & O'Brien, 1993). A consistent and clear conclusion of social science research is of these factors, the warning message itself is one of the most important factors that influences the effectiveness of the warning system (Mileti & Sorensen, 1990). Unfortunately, one or more of the important attributes required of warning messages (specificity, consistency, certainty, accuracy, clarity) is usually deficient or missing during a crisis. Responding authorities would do well to recognize this possibility. Five topics are important when constructing a warning message: the hazard or risk, guidance, location, time, and source. The warning message must contain information about the impending hazard with sufficient simple detail that the public can understand the characteristics of the hazard from which they need to protect themselves.

Emergency management research (e.g., Perry 1985) has identified three general variables which appear crucial to citizens' evacuation decision-making:

- the definition of the threat as real (i.e., the development of a belief in the warning);
- the level of perceived personal risk (belief about the personal consequences of the disaster impact); and
- the presence of an adaptive plan (being acquainted with and believing in the response including means of evacuation and of sheltering).

These points reinforce the need for community participation and the provision of mutual information. In addition, research (Drabek, 1986) shows three social variables are important with respect to evacuation performance and need to be addressed in evacuation planning; these include family context, level of community involvement, and cultural factors. We would add that the school context is an important factor here as well and expand on this in Chapter 6.

Response to the Disaster Itself

Response to a disaster involves coordinating and mobilizing resources to attend to a variety of activities that include sheltering and evacuation, search and rescue, police and fire activities, physical and psychological first aid, continuing assessment for ongoing threats and damage and other emergency management activities (Haddow & Bullock, 2003; Peek & Mileti, 2002; Tierney et al., 2001; see also Chapter 6).

In terms of how the public itself responds to disasters, Perry and Lindell (2003) state clearly that the idea of mass panic, shock, passivity, and social disorganization during a disaster, popularized in the mass media, is unwarranted. What the evidence does say is that none of these patterns reflect the majority response. People in general tend to act in their best interest and most respond not only rationally, but constructively. Thus, most citizens respond to disasters in prosocial fashion. For example, the first to try to rescue or assist people affected by a hazard are generally those who are not affected. In addition, and contrary to what might be popular belief, crime actually tends to reduce following a disaster (Tierney et al., 2001) and antisocial behavior such as looting and rioting is relatively rare. In fact, there has never been martial law declared after a natural disaster in the United States.

What does appear to happen in fact is that the public do tend to converge on disaster sites not with ill behavior in mind but with offers of assistance. In fact, as a salient example, after the 9/11 disaster, there were approximately 9000 crisis and grief counselors who descended on New York City (Kadet, 2002).[1] For those

---

[1] Whether or not such crisis counselling actually assists is a matter taken up in Chapter 7.

who are affected directly by a disaster, the majority tend to seek information and resources that will assist in their coping with the effects of the disaster. Of course, one major form of support is often from federal, state, and local governments and non-governmental organizations (NGO). Tierney et al. (2001) summarize nicely the general findings:

> The picture that emerges of disaster victims is one of responsible activism, attempting self-care, supporting neighbors, and ameliorating the situation as best they understand it, using whatever resources available. Victims are typically supported in these endeavors (not only) by official organizations and resources, but also by contributions from other households not directly affected by the event (p. 50).

During a disaster, there appears to be a shift in social responding in affected communities: an increase in overall cohesion and support between victims and non-victims. In addition, the convergence of aid offered to affected communities from outside organizations and individuals offers resources to emergency managers to help deal with the crisis. However, this convergence of assistance can also produce difficulties. For example, some forms of assistance are simply not needed. In such cases, they can then stretch resources available for necessary emergency management coordination (e.g., Kartez & Lindell, 1989). Such findings have obvious implications for planning for a hazard whether in a school or other community setting.

Prosocial responding in such situations has been referred to as based on therapeutic, or altruistic, community influences: "(response to disasters are characterized by an) outpouring of altruistic . . . behaviour beginning with mass rescue . . ." (Barton, 1969, p. 206). In fact, disasters have been shown to lead to the emergence of new groups based on some common cause (Peek & Mileti, 2002). However, as pointed out by Perry and Lindell (2003), the phenomenon of overall community and political cohesiveness may have a temporary quality. The actual length of time has not been researched adequately to make any definitive conclusions as to specific timeframes. However, Perry and Lindell do point out that after 9/11 that social and political conflict began to arise within approximately 6 months after the attacks. Such a phenomenon was also seen following some recent floods (Ronan et al., 2005). The point here is that planning for hazardous events does need to take into account, and perhaps capitalize on, this altruistic phenomenon in the short-term and plan for its possible cessation in the longer term.

Psychological Effects on Communities and Individuals Including Youth and Families

When people do have problems following a hazard, they tend to be of the following major types identified in the biggest review to date (Norris et al., 2002):

(a) specific forms of distress: primarily anxiety-based symptoms including those of acute and posttraumatic stress disorder (ASD, SPTSD); and depression and grief reactions; (b) general forms of distress (e.g., heightened stress levels); (c) health-related problems (e.g., somatic complaints, sleep disruption is common); (d) other more chronic problems including secondary stressors (e.g., family conflict, work-related and financial problems; continued disruption to recovery); (e) loss of social support and normal coping skills (i.e., psychosocial resource loss); and, identified in a category of its own, (f) specific problems for youth (e.g., clinginess in younger children).

In terms of the effects of hazards on those in any given community, a large scale meta-analysis was done well over 10 years ago (Rubonis & Bickman, 1991) that reviewed all available quantitative studies that had been done from 1943 through 1990. The main findings of that study were first that the effects of disasters were highly heterogenous. However, some generalizations were possible. First, across the 52 studies included, findings indicated a 17% psychiatric incidence rate.

Additionally, some participant and disaster characteristics were seen to increase the risk of disaster-related mental health problems. If victims were female, if the disaster had more deaths, and if the disaster was caused by natural, versus human, means, then the risk of problems was seen to increase. However, a more recent study (Norris et al., 2002; see also Watson et al., 2003) looking at a larger pool of studies (n = 160 samples of victims) quite clearly demonstrated that in terms of severity, mass violence had by far the most severe effect (67% of samples "severely" affected) followed by technological (39%) and natural disasters (34%), respectively.

A point of agreement between both of these reviews was that the passage of time appears to help people report reduced distress. However, as reported by Norris et al. (2002), the change for some was not necessarily linear:

> ... many victims and survivors reported initial improvement, followed by a period of stabilization or worsening, followed by later improvement. Symptoms usually peaked in the first year and were less prevalent thereafter, leaving only a minority of communities and individuals substantially impaired. The first anniversary was generally associated with intensification of distress and increased use of mental health services. Levels of symptoms in ... early phases (predicted) symptoms in later phases. Delayed onset of ... disorders were rare (Watson et al., 2003).

Thus, some but certainly not all people are affected by disaster. The more hazardous the effects, the more problems appear to accrue. However, it does also appear clear from early and more recent research that the process of normal reactions to a disaster may follow a natural course of resolution for the majority of people. In other words, the grandmotherly adage that "time heals" has evidence based support (e.g., Gist & Devilly, 2002). In fact, following the September 11th attacks, the numbers in New York City initially meeting the criteria for a diagnosis of PTSD (7.5 % of a sample of 1008 adults living south of 110th Street; 20% of those in that sample living nearer the disaster, below Canal Street; Galea, Boscarino, Resnick, & Vlahov, 2002 had fallen substantially (by approximately two-thirds) over a period of 4 months (Galea et al., 2002). Other research has found a similar course (e.g., Cook & Bickman, 1990; Rubonis & Bickman, 1991; Salzer & Bickman, 1999). In our own research (Ronan & Johnston, 1999), we found that a two month interval following a hazard was seen to be quite helpful to the majority of youth in terms of their self-reported PTSD-related distress. Distress-related scores were seen to drop by an average of 33% (.80 of a standard deviation) in that particular study.

However, it is also the case that in that same study (Ronan & Johnston, 1999), active coping ability was not seen to increase by nearly the same proportion as the distress decreased. In fact, in one of the schools under study, coping scores actually deteriorated across the 2 month time interval. In addition, time is clearly not healing for all (e.g., Amir & Lev-Wiesel, 2003; Galea et al., 2002).

Factors That Promote and Hinder Natural Resolution

Who exactly is more vulnerable to the effects of disasters? In addition, who is more resilient? A number of factors have been identified that appear to promote, and complicate, natural recovery from hazard-related traumatic events, both in terms of reducing distress as well as assisting with coping. As seen in Table 2.3, a whole range of factors accumulated in a review by Don Meichenbaum include factors related to characteristics of the (a) Response phase ("within" the hazard), (b) pre-hazard environment (Readiness phase), and (c) post-disaster (Recovery phase) (Meichenbaum, 1997).

Other reviews cited earlier (Norris et al., 2002; Rubonis & Bickman, 1991) have identified a smaller set of factors that appear to be most important. In Rubonis & Bickman(1991), the factors that increased vulnerability were being female and the hazard causing more deaths. The Norris et al. (2002) review confirmed these factors increase vulnerability and added to that list:

- female;
- more injuries and deaths;
- youth;
- exposed to disaster in a developing (versus developed) country;
- experienced mass violence (versus technological or natural disasters);
- were primary victims (versus rescue and recovery workers who tended to demonstrate resilience).

TABLE 2.3. List of Factors Identified as Affecting Recovery From a Disaster
(Meichenbaum, 1997).

I. CHARACTERISTICS OF THE DISASTER

Objective factors directly affecting the "victim" and "significant others"

1. Proximity to disaster and duration
   of the stressor

   Was the individual close or "relatively" close to the
   site of the disaster? Did the individual experience a
   "narrow escape?" (The greater the proximity, intensity
   and duration, the poorer the level of adjustment).

2. Degree of physical harm or injury
   to the "victim".

   Was the individual physically injured?

3. Intentionality of injury or harm along a
   "continuum of deliberateness"

   Was the individual injured "on purpose"?

4. Witness violence

   Did the individual witness physical violence?

5. Witness violent or sudden death of
   others—like one's loved one or of a
   child or friend

   Did the individual witness the death of a
   "significant other"? Was there violent or sudden
   death to loved ones? Has the parent lost a child?
   Did the individual helplessly witness such deaths?

6. Exposure to grotesque or mutilating
   deaths of others—exposure to mass
   deaths or human remains

   Was the individual exposed to grotesque sights,
   sounds and smells, (e.g., mutilated and severed
   bodies)? Was the individual exposed to scenes of
   death and destruction? If there was injury or death,
   was there disfigurement, mutilation and other
   grotesque sights? Was the individual exposed to
   mutilated or burned bodies? Was the individual
   exposed to mass deaths or mass dying? Was the
   individual exposed to traumatic events that were
   vivid and emotionally powerful? Were children
   among the injured and dead? Does the individual
   identify with the victims?

7. Degree of property damage to "victim"
   and others ($5,000+)

   Did the individual experience a substantial degree of
   property damage to the point where his/her home is
   uninhabitable? Is the individual living in make-shift
   quarters? Was there sudden and severe property loss
   to others, as well? Will the property damage take a
   long time to repair? Is the landscape devastated?

8. Learning of one's exposure to further
   potential threats

   Is the individual or group at continued "high risk"
   of future stressors?

9. Irreversibility of resource losses
   (prolonged environmental disruption)

   Is the individual, family, group *unable* to reverse
   losses (i.e., failure to recover lost possessions,
   property, job, income, and other personal losses)? Is
   there continual displacement? Is there loss of both
   home *and* job or livelihood?

TABLE 2.3. *(Continued)*

10. Escape blocked or experience impossible choices	Was escape blocked for the individual? Was the individual faced with impossible choices such as helping others at great risk to one's own survival?
11. Constant reminders—remain in or near epicentre	Are there constant reminders of the accident or traumatic events? Is there an absence of a "safety signal"?"
12. Signs of injury	Is the impact of the traumatic event evident to the individual, but "invisible" or not readily noticeable to others?
13. Involve noxious agents	Was the individual or loved ones exposed to noxious agents or experienced continuing threat from potential toxicity or radiation? Are there continuing concerns and uncertainty about possible long-term health consequences?
14. Degree of physical injury and death to others and loved ones	Was there violent, sudden or severe injury or death to a "loved one," or friend or neighbour (e.g., number of friends killed)? Did the individual have to wait a prolonged period to hear about the fate of a loved one?
15. How information of death was conveyed	If there was death that was not witnessed was the news of the death conveyed in a non-supportive fashion? Not told why he/she cannot view body of significant other?
16. Description of social supports—both immediate and long-term	(i) Was the individual separated from family members during or immediately after the disaster? (ii) Was there significant disruption of social supports and kin networks with accompanying loss of proximity to friends and relatives?

"Subjective" factors related to the "victim" and "significant others"

17. Perception of the disaster	(i) Was the disaster viewed as unexpected, unpredictable, and sudden, as compared to a predictable disaster (e.g., seasonal flooding)? (ii) Was the threat *not* known to exist?
18. Perception of the "intensity" of threat to life or bodily integrity to self or family	Did the disaster cause "threat" to life survival or to physical integrity? Is the traumatic event perceived as being continually threatening to one's life or well-being or to his/her loved ones?
19. Perception of "psychological" and "physical" demands	Did the disaster cause excessive demands and entail extended exposure?

(Continued)

TABLE 2.3. *(Continued)*

20. Perception of cause of the disaster	Did the individual(s) perceive the disaster as being due to callousness . . . irresponsibility . . . greed . . . stupidity? Does the individual(s) feel the disaster was preventable and controllable? Is there someone to blame?
21. Perception of preparation	Did the individual(s) feel unprepared for the disaster? Was there lack of training for such disasters? Was there an opportunity to warn potential victims ahead of time, so they could take precautions, but the warning was not given? Were the potential victims unable to take precautions after the warning? Did the individual fail to respond to anticipatory warnings? Could the event have been prevented or the injury/destruction reduced?
22. Perception of lack of personal control	Does the individual feel a loss of control over social processes that are generally perceived as being in control? . . . Does the disaster represent a breakdown in a system that is *not* supposed to falter? Does the individual experience a loss of personal control?
23. Perception of assistance offered	Did the individual offer assistance to others that proved to be unhelpful . . . futile . . . or even made things worse (e.g., further property loss)?
24. Perception of personal responsibility—blame self	Does the individual see himself/herself as being in a role that resulted in injury or death to others because of what he/she did or failed to do?
25. Perception of social supports	Does the individual(s) feel he/she has no, or few, family members, friends, neighbours to turn to for help? Did the disaster interfere with peer support?

II. CHARACTERISTICS OF THE POST-DISASTER RESPONSE

Reactions of the Individual

26. Intense initial emotional reactions to disaster. For example, symptomatic response/panic anxiety/ dissociation/ sadness/depression	In the immediate aftermath of the traumatic event did the individual develop high levels of anxiety and/or evidence dissociative reactions? In children did they evidence being sad, grieving over potential and realised losses, feel alone during and immediately after the traumatic event? Does the individual experience the "pressure" of PTSD symptoms?
27. Feelings of helplessness	Did the individual experience terror and feel helpless and powerless during and after the event?
28. Symptomatic responses/sleep disturbance/insomnia/agitation	In subsequent weeks following the disaster, did the individual evidence insomnia or agitation?

TABLE 2.3. *(Continued)*

29. Presence of continual intrusive ideation	a) Does the individual have persistent intrusive thoughts, images, dreams, and/or nightmares of the traumatic experience? b) Does the individual continue to repetitively "relive" and re-experience the event and its aftermath? (Note, 3 months following the event is usually taken as a guidepost when such intrusive symptoms should become less frequent and less disruptive)
30. Degree of bereavement	Is the individual acquainted with the victims? Is the individual grieving the loss of significant others?
31. Presence of evidence to "work through" and "resolve" trauma	Is the individual having difficulty "integrating" or constructing "a new world view," or having difficulty "moving beyond" this event (i.e., a constructive resolution)? Does the individual, family or group *lack* a coherent framework (e.g., religious or philosophical outlook) that would help make sense of what has happened? Is the individual continuing to "search for meaning" by pursuing the answer to "why" questions, for which there are no acceptable answers?
32. Self-disclosure opportunities	Is the individual unable or unwilling to talk with others about the trauma and his/her reactions?

Reactions involving significant others—environment recovery factors

33. Opportunity for self-disclosure, working through and resolution	Does the individual think about the upheaval a good deal, but have limited access or opportunity to share his/her feelings and thoughts with others?
34. Lack of social support	Are kin or neighbours/friends unavailable to provide material and social support? Has the family failed to share their different experiences about the disaster?
35. Extent of dislocation or displacement (move often and move furthest away against one's will—involuntary relocation)	Was (Is) the individual and his/her family placed in an unfamiliar environment due to the disaster (dislocated)? Is the nuclear family still apart? Does the relocation plan fail to take into consideration family or neighbourhood patterns and wishes? Was relocation done arbitrarily? (What is the length of time in so-called "temporary housing?")
36. Disruption social support	Was there significant disruption of social support and kin networks with accompanying loss of proximity to friends and relatives?
37. Impact of disaster on social support providers	Are the kinfolk or neighbours/friends who are providing support also "victims" of the disaster or "victims" of its aftermath?

(Continued)

TABLE 2.3. *(Continued)*

38. Stress of receiving social support	Has the evacuee individual or family "worn out his/her welcome" with the host family (e.g., stayed longer than 1 month)?
39. Resumption of normal routines—exposure to continued adversities such as financial strain, lack of transportation, residential displacement, jobless)	Has the individual and his/her family and community been unable to re-establish "normal" routines (e.g., sleeping arrangements, communication, transportation arrangements, work and school schedules)? Is there still dislocation and unemployment? Has the individual or group failed to engage in any proactive actions (e.g., attempts to change things)?
40. Stress reactions of significant others	Did the parent(s) evidence exaggerated emotional response at the time of the disaster or at the reunion? Do "significant others" (e.g., parents) evidence continual distress? Is the individual exposed to a social network of negative rumours that acts like a stress contagion or what has been called a "pressure cooker effect"? Are parents intolerant of their child's proclivity to engage in regressive behaviour?
41. Community efforts at rebuilding and social support—evidence of community solidarity, group cohesion and a common purpose and rapid disaster relief	Has the community failed to organise efforts to rebuild or cope in some *acceptable* fashion? Does the community evidence little concern and lack a supportive response? Is there an absence of any temporary community near the disaster site for victim families? Has the group or community *failed to* engage in any group bereavement or memorial service (i.e., did *not* provide ritual healing ceremonies)? Is there disruption in community life and routines? Is there a shortage of food and fuel and health care services? Is there a lack of counselling?
42. Nature of information	Is the information following the disaster seen as confusing, inconsistent or contradictory? Is there an absence of an ascribed individual or designated group who gathers and disseminates information to combat negative rumours?
43. Nature of designated leadership	Are the authorities in charge seen as being untrustworthy, secretive, and inconsistent, and as a result suffering from a loss of credibility, leading to general mistrust?
44. Mitigating factors to recovery	Is the recovery process being hampered by extensive media coverage, litigation hearings, difficulty over insurance claims, unavailability of contractors/repairmen/storekeepers or dispute with authorities about recovery procedures such as decontamination, lack of information about permanent housing, long term loans, and the like?

TABLE 2.3. *(Continued)*

45. How community views victim(s)—stigmatisation	Does the community (society) view the individual ("victim") who has gone through the traumatic events in a "negative" fashion? Is there a "stigma" attached to asking for help? Does the individual fail to feel part of the community at large?
46. Secondary victimisation	Did the individual experience "secondary victimisation" (e.g., from agencies such as police, doctors, courts, insurance companies)? Has the individual experienced a loss in the market value of his/her home as a result of the disaster?

III. CHARACTERISTICS OF THE INDIVIDUAL AND GROUP

47. High risk factors – Is the individual a member of a group who lives on the "margin" of society or is likely to be "overlooked" or "forgotten" (e.g., geographically isolated, frail and elderly, homeless, physically or mentally ill, lack financial or social resources.	Is the individual at particular risk because he/she is a single parent, middle aged with responsibility to both children and parents, frailed elderly, or from a lower SES level, or a child separated from his/her family as an immediate aftermath of the disaster? Is the individual or parent unemployed or work for low wages? Is the individual single, widowed, divorced? Is the child of a single, divorced or separated parent? Does the child not reside with a family member?
48. Prior history of adjustment problems to stressors and other traumatic events	Did the individual and family members adjust poorly to prior major losses and stressors?
49. Prior history of mental illness (e.g., anxiety, depression, substance abuse)	Does the individual have a history of mental illness? For example, is there a personal or family history of anxiety disorders? In children is there evidence of high trait anxiety prior to the disaster?
50. Presence of comorbidity	Is the individual evidencing anxiety, phobias, depression, addictive behaviours and somatisation?
51. Prior exposure, to traumatic events, anniversary effects, reactive unresolved conflicts (e.g., prior violent crime victimisation)	Were the prior stressors that influenced the present reactions to the disaster (e.g., anniversary effects), or exposure to prior stressful events? Did the events reactivate prior unresolved conflicts and reactions from prior victimisation?
52. Premorbid evidence marital and familial distress	Was there marital or familial discord prior to the disaster?
53. Family vulnerability	Is the family "vulnerable" as evident in the "pile-up" of family life changes and demands? Does the family have a history of irritability with each other, depression, despair and family instability?
54. Family style of communicating	Do the family members engage in what are called "hot reactions", tending to blow-up small events into larger crises, use language that is blaming, critical, inflames reactions, and other similar "high expressed emotional" behaviours (e.g., being overprotective unwittingly reinforcing overdependent behaviours)?

(Continued)

TABLE 2.3. *(Continued)*

55. Exposure to sustained anticipatory alerts	Was the individual or group exposed to sustained anticipatory alerts?
56. Degree of preparedness	Does the individual/group/community *lack* experience and/or training in dealing with such traumatic events (disasters)? Has the individual been assigned (as compared to volunteering) for this recovery work or involuntarily assigned to live in this residential area? Is the individual or group unable to use rescue skills that he/she was trained for?
57. Exposure to low magnitude pre-existing non-traumatic, stressful life events in the last year	Was the individual (family, group) exposed to a series of low magnitude stressful events in the last year?
58. Exposure to traumatic events over the course of a lifetime	Was the individual (family, group) exposed to a series of traumatic events over the course of a lifetime?

Source: Adapted from Meichenbaum (1997). Copyright John Wiley & Sons Limited and reprinted with permission.

For youth, the most important factors according to the large scale Norris et al (2002) review were family factors. For example, in research of our own as well as others, there is a significant relationship that has been found between children's and parent's levels of hazard-related distress (e.g., Ronan, 1997a; Huzziff & Ronan, 1999; see also Norris et al., 2002), including after the September 11 attacks (Hock, Hart, Kang, & Lutz, 2004). Families are often a main source of support that promotes natural recovery from the effects of a disaster for many. However, for children, they can be sources of added stress if parents are themselves unable to regulate any of their own distress and conflict. For example, after a volcanic eruption, youth were seen to cope less adequately with stimuli related to the eruption both initially and over time if they (a) perceived their parents to be upset about the eruptions and (b) if there were upsetting home-based discussions about the eruptions (Huzziff & Ronan, 1999). Overall, parent's hazard-related distress appears as a particularly prominent, perhaps the most prominent, risk factor for childhood distress (Norris et al., 2002). Other parenting factors increasing risk include: parental psychopathology, higher levels of irritability, and lower levels of supportive parenting. While parents' distress appears to be most important here, risk does appear to increase in the presence of a number of family factors. In general, significant distress in other family members, conflict in the family, and a lack of a supportive atmosphere in the home are all risk factors. More generally, research on the overall well-being of youth have found that children benefit from consistent, predictable routines that are established by adults; consequently, when useful routines break down at home or at school, whether following a hazard or at other times, youth are likely to be at more risk for problematic functioning.

Given the fundamentally important role of parents, family, and school-based factors, it is important to understand more clearly what specifically puts adults at increased risk for problems following a disaster. Thus, in addition to the factors described earlier, other specific factors have been identified that make adults more vulnerable (Norris et al., 2002):

- more severe exposure (particularly life threat, injury, devastating loss);
- middle age (40-60 years of age);
- ethnic minority status;
- being in a family or relationship versus being single;
- prior psychological problems;
- little experience relevant to coping with a disaster;
- additional (secondary) stressors (acute or chronic);
- coping style (avoidance coping, blaming) and beliefs (lack of hope/ optimism, low self-efficacy/perceived control, low level of hardiness)
- deteriorating, weak social resources (perceived and actual social support, social connectedness).

For youth, similar specific factors including more severe exposure (e.g., direct exposure, life threat, injury, disruption), ethnic minority status, additional stressors, reduced social support, and inadequate coping have also been found to predict more distressed functioning (Huzziff & Ronan, 1999; LaGreca et al., 1996; Ronan, 1997a; Ronan & Johnston, 2003). Thus, attention to these factors through various naturally occurring as well as designed support services would be thought to be useful for youth. However, attention first to family factors appears paramount, particularly in the immediate aftermath of a hazard.

The aforementioned risk and protective factors take on more importance in the face of disasters that produce the following community level impacts: (a) injury and death, (b) loss and destruction of property that is greater than the resources (e.g., financial) available to a community, (c) breakdown in social support available in a community, and (d) the event is perceived to involve some form of human intent (e.g., neglect, maliciousness). In fact, when none of these factors are present, the risk for more than transient, normal reactions is greatly reduced. The more specific factors that appear to raise the risk of adverse, longer term reactions are when at least two of the following occur: (a) extreme property damage across a community, (b) serious financial problems that linger, (c) human factors causing the hazard, with intent being the most pernicious factor, and (d) widespread trauma based on injuries, deaths, and perception of life threat (Norris et al., 2002).

Thus, under various conditions that affect communities, families, and individuals, the expected normal recovery processes can be interrupted or stalled.

When this happens, people can develop longer term problems of the sort described earlier. Younger children may become clingier, dependent, or have temper tantrums. Children or adolescents may show symptoms of anxiety (e.g., PTSD symptoms) or depression; others may engage in minor forms of disruptive behaviour. Adults may also show problems with stress, anxiety, and depression and other problems. These initial disruptions when coupled with other forms of disruption (e.g, physical effects of the hazard; other secondary stressors that develop) then can begin to create a vicious cycle. The first step to interrupting this cycle is to try and assist people with normal recovery: to help them help themselves. When this is not possible, then more direct forms of help are called for that take into account the factors described in this chapter.

In Chapter 7, we return to this topic as we discuss interventions in school and community settings for youth and families following a hazardous event. However, and importantly from a prevention-based perspective, knowledge of the factors reviewed in this section can assist school and community-based professionals in planning education campaigns prior to a hazard, during the Readiness and Risk Reduction phase. These factors can be incorporated into programs designed to equip schools, youth, and families to be both physically as well as emotionally prepared to cope with and bounce back from a disaster or hazardous event.

Chapter 3

Community Resilience
The Role for Schools, Youth, and Families

As reviewed in Chapter 2, education campaigns and interventions have been found to assist people and households to prepare for and respond to hazards. However, there also appear to be a number of predictors of better preparedness and response. These include the idea of being bonded to, or embedded within, a community. Another predictor of increased preparedness is having children in the household (e.g., Ronan et al., 1998). Additionally, a predictor of vulnerability to the effects of hazards and mass violence is youth and family status. Given such predictors, it appears clear that an increased focus on incorporating hazards education materials within a school's curricula and linking that learning at school with family-, home-, and community-based action has the potential to have immediate, as well as longer term impact, within a community.

According to some recent census figures (U.S. Census, 1998), approximately 50% of household in the United States have youth under age 18. Similar figures are apparent for a number of other countries (e.g., New Zealand, 60%, New Zealand Census, 2000). Consequently, if schools themselves were to incorporate hazards curricula that included such activities as homework exercises that involved discussions and activities with parents or caregivers (e.g., Ronan & Johnston, 2003), the potential for an immediate impact in a very large number of households is obvious. Of course, given what we referred to in Chapter 2 as the half-life of education programs (e.g., Mileti, 1999), any impact produced would need to be reinforced over the longer term. However, that every adult has attended school at some stage in their life, the school setting is perhaps the ideal place to set the necessary foundation for long term impact in this area. In fact, schools represent a potentially ideal setting for dissemination of risk-based education programs (Slovic et al., 1981).

However, given that this potential has yet to be realized, questions emerge around such issues as to how to get such curricula incorporated into a school's overall program of study. Many different education campaigns often compete for limited space in the classroom. Perhaps a more basic issue yet is how to convince educators and administrators that hazards curricula is worthy of a place in what is routinely an already crowded schedule. Given a school engaging the idea, another question that emerges is how best to deliver such a program? What is the content, how, when, and by whom is it delivered, does it require additional training and ongoing monitoring? Who assumes accountability for its effectiveness?

This chapter begins to address these questions. First, a discussion, including a review of relevant research, is undertaken to highlight some of the potential of hazards education programs being included in school and home settings. We next then begin to consider the content, sequence, and delivery of such programs. This includes the "how to" of linking the learning from school with child- and family-based activities at home and within the larger community. Next, we address the fundamental issue of how to engage a school community and help them to assimilate hazards education materials within their setting. Then, we look into the future and discuss the longer term impact of this approach and the research necessary to help realize fully its potential. Finally, the SS4R model is presented and discussed.

THE POTENTIAL OF HAZARDS EDUCATION IN THE SHORT-TERM

As a beginning to this section, it must be said that this area of research and practice is still in its early days. Little systematic research has been carried out prior to hazardous events that involve education efforts with youth and families specifically. Research there has tended to focus on "household" preparedness and more on public education campaigns. More specific health research has been carried out following hazardous events, mainly on the effects of hazards in the mental health area (see Chapter 2). However, here again, very little research has been carried out in terms of education and intervention effectiveness, though much advice has been offered in the literature.

Readiness and Risk Mitigation

Our research team began to look into the area of hazards education for youth and families in school and community settings following a volcanic eruption in 1995.

We look at various research questions and findings related to that program of study in the Response and Recovery section that follows. However, as relates here, that initial prospective study served as an impetus to consider the value of doing earlier, prevention-based intervention in community settings including schools and with youth and families. Part of the rationale was that we know that education prior to hazards has been shown to assist adults and communities prepare more effectively for a hazard. In addition, while public education efforts have been shown to produce increased preparedness in communities (e.g., Tierney, Lindell, & Perry, 2001), the overall and sustained preparedness of a community has continued to fall short of expectations. Related, calls by the participants in the second Assessment of Research and Applications on Natural Disasters for more innovative and holistic models of hazards education and delivery (Mileti, 1999) have served as further impetus. Following Slovic et al. (1981), one main piece of an overall effort to establishing more sustainability and resilience in communities in the future involves school communities. In particular, we are clear that the vision of communities in the future engaging a resilience-based framework starts in childhood. Linked to this idea in the shorter term, as children begin to be exposed to such thinking, there is no doubt that they can then influence their own families as documented in the next few sections. In a more practical fashion, schoolchildren are potentially useful conduits for helping motivate their parents. Families also link to many others in a community. There is clearly much more potential here. However, research is necessary to begin to tap into and assess this potential. The initial research that has been done in this area is now reviewed, starting with Readiness and Risk Reduction.

Correlational Research

The research carried out thus far in this area has in fact confirmed that hazards education programs for youth are beneficial in a number of ways. First, we know that children's increased knowledge related to hazards (e.g., knowing specific emergency preparedness and response activities) is related to more realistic risk perceptions, lower levels of hazard-related fear, and lower levels of perceived hazard-related fear in their parents (Ronan et al., 2001). On the other hand, unrealistic risk perceptions (perceiving low frequency events at a higher frequency) are related to higher levels of fear, higher levels of perceived parental fear, and less confidence in the ability to cope with a future hazard.

Thus, increasing knowledge through education programs would be thought to assist youth in a variety of ways. That has indeed been the case. For example, in our first large scale study in the risk mitigation and readiness area, over 400 participants (aged 5 to 13) filled out a self-report measure that assessed a wide array of hazards relevant information (Ronan & Johnston, 1997; Ronan, Johnston, Fairley, & Daly, 2001). The areas assessed included awareness of hazards, risk perceptions, and knowledge. We found that hazards education programs helped youth increase hazards awareness and knowledge. Another benefit for those in education programs was seen in the area of risk perceptions.

As a salient example, educated children here were seen to have more realistic risk perceptions (i.e., endorsed low frequency events at lower rates). Children involved in education programs also tended to rate the likelihood of physical risk (i.e., likelihood that a hazard might "hurt you") as greater than those not involved in hazards education. Such a finding might be a concern, particularly if it were related to high levels of fear or distress. However, we found that these same children reporting educational involvement also reported fear of hazards at a much reduced rate compared to those not involved in any education program by over a factor of 2: 12% versus 28% reported being "often scared" when thinking or talking about hazards, respectively Similarly, we also found that the educated youth reported that they perceived their parents to be hazards fearful at a much reduced rate. In response to the question "do your parents get upset talking about hazards, 9% of the educated versus 22% of the uneducated youth responded 'yes'. As reviewed in Chapter 2, we know that parents' fears and stress levels in relation to a hazard's occurrence (as well as more generally) can have a significant impact on their child's functioning (e.g., Allen & Rosse, 1998; Ronan, 1997a). We also know that when fears or other problems are continually avoided, problems tend to arise. By contrast, talking about and dealing directly with fears, particularly in supportive contexts, has been shown to be useful (Ronan, 1997a; Ronan & Deane, 1998). Given this finding, it was no surprise that the educated group of youth reported more interaction with parents (e.g., more discussion) compared to the youth not involved. Thus, initial findings from this research indicate that promoting guided interaction has the potential to have benefits for youth.

Educated youth in this study also had much higher levels of factual knowledge about mitigation and emergency response. Finally, being involved in more than one education program was seen to have significant benefit: hazards knowledge overall increased by a factor of 2 for those involved in 2 or more programs compared to those involved in only 1 program. While these benefits were encouraging in this initial study (Ronan et al., 2001), we did not find any support for education program involvement as being related to increased preparedness at home. However, that research had some relevant limitations: reliance on child self-report only (versus including parent report) and a low number of preparedness items assessed.

To overcome these limitations, our next study (Ronan & Johnston, 2001) included separate child and parent reports as well as a larger pool of preparedness items from which to choose. The participants here were 560 school children and their parents or caregivers in an area subject to a wide range of hazards including floods, fires, cyclones, tsunamis, volcanic eruptions, earthquakes and chemical spills. Child participants filled out a measure similar to that included in our first study that had added to it a number of additional preparedness, planning, and practice items (see Table 2.2 in Chapter 2). Parents were also asked to fill out a questionnaire that assessed whether any of these adjustments had been carried out at home.

A main finding of this study was that, similar to our first study, education involvement had a positive impact on awareness, risk perceptions, and hazards knowledge. Further, it also found that adjustments (both child- and parent-reported) were increased as a function of youths' hazards education involvement. Further, households exposed to education on readiness reported an increased number of both simple and more effortful adjustments (e.g., adding lips to shelves, learning to put out fires, learning first aid, having home inspected for earthquake resistance, securing the house foundation) compared to those households not exposed to education. An additional aspect to this study was identifying education factors that predicted increased adjustment activities. Across child- and parent-reported adjustments, four factors emerged that predicted increased preparedness at home: (a) hazards knowledge, (b) more recent involvement in an educational program, (c) greater number of programs, and (d) increased interaction between child and parent.

While this study did not find a beneficial effect of education on emotional factors, it also did not find any negative emotional impact. We feel it is important for research in this area to document whether education efforts in this area negatively sensitize youth. One reason is that research has indicated that fear of disasters is often one of the major fears throughout childhood (e.g., Ollendick, 1983). When engaging in education efforts, those carrying out such programs need to be sure they are not creating problems or exacerbating already held fears. Thus, it is reassuring that while educated youth in this study reported some increased physical risk perceptions (likelihood of injury), they didn't report being more hazard fearful overall. Again, this underscores our general belief that exposing youth to hazards in a realistic fashion does not have to be distressing.

Other correlational studies have been initiated and carried out by people in our collaborative network—Caroline Driedger and others in the state of Washington, Chris Gregg, Bruce Houghton and others in Hawaii, and Kirsten Finnis and others in New Zealand (e.g., Finnis, Standring, Johnston, & Ronan, 2004; Gregg, Houghton, Johnston, Paton, & Swanson, 2004; Johnston, Paton, Driedger, Houghton, & Ronan, 2001). Overall, taken together, these studies have similarly provided findings supportive of the value of educating youth and families. Another recent survey-based study in Japan found that while school knowledge-based education programs were determined to be useful, additional activities, including family and community education, were more important for converting knowledge to action (Shaw, Shiwaku, Kobayashi, & Kobayashi, 2003). Later in the chapter, such ideas are expanded on in the SS4R model. However, next, we look at the role of linking school education with family education and action using an experimental design.

Experimental Research

To our knowledge, only one study has been carried out in this area. However, the study is reviewed in its own section to highlight our bias towards the evolution of this area being contingent on both sound practice and good science.

Our most recent study to date (Ronan & Johnston, 2003) involved a quasi-experimental methodology and followed from our correlational research. This study included 219 youth (ages 11 to 13 years) and their parents. Youth were randomly assigned, based on classroom, to one of two conditions. The first was designated Usual Conditions (UC) and the second, Emergency Management (EM). The UC condition consisted of a classroom based reading and discussion program held over 6 weeks that focused on hazards and disasters. The EM condition supplemented the reading and discussion with explicit focus on integrated emergency management and readiness and risk reduction themes. In particular, this condition provided specific guidance to the youth on hazard mitigation and emergency responding. It also explicitly guided youth to interact with their parents in the form of a homework discussion-based exercise aimed at increasing home-based preparedness activities.

The emergency management-focused guidance provided to the youth in the EM condition was in the form of information that youth could independently carry out (e.g., emergency response protective behaviors) and those that relied more heavily on adult participation (e.g., home- and family-based adjustments). The homework exercise included youth bringing home material that provided (a) a basis for discussions about what could be done at home to make the home more hazard-resilient, (b) a form to be filled out to better ensure discussions actually did take place, and (c) filling out the form as the family's "public statement of commitment" to carry out some adjustment activities immediately or in the near term. The form itself included a range of adjustments and the youth and parents were asked to indicate whether that adjustment had been carried out or whether they intended to carry it out. The other task was to identify two activities from that list that they would be most capable of carrying out in the "next week or two". This form was then brought back to school and used for more classroom discussion on mitigation, preparedness, and response.

Prior to the program's commencement and once again when the program was finished, children and parents separately filled out relevant measures to assess change over the course of the programs. Youth and parents filled out measures used in our previous research (see previous section, Ronan & Johnston, 2001). Overall, findings were quite clear: being exposed to hazards in a classroom setting in general (i.e., without regard to specific condition) was useful in increasing resilience both in youth and within the family and home in both problem- and emotion-focused areas. With respect to problem-focused coping, findings indicated large intervention-produced effect sizes for home-based adjustments. Both youth and parents reported a relatively large number of adjustments carried out between pre- and post-test (overall average increase of just over 4 adjustments based on child- (4.2) and parent-report (4.1)). Youth also reported significantly increased hazards-related knowledge from pre- to post-test. Similarly, in the emotion-focused domain, youths' hazard-related fear was seen to reduce significantly as was their perception of parental hazard-related fear.

In addition to the overall benefit of hazards programs generally, all of the problem-focused factors were seen to improve significantly more following the EM versus the UC condition. This finding supported our hypothesis that targeting these areas would produce additional benefits. However, it is also worth remembering that the reading and discussion program alone (UC) was sufficient to produce beneficial change in the problem-focused areas. Later, in the SS4R section, we consider the possible reasons for this finding. In addition, while the EM and UC condition both produced significant change in the emotional factors, no differences were seen between these conditions in the amount of change produced on these factors. As opposed to the problem-focused area, the EM condition did not specifically target emotional factors. While it was thought that a more specific focus on adjustments and knowledge would increase a sense of emotional control, no explicit information was included in the EM condition to assist directly with emotional coping. Given the role that such factors play in response and recovery (see Chapter 2), this is an area that has future potential.

As a consequence of these findings, support was found overall for exposing youth, and their parents, to information about hazards. The findings also by implication support adults' willingness to discuss hazards with youth versus avoiding such discussions. For example, if a young person perceives parents to be distressed or upset about hazards, one way to clarify is for parents or teachers to provide a "coping model" (Bandura, 1986). In other words, having discussions with the child about their own feelings, and how they cope with them and use them adaptively, can assist children in a variety of ways. Consequently, for local or media-covered disasters, children will often be privy to some information. Adults who try to protect children, and with the best of intentions, avoid discussions, may unintentionally exacerbate rather than reduce any fears that a child might be harboring (e.g., Ronan, 1997a).

A lack of discussion has the potential to reinforce and increase uncertainty about any information already received. Children may also begin to develop inaccurate perceptions about how parents, teachers, and other relevant adults are actually feeling about the hazard and how they are coping with those feelings. Related to this idea, youth rely on adults to solve a variety of problems. Clearly, a willingness to discuss hazards—in child-friendly ways—are part of that overall ethos. Later in this chapter, we expand on the ideas of interactive models in our discussion of the SS4R education and intervention model.

RESPONSE AND RECOVERY

Almost no research has looked into the effectiveness of school-based (or other) education or intervention programs for youth and families following a hazard. In fact, to our knowledge, only a few studies have looked at the effectiveness of intervention. On the other hand, a number of studies have looked at youth's reactions to hazards and disasters. As reviewed more comprehensively in Chapter 2, the main findings here (Ronan & Johnston, 2001) include the idea that a combination of factors appears to contribute to child and adolescent responses. Consistent with some of the major findings in the adult literature (Long, Ronan, & Perreira-Laird, 1998), the following factors have been implicated: (a) direct exposure including the perception of physical peril; (b) demographic factors (e.g., younger age, females) and other pre-existing features (e.g., medical conditions; mental health problems); (c) coping style and ability including individual coping and availability of support from others; (d) the cumulative effect of other major stressors following a hazard (Huzziff & Ronan, 1999; LaGreca et al., 1996; Ronan, 1997; Vernberg et al., 1996). However, while these factors are important, and as we continue to stress, parent's reactions and family factors appear to have a pivotal influence on youth's ability to cope effectively.

As introduced in the previous section, we also know from other research that included in the major fears of childhood are often the threat of disasters. Consequently, when a hazard does occur, the unspoken fear of a child may have been realized. Thus, even in the case of a relatively benign hazard, some children are quite likely to perceive that hazard differently than would adults. As an example, the eruption of Mount Ruapehu (New Zealand) in 1995 was a small scale event with no loss of human life. Despite media reports emphasizing interviews with adults claiming no one was overly affected, our 7-month longitudinal research findings indicated otherwise for youth (e.g., Huzziff & Ronan, 1999; Ronan, 1997a, 1997b; Ronan & Johnston, 1999).

It did appear that most of the approximately 200 children from three primary schools located near the volcano coped effectively in the immediate aftermath of the event (Ronan et al., 2000). However, a significant minority (c. 25 %) reported moderate to severe indications of distress related directly to the eruptions. Of this group, about 40% of them (i.e., approximately 10% overall) would have been considered to be distressed enough potentially to warrant a diagnosis of Post-Traumatic Stress Disorder (PTSD)[1] (Ronan, 1997b). In keeping with general findings in the literature, it was also the case that more vulnerable children in the sample (e.g., those with asthma, younger children) fared worse (Ronan, 1997a, b). In addition, other factors predicted a lesser ability to cope with the aftermath of the eruption (Huzziff & Ronan, 1999). These included negative thoughts (e.g., "I thought my world was coming to an end") as well as parent factors. Both negatively valenced discussions about the eruptions at home as well as the perception of parental upset about the eruptions predicted coping problems for youth (see also Ronan, 1997a).

---

[1] Posttraumatic Stress Disorder (PTSD) is a mental health disorder that results from witnessing an event, such as a hazard or disaster that is particularly distressing and produces a cluster of symptoms that includes re-experiencing phenomena (e.g., flashbacks, nightmares), psychic numbing /avoidance, and hyperarousal. Related to this disorder, Acute Stress Disorder is similar symptoms that are limited to a shorter time frame (American Psychiatric Association, 2000). We provided more information on this disorder in Chapter 2 and again in Chapter 7.

Indeed, 15% of the parents involved in this study also reported some level of distress related to the eruptions (Ronan et al., 2000).

Intervention Research Following a Hazard

As introduced earlier, many intervention models are available. A quick look in any search engine will uncover a tremendous variety of school-based, youth-, and family-based intervention approaches (see also LaGreca, et al., 1994; Long, Ronan, & Perreira-Laird, 1998; Saylor, 1993;). However, very little research has assessed the possible merits of these disaster focused programs. By contrast, a good amount of research in the past decade and a half has assessed the efficacy of interventions for youth and families experiencing a range of anxiety problems, including PTSD (Feather & Ronan, 2005; Kendall, Chansky, Kortlander, Kim, Ronan, Sessa, & Siqueland, 1992; McMurray & Ronan, 2005; Ronan & Deane, 1998). This includes recent meta-analyses (Huzziff & Ronan, 2005; McMurray & Ronan, 2005) that have confirmed the overall effectiveness of behaviorally-based and cognitive-behavioral (CBT) interventions (see Chapter 7 for full description).

We empirically tested an intervention based on representative behavioral and CBT models following the volcanic eruption (Ronan & Johnston, 1999). That study involved 113 youth between the ages of 7 and 13 who attended the three primary schools all within about 7 miles (11 kilometers) of the base of a volcano that erupted in September, 1995. Children in the study were randomly assigned based on school to one of two conditions both consisting of 1 hour interventions: video-based exposure and normalizing (VE) and a cognitive-behavioral (CB) intervention. The VE condition involved a presentation by a volcanologist (second author) accompanied by a 20-minute video of the eruption. In addition to discussing the general science, matters of safety in relation to the science were also presented. For example, potentially erroneous beliefs about the effects of volcanic products (e.g., lahars, ashfall) were dispelled. A clinical psychologist (senior author) presented additional information about normal fears and other features of the physical science from a layperson's reaction. The intention here was to normalize fears as well as control for time (i.e., the amount spent in the CB intervention).

The CB intervention included all features of the VE approach (exposure, normalizing of fears, science information) and some additional features of a CB approach. The main vehicle here was a "coping modeling" approach. That is, the intent here was to demonstrate, or model, coping with adverse (as well as normal) effects of the eruptions. This included modeling problem-solving strategies (e.g., how to modify negative self-talk, how to seek information and support) and the idea of self-reinforcement (e.g., praising oneself for engaging in problem-solving attempts). One area modeled was how to problem-solve and seek information to confirm or deny the erroneous belief that ash was poisoning the water supply. The foundation for this intervention comes from a treatment approach that the first author helped develop in the late 1980s and has been involved with for over 15 years (e.g., Kendall et al., 1992; Ronan & Deane, 1998).

The study itself involved 4 separate assessments done over a 7-month interval. Two assessments were carried out prior to the intervention, 1 and 3 months following the initial eruption. The second two assessments were carried out (a) immediately after the intervention and (b) 4 months later (i.e., 7 months following the initial eruption). The purpose of the first two assessments was to assess the effect of time on participants' self-reported levels of eruption-related distress (PTSD related features) and coping ability (with stimuli related to the eruptions). The second two assessments were used to assess the immediate effectiveness of the intervention as well as longer-term functioning of the youth involved.

The overall findings of this study indicated that both interventions were seen to be effective and not significantly different from each other in terms of effectiveness. In terms of effect sizes (ES), and for those children who were deemed distressed outside the normal range (n = 69), and as initially described in Chapter 2, time was seen to produce an average ES (Cohen's d) of .80 on PTSD-related distress; the interventions, an average ES of .52. In terms of coping with stimuli related to the eruptions, time produced an average ES of .22; the interventions, an average ES of .31. In other words, the coping ability of youth was seen to change more following the intervention than it had during the 2 month preceding interval (.22 versus .31). By contrast, PTSD distress scores changed more during the 2 month pre-treatment interval than following intervention (.80 versus .55). That time is more of an ally for distress symptoms than for active coping ability was confirmed during the 4 month follow-up interval following intervention. That is, PTSD scores continued to decrease whereas coping scores were maintained but did not continue to change (i.e., continued to reflect post-treatment improvement only). In addition, the PTSD and coping scores of the children who participated were compared with another group of children not involved in the intervention at the follow-up interval. Compared to the untreated children, the treated group scores were both significantly different in the directions hypothesized. In this study, and perhaps because of the relatively benign nature of the disaster, no additional intervention was deemed necessary based on the final assessment. We expand on this study and place it in the context of a sequenced intervention approach in Chapter 7. We describe the philosophy of a sequenced approach later in this chapter.

Based on these findings, the speculation in the literature (e.g., LaGreca et al., 1996; Long et al., 1998; Saylor, 1993) that school- and behaviorally-based interventions can be effective was confirmed. However, given the wide variety of intervention models on offer in the literature and on the worldwide web, it is important for practitioners to be able to sort out what programs, or what elements of what programs, will work best in school settings, for youth, for families. Thus, while the potential has been confirmed, more research establishing what programs, and what components, are best for what youth under what conditions is clearly necessary. That said, it does not preclude us from helping sort the "wheat from the chaff" in subsequent chapters to begin to establish what at this point constitutes evidence-based programs in this area. In those chapters, we will turn to related literature to begin to establish what education or intervention factors appear to have most promise. In the SS4R section, we consider what school, youth, and family factors are best attended to first, and what practitioner qualities might help produce maximal gains for schools, youth, and families. In Chapter 7, we discuss how evidence-based interventions can be carried out from the time of the hazard and how to maximize available resources for those efforts.

THE POTENTIAL OF HAZARDS EDUCATION IN THE LONGER-TERM

Through the research carried out to date, there is little doubt about the potential of school-based programs as playing perhaps even a key role in promoting community resilience to hazards. Based on this potential, the next question that arises is how best to harness this potential in the best interests of schools, youth, families, and the wider community. We agree with the main thrust of Dennis Mileti and our other colleagues in the field (Mileti, 1999; Tierney et al., 2001) that a shift in thinking is necessary to embed the idea of resilience to disasters within a larger context. One of the main themes of that shift is moving from linear to more integrated models. While school-based programs certainly do not represent the panacea here, they most certainly represent a relatively untapped resource. To begin to consider the longer term potential of schools as a platform for assisting the inculcation of such thinking, we begin first where we left off in the previous section. Standalone programs in schools have their place in the future. Given that a six week one period per day reading and discussion program produced an average increase of four adjustments per household is encouraging. However, we feel that this only highlights what is a greater potential for longer term and sustained impact. Through education efforts, an ethos of hazards sustainability can be embedded within youth, within families, and within schools and communities (see Table 3.1). We provide more detail on this longer term potential in the next section on SS4R practice principles and chapters that follow.

TABLE 3.1. Education across the 4R's: The Move toward Integration

I. Standalone Programs
  A. The role for risk and protective factors
  B. Use of evidence from literature on Readiness, Response and Recovery
  C. Use of evidence from related literature (psychology, education, others)
  D. The role for theory

II. A Move Toward Integration
  A. Integrating material within the wider curricula
  B. Increased links with family and home
  C. Links with the community
  D. Putting it together: a central role for schools in community efforts

TARGETING RESPONSE AND RECOVERY THROUGH READINESS: THE STRENGTHENING SYSTEMS 4R PREVENTION MODEL

The first aim of our SS4R model is to prevent problems from occurring. Consequently, this prevention-based model assumes that the best interventions are carried out prior to a hazard's occurrence and equip the community with the means necessary to cope with response and recovery. Therefore, in line with a hazards sustainability model, we emphasize readiness-based educational programs that link schools with families and link schools and families with other community initiatives. Readiness-based public and school education programs to date have routinely focused on assisting households and others in a community to prepare physically for a hazardous event. Stockpiling food and water, having emergency plans, making structural modifications to buildings, buying insurance and many other adjustments are intended primarily to help people mitigate physical risk. Of course, physical problems do most certainly occur following a hazard (e.g., injuries, deaths, property damage, lifeline disruption). However, major psychosocial difficulties also occur including anxiety (e.g., PTSD), grief and depression, the development of secondary stressors, a reduction in social support, an increase in coping strategies that are unhelpful, and a loss of various routines. Further, as discussed at more length in Chapter 7, we know that there is a relationship between problem- and emotion-focused coping. For example, when distress is high or when one is depressed and without energy, in either case it can be very difficult to carry out those activities and tasks that can assist physical recovery efforts.

Consequently, readiness campaigns that consider incorporating such findings to help people be equipped both physically as well as psychosocially would be thought to be more effective in helping people with increased confidence in their ability to cope when a hazardous event does occur (see Chapter 5). Such confidence, or self-efficacy, would then be thought to equip people to cope more effectively when disaster does strike. However, a more primary problem related to low preparedness has to do with low levels of concern about risks and a range of beliefs that can reduce concern.

The Problem of Motivation and Intention

As reviewed in Chapter 2, a primary problem in the area of hazards readiness and recovery relates to almost universally low levels of preparation prior to a hazard by individuals, households, and organizations, even in high hazard areas. Given low levels of readiness, it is then no surprise that most research demonstrates less than adequate or coordinated responses to large scale events. Given these problems, recovery from a hazardous event can be made more complicated when those who most require assistance are not equipped psychologically to help themselves and may in fact not come forward for assistance. Given the link between emotion- and problem-focused coping (Lazarus & Folkman, 1984; Lazarus, 1999), people are better able to engage in problem-solving activities, including various forms of physical recovery, when they are better equipped emotionally.

As detailed earlier, links have also been established between parent and child emotional well-being and outcomes. For example, when parents have emotional difficulties, their youth's emotional behavioral functioning may be compromised. For example, youth who have emotional and behavioral problems are more likely to have mothers and fathers with emotional and behavioral problems. For example, when children have problems, parents' decision-making and problem-solving has been found to mirror the child's difficulty. Relevant to the current discussion, parents of anxious children tend more often to reinforce avoidant solutions to problems (e.g., Dadds, Bennett, & Ropee, 1996; Dadds, 2002). They also tend to be over controlling or overprotective (Siqueland, Sternberg, & Kendall, 1996; Stuart & Ronan, 2005). Thus, the fact that parenting and family factors predict childhood distress following a hazard is no great surprise. However, those families that might be most prone to problems, including those with parent and child emotional difficulties and a whole host of other factors identified in the psychological literature, may also be less likely to prepare for them. For example, in families where anxiety is more pronounced, and as just introduced, families appear to engage in problem-solving that is at times characterized more by avoidance than approach. Obviously, this is a coping style not best suited to getting ready for a potentially stressful event. Another example here is that families with lesser means may feel that preparation is beyond their resources (e.g., Tierney et al., 2001).

Even for those families without any identified psychosocial, financial, or other difficulties, the idea of preparing for an event that may or may not occur at some unidentified time in the future really leads to the question not of why do most people not prepare to wondering about "why do some people actually prepare?" As reviewed in Chapter 2 and earlier in this chapter, a growing list of programs and factors has been compiled that begin to answer that question. Those risk and protective factors are those that should be considered in any program that we undertake. Additionally, as seen earlier, continuing efforts to encourage the public to prepare are worthwhile. Education programs in school and community settings to date have produced results encouraging enough to continue to focus attention on how better to do the job.

However, even if we take into account all risk and protective factors in any given education program, rates of preparation are still likely to be relatively low. Various means have been introduced over time to explain this phenomenon, including the idea that communities often have not fully considered the value of preparing. The idea of incorporating along with the "how to prepare" messages, emphasizing the value of preparatory activities (e.g., to protect children, lives, property, financial investment; its value for other purposes) appears to have merit. As seen in Chapter 2, such values are related to increased behavioral intentions as well as actually engaging in the behaviors themselves (i.e., adjustment adoption activities) (e.g., Lindell & Whitney, 2000). In addition, if people intend or plan to do something, it is much more likely they will eventually do it (e.g., Paton, 2003).

To put this last idea into other words, people may consider or make changes in accord with their "stage of change." The Stage of Change model (Prochasha et al., 1992) posits that people who are posed with a problem will be at different points in the change continuum: ranging from not considering taking any action at all in an area (i.e., precontemplative stage) to considering taking some action (contemplative stage) to actually taking action (action stage) to solve that problem. While change happens naturally for some problems and some people, for other it does not. In fact, even with very good reasons for changing (e.g., life threatening conditions exacerbated by lifestyle), people will resist making necessary adjustments (e.g., stop smoking, diet and exercise more) (Miller & Rollnick, 2002). Consequently, the idea that occasional public or school education campaigns are going to lead to long-term behavioral change in a community that is dealing with much more in the way of pressing concerns is an unfounded notion.

The links between beginning to think about a possible change, intention to change, and actual change behavior assumes a few factors. First is the idea of increased awareness that there might even be a problem (e.g., hazard awareness). Second is the idea that the problem is important enough to continue to attend to and consider (e.g., personalized risk perception); and that it is pressing enough to produce an emotional reaction (e.g., "hazard concern"; anxiety) that activates thoughts of making a change (e.g., Paton et al., 2001; Tierney et al., 2001).

In their work on motivating people to make change, Miller and Rollnick (2002) talk about this sequence as being "willing, able, and ready." The first factor, willingness, has to do with how much a person wants to change. They talk about the idea of a discrepancy between a desirable state of affairs and one's current status. To enhance a person's willingness to change, the idea of developing and resolving discrepancy is designed to help a person see more clearly the value of making a change.

The second element, ability, has to do with a person's confidence that change can be brought about. Two main elements are implicated here: general efficacy (i.e, that the course of action (e.g., adjustment) will work) and self-efficacy (i.e., that they believe they can carry out that course of action). Finally, the third element, readiness, reflects that the perceived importance of change (willingness) and confidence (ability) are by themselves insufficient. This is best captured in the idea of "I'll do it tomorrow." Thus, readiness is intended to capture the idea of prioritization of change. Thus, for change to occur, people need to feel not only that it is important to change and that that they can make the change (i.e., contemplative stage), but that they also need to have the feeling that they need to do it now (action stage).

Thus, in terms of activating, or triggering, intentions and change, the idea is to promote increased emotional investment and reflection (e.g., through developing a discrepancy between goals and current status; weighing up the pros and cons of change; activation of hope and other emotions). This process summarized by Miller and Rollnick (2002):

> It is discrepancy that underlies the perceived importance of change: no discrepancy, no motivation. The discrepancy is generally between present status and a desired goal, between what is happening and how one would want things to be (one's goals). Note that this is the difference between two *perceptions*, and the degree of discrepancy (also a perception) is affected by a change in either. The larger the discrepancy, the greater the importance of change. . . . So the challenge is to first intensify and then resolve ambivalence by developing discrepancy between the actual present and the desired future.

In Miller and Rollnick's view, ambivalence and discrepancy are not obstacles to change but what makes change possible. How this happens is through what is referred to as "change talk." Change talk refers to discussions—motivating discussions and a person's self-talk—that reflect reasons for making a change. The types of change talk include:

- disadvantages of the status quo;
- advantages of change;
- optimism for change (including general and self-efficacy);
- intention or commitment to change.

As the decisional balance starts to move in the direction of favoring change, the change talk can then begin to reflect more commitment to a change in behavior. In this way, this approach is designed to elicit a person's own intrinsic motivation versus that which is imposed by external means (e.g., statutory requirements, monetary reasons, pressure imposed by others in a social or organizational network). However, as a relevant aside, we agree with Miller and Rollnick's view that both means of change are not mutually exclusive. As discussed in Chapter 5, mandated building codes and land use plans can sit alongside an individual's or family's willingness to do additional activities deemed to be in their own best interest.

Consequently, this SS4R principle assumes that risk communication and hazards education and intervention programs that are better able to elicit intrinsic motivation to change are more likely to produce initial as well as longer-lasting change. In the case of the initial work of a hazards education program in the short term as discussed earlier, there is already some built-in motivation likely to be apparent for many. That is, a finding reviewed in Chapter 2 is that households that have children tend to prepare for a hazard more often than those households without children. Why this is so has never been specified. However, it is not too much of a leap to assume that having children in a household at least for some would increase discrepancy of the sort that we have been discussing: between a current status (unprepared) juxtaposed against a value (to protect children) and related goal state (prepare in order to protect children and the household).

In general support of that idea, as reviewed in Chapter 2, Lindell and Whitney (2000) found that efficacy perceptions—including the belief that adjustments would be effective in (a) protecting people and (b) protecting property—were correlated with actual adjustment adoption. In fact, this cluster of beliefs was the most strongly correlated of all the factors measure in their study with both adoption as well as intention to adopt. In other words, the belief that engaging in an adjustment would protect people and households makes it more likely that people will consider as well as engage in change-related behavior. By contrast, beliefs about inconvenience attributes (cost, skill, time, effort, and needing cooperation from others) were not related to intentions or actual adjustment adoption nor were risk perceptions (belief that a damaging earthquake would occur within 5 years). In other words, the value of protecting persons and protecting property may outweigh the disadvantages of such activities as well as beliefs about a hazard's immediacy.

Our studies have also found that promoting increased interaction between youth and families as a result of hazards education improves home preparedness (Ronan & Johnston, 2001, 2003). In our later study, as detailed earlier, children in the 6 week interactive condition (Emergency Management (EM) condition) were asked to bring a homework exercise with them and talk with their parents about whether a list of 23 adjustment activities had been carried out, whether they intended to carry them out, and to pick from the list two activities they felt they were most capable of doing within the next week or two. They were then asked to bring the form back for classroom based discussions that focused, amongst other things, on specifics having to do with risk mitigation and emergency preparedness. Predictably, as reported by youth and separately by parents, this group was seen to have more change in adoption of home-based adjustments compared to that reported by the Usual Conditions (UC) group from pre- to post-test. However, while the difference in the magnitude of change was significant between groups, the Usual Condition group also reported significant changes across the pre- to post-test interval. In fact, whereas the EM condition reported an increase from 5.8 to 11.2 (child-reported mean change of 5.4 adjustments) and 10.3 to 14.7 (parent; mean change, 4.4), the UC condition reported a change from 7.00 to 10.07 (child; 3.1) and 9.9 to 13.4 (parent; 3.5). Thus, in using the parent report as a benchmark here, there was a magnitude difference of less than one adjustment per household reported (i.e., 4.4 versus 3.5). In addition, for those more statistically inclined, the standard deviations across parent-reported conditions were virtually identical meaning that variability in responding was similar across groups.

The upshot as relates here is that:

> . . . [while] it is unclear what produced these benefits . . . , it is the case that children, and their parents, in both conditions filled out the hazard adjustment measure prior to the start of each program. Such initial exposure may have initiated increased communication and activity at home and school that may have been reflected in (increased adjustment adoption) (Ronan & Johnston, 2003, p. 1018).

The issue then to be considered is if this premise is true, what was it specifi-cally about this exposure to preparation materials that motivated changes? Our premise is that one candidate is most certainly the creation of a discrepancy for both child and parent. For youth, such a discrepancy may have come from perceiv-ing an expectation from school, from peers, and perhaps from their own sense of safety. For parents, we would suggest that the primary candidate there is the same as was found in Lindell and Whitney—a discrepancy between current household status and the value or goal state of being able to protect their household and the people within it (i.e., their children and themselves). Alternatively, the motivation might simply be initiated by indulging a child who has come home from school full of enthusiasm for having a family emergency plan, for having food, water and other materials necessary for 72 hours, for strapping the water heater, and so forth.

We would add that the premise for motivation as a key issue holds for response and recovery. Those who need help may not be motivated to engage with help providers owing to avoidance coping (e.g., withdrawal, isolation) and other factors (e.g., lack of energy, stigma). They too may benefit from efforts aimed at assisting them to see a discrepancy between their current state (e.g., distress) and other end states (e.g., their own and their children's, spouse's, and family's welfare) as well as outreach (see Chapter 7).

Links between Systems: Strengthening Interactions

Compatible with a local hazards sustainability model, another main principle in our model targets strengthening links first between various aspects of a community with respect to hazards education and intervention across the 4Rs. It is our firm contention that the school-youth-family linkages can be linked in with other vital networks in a community. In Chapter 4, we look at a mapping of these linkages and point out more specifically the role for the school-youth-family linkage that this book emphasizes. In our model, we assume that the first links have to be estab-lished and strengthened within the school community including between the school and its youth. Such initial linkages when well established are first and foremost thought to be working as a primary prevention for future hazards management in a local community. In other words, helping inculcate a hazards sus-tainability model within the adults of tomorrow is a first step. Of course, singular education programs are unlikely to produce long-term benefit as was documented in Chapter 2. With education programs having a certain half-life, it is vital to think about sustaining efforts over time in school and community settings. How to do this we take up in later chapters.

However, the school-youth linkage also is intended to have more immediate benefits. For example, as reviewed earlier, education has been found to increase hazards knowledge. In turn, hazards knowledge including that related to emer-gency preparedness has been shown to be related to additional benefits (e.g., lower levels of hazards related fear, more accurate risk perceptions). In addition, those youth involved in hazards education in two of our studies, including our experimental study, reported perceiving lower levels of hazard related fear in their parents (Ronan et al., 2001; Ronan & Johnston, 2003). Thus, the school-youth linkage has an important role to play both currently and for the future.

Following this most basic linkage, our model then moves outward first to home and then to other community-based stakeholders in what might be referred to as a "spreading activation network." With respect to the first such linkage, with the home and family, we have reviewed research that demonstrates that potential. However, those programs might be improved through the inclusion of some additional evidence-based features. This includes features designed to assist with home-based preparedness as well as to promote links between the family setting and other community systems. With respect to moving outward from the school-youth-family, the idea is to establish various linkages or partnerships between the child and community, school and community, family and community. How these linkages might look in practice we begin to address in Chapter 4. This includes addressing a real life example of such linkages established through a preparedness program done in Orting, Washington, some related research, and some additional initiatives.

Multiple-Gating Stepped Care Approach to Prevention and Service Delivery

The main idea here is to be able to do "more with less" (Davison, 2000). The two related notions of multiple gating and stepped care involve, respectively, parsimonious allocation of assessment (e.g., Hinshaw, March, & Abikoff, 1997) and intervention resources (e.g., Haaga, 2000). Given the fact that communities' resources are often stretched even during non-hazard times, a large scale event can make meager resources more scant yet (e.g., Tierney et al., 2001). The ability to access financial and other necessary resources represents an ongoing concern for those involved in various aspects of emergency management (e.g., Haddow & Bullock, 2003). Of course, this includes most aspects of a community: government agencies, non-governmental agencies, search and rescue, fire, police, military, and others including schools.

A multiple-gating, stepped care (MGSC) model of assessment and intervention is designed specifically to capitalize on those resources that are available to address needs within a community potentially affected by problems including hazards (e.g., Johnston & Ronan, 2000; Ronan et al., 2005). The model itself involves the following components: (a) assessment using multiple gates, (b) interventions that are sequenced and start at a more basic levels and move progressively to those that are more intensive and family and individually-focused, and a (c) self-correcting feature designed to assist those not helped at earlier gates. This self-correcting idea is summarized by Davison (2000): "[a]n inherent feature and advantage of (MGSC) is that it self-corrects; that is, it forces one to monitor constantly the effects of one's interventions and to adjust subsequent strategies based on what has just happened" (p. 582).

The idea here of course is to assess whether basic forms of assistance, requiring relatively minimal resourcing, can help larger groups of people. While the ideas for this model are based on assisting those who have already developed problems, it is readily applicable to a prevention model of care. In the readiness phase, as discussed in later chapters, this would include sequencing education programs across time and starting with simple messages for younger children. However, at the same time, these simple messages can be linked with interactive material designed to help motivate parents to participate in the child's learning as well as encouraging home-based readiness activities.

Similarly, during response and recovery, examples of basic forms of intervention would include self-help information (e.g., emergency management guidelines; simple ways of coping and seeking assistance) provided through various forms of community level and support-based assistance (e.g., "therapy by walking around" (see Chapter 7), videotapes, television broadcasts, newspapers, radio, computer programs, classrooms, books). Another example, requiring more resourcing but still representing an early gate, would be larger group- or school-based interventions carried out by teachers or perhaps others (e.g., emergency management professionals, school psychologists, scientists). At each successive step, or gate, the job is to be able to identify those who have not been assisted and to increase the resourcing necessary to provide adequate assistance to the majority of those people. This iterative, self-corrective process then is intended to continue until all in the targeted catchments have been provided adequate assistance.

The Practitioner as Scientist I: Accountability and Evaluation of Helping Efforts

Practitioners are not always held accountable for outcomes in education and intervention programs. In working with children and families with psychosocial problems, no accountability for producing desirable outcomes is the norm. Rather, here, the expectations usually focus on number of "contact hours" spent with children and families. Similarly, in helping communities prepare for emergencies, research on the effectiveness of those efforts is undertaken by a few but certainly not the majority.

While larger scale research of the sort reviewed in this book is certainly necessary, it is important here to emphasise that we value a "local science" model of service delivery, which in fact is an integral feature of a MGSC approach (Ronan, Finnis, & Johnston, 2005). In other words, we believe it is vital to helping efforts that progress is actually measured, day-to-day, child-by-child, family-by-family, school-by-school, community-by-community, and program-by-program. Given low levels of accountability for producing outcomes both generally and with respect to the 4Rs, ongoing measurement of progress has a number of advantages. First, and foremost, it increases accountability for the change process. Given that helping efforts are designed to encourage various approach-based coping skills in youth, families, schools, and the community, we are also obliged to do similarly with respect to our own practice.

In doing so, it also provides the recipients of services or education programs (e.g., a community, a school, a family, a child) with tangible feedback about those helping efforts. Ongoing evaluation also provides useful information about whether current forms of assistance are "hitting the mark." If they are not, then we are able to adjust services accordingly. In this way, it can serve as a proxy for assessing the integrity, or fidelity, of service delivery (i.e., being carried out in the manner intended). In relation to this point, given the role of expectations in the change process (i.e., those with more hope and confidence do better), a willingness to engage in monitoring and assume increased accountability would be thought to increase recipients', and perhaps even our own, confidence in services being delivered. Finally, a MGSC model rests on ongoing assessment to identify who is getting assistance, and who may not be responding, at a particular step of the intervention continuum.

Potential disadvantages include what may be perceived as a need for evaluation procedures and personnel that tax current resources. We would emphasize here that a main idea of the practitioner as local scientist is to keep it relatively simple and within resource capacity. Pragmatic forms of evaluation can be used with effectiveness—and, we would add, are most certainly better than no evaluation whatsoever. More detail is provided in later chapters on the steps in a stepped care program prior to, during, and following a hazardous event. For now, and put simply, we strongly recommend this as part of usual practice. Such evaluation efforts are not only possible for busy practitioners, but that they are also part of truly quality service delivery.

The Practitioner as Scientist II: Follow the Evidence

In a scientist-practitioner model, one responsibility relates to the idea of local science as described in the previous section. Another integral component relates to the value of the practitioner looking towards the research literature to inform practice. Similar in a number of professions, the gold standard dictating "best practice" in those professions has often been the randomized, controlled clinical trial. However, more recent discussions in the literature have pointed to other methodologies—including correlational—as informing practice. We do agree that the gold standard in this field should rest in experimental, and longitudinal, forms of research (see Chapter 9). However, the main form of research across the 4Rs to date has been correlational and cross-sectional. Given a dearth of experimental research, we do value greatly the accumulating databases that are reviewed in this book as they represent the core of our own educational and intervention practice. We would go so far as to say that practitioners who do not consider the evidence when designing education and intervention programs are reneging on their professional responsibility. In addition, research has demonstrated that professionals tend to drift away from keeping current with the research literature after they finish their professional training programs. In fact, it is our guess that those of you who are already in practice and reading this have not succumbed to this tendency. Therefore, it is imperative that you keep the message of evidence-based practice at the forefront of your own practice, that you continue to advocate for its use, and, if you are a student, that you make that continuing commitment to its role in your own practice.

The Role of the Messenger

As described in Chapter 2, the characteristics of the risk communication message and the recipient are important features that determine whether a message is taken up. However, we would add, based on research in educational and psychological areas, that characteristics of the messenger are highly important. For example, in mental health research, interventions are found to be more effective when they are delivered by practitioners who are perceived as likable and friendly. In addition, those who are better able to provide structure and specifics to the intervention (e.g., setting a specific agenda, use of homework), while remaining flexible to individual needs, are also better able to produce outcomes (e.g., Chu & Kendall, 2004; Kazantzis, Deane, & Ronan, 2000). Finally, and particularly important in the current context, those practitioners who are able to instil hope in those with whom they work are also likely to have the person be more motivated, engage more readily with the intervention, and experience better outcomes (e.g., Clarkin & Levy, 2004). Hope is related to an emerging optimism that fuels motivation to change as discussed earlier. Whereas pessimism is related to feelings that can be characterized by low levels of energy and activity (e.g., depression), optimism and hope are those that are linked with more of an energizing function that can provide additional fuel for the intention and change process. In fact, we know that readiness to change and higher activity levels are predictors of benefits for people trying to change (Chu & Kendall, 2004; Clarkin & Levy, 2004). Thus, the matter of practitioners instilling optimism and hope, engaging in positive forms of change talk, and, very importantly, believing in their approach and in their ability to make a difference, is not discussed often in the readiness and recovery literature. However, we think that, along with using specific forms of guidance, multiple and consistent messages, linking with other trusted sources (Mileti, 1999) and other factors (see Chaper 2 and first sections of Chapter 3), it is vital to embody certain qualities that are more likely to lead to change in school, family, and community contexts. These are high levels of activity, optimism, believing in the messages being promoted, a commitment to quality control, and a belief in the capacity for people to make change.

TABLE 3.2. The SS4R Approach to Hazards Education: Motivating, Engaging, and Priming the Community to Think About, Talk About, and Do

---

Principles

1. *First motivate and engage, then do*
   a. encourage intention formation: a role for concern, promote efficacy of adjustments, the role of promoting and resolving discrepancy
   b. be specific, consistent, use multiple media
   c. be interactive
   d. emphasize specific forms of doing across time; developmentally-based programming
   e. the role for hope and active participation
   f. the role of the messenger/practitioner
2. Encourage links within and between systems: *interactive community problem solving approach*
   a. multidisciplinary efforts; problem-solving model
   b. education efforts (i.e., school-student link; schools linking with families through youth; youth-family link; school-community link; family-community link; youth-community link)
3. *Evidence-based practice:* target risk and protective factors; integrating research evidence into practice; evaluate practice
4. Target response and recovery through readiness: *prevention as primary*
5. *Multiple Gating Stepped Care* (MGSC) approach to service delivery
   a. MGSC model of prevention and intervention
   b. Accountability for outcomes and the role for pragmatic evaluation
6. Promote problem- and emotion-focused coping; *linking physical and psychosocial factors* in planning, response, and recovery
   a. develop approach versus avoidance coping, sense of self-efficacy, positive outcome expectancies
   b. children's reliance on adult models and adult coping; role of support from others in a community
7. *Messenger attributes and support:* motivation and engagement abilities; leaderships skills; good communication skills; high activity levels; providing hope on evidence foundation; flexibility; relationship and structuring skills; high levels of personal accountability; support those involved through recognition and providing for personal skill development.

The basic features of our model are summarized in Table 3.2.

As we turn to Chapter 4, another attribute that we consider essential is the ability to develop collaborative relationships with a variety of others in a school and community, including other professional disciplines.

Chapter 4

Community Resilience
A Partnership and Multidisciplinary Perspective

In terms of the foundation necessary to help communities prepare, we have reviewed information on the evidence basis, including the role for schools, youth, and families. As additionally emphasized in Chapter 3, the first step is to deal directly with the problem of low levels of preparedness by focusing directly on motivation and engagement. Once motivated, those targeted in education and intervention programs then have a greater likelihood of moving from passive recipients to active participants in engaging with educational and intervention material. To get this process started, the first step is to develop collaborative partnerships to begin to build motivational momentum. Multidisciplinary collaborations also have the potential to maximize content and delivery of linked school and community programs (Ronan et al., 2000).

Prior to talking specifically about the partnership role for schools, youth, and families, background material on multidisciplinary features of disaster management is provided to give a context to the idea of partnerships.

MULTI-ORGANIZATIONAL AND MULTIDISCIPLINARY APPROACHES TO DISASTER MANAGEMENT

The management of complex emergencies and disasters has highlighted the need for multiorganizational and multidisciplinary inputs into the decision making process within schools and local communities. In an integrated emergency management (IEM) environment, inter-agency communication is necessary to facilitate the understanding of complex, dynamic and evolving emergencies, and to provide information for decision making (Paton et al., 1998). By their very nature, disasters create a decision environment that is complex and which differs substantially from that within which decision expertise and support systems develop (Flin, 1996). Emergency managers and other decision makers can be called upon to deal with inadequately defined, changing, and sometimes competing, goals under considerable time and physical pressures. It can also involve making decisions in multi-jurisdictional and multi-agency contexts where the necessary expertise is dispersed geographically (Paton et al, 1999; Galley et al., 2004).

While some communication and decision-making problems emanate from the hazard effects themselves (e.g., flood waters interrupting communications equipment), inadequate crisis management systems—particularly in relationship to an organization's ability to access, interpret and utilise scientific information—are often a problem (Ronan et al., 2000). An example of this was illustrated by the lack of warning given to residents of eastern Washington (U.S.A.) after the May 1980 eruption of Mount St. Helens of the impending ash falls (Saarinen & Sell, 1985). The 1980 eruption of Mount St Helens was the most significant eruption in the United States this century, killing 57 people and causing in excess of US$ 1 billion in damage (Lipman & Mullineaux, 1981). On 20 March 1980, a sequence of earthquakes was recorded beneath Mount St Helens, ending 123 years of quiescence. Seven days later steam explosions commenced at the summit and over the next two months earthquakes and minor steam eruptions continued, accompanied by growth of the volcano's north flank. At 8:32 am (local time) on 18 May 1980, an earthquake-triggered collapse removed much of the north flank of the cone to form a massive avalanche (i.e., debris avalanche) that travelled 18 km downstream and was followed by an explosive (lateral) blast, devastating an area of 600 km^2. Lahars were generated by the rapid melting of snow and ice and flowed down a number of valleys. The eruption continued for 9 hours, with the column reaching 15 miles (25 km) in height. Heavy ash falls occurred over much of northern USA. The city of Yakima is approximately 10 miles (135 km) from Mt St Helens, with a population of around 50, 000, received about 10 mm of sand-sized ash on 18 May 1980. This caused the city to undertake a major clean-up operation and resulted in severe problems to its sewage system (Johnston, 1997). Prior to the eruption, the city had made no provision for dealing with the possible impacts of ash fall despite the release of information and a warning from the USGS that Mount St Helens posed a significant threat (Crandell & Mullineaux, 1978). Most officials reported not receiving the published material describing the potential threat until after the ash falls had occurred (Johnston, 1997). This story was repeated in many communities across Washington and Montana (Warwick et al., 1981, Saarinen & Sell, 1985).

The technical difficulties in accessing and utilizing information, commonly reported by response agencies and the public, may reflect inadequacies in the

FIGURE 4.1. Clean-up operations after only 1 centimetre of ash fall in Yakima, USA, following the 1980 Mt St Helens eruption (photo City of Yakima).

nature, content and timing of the data furnished by scientific agencies. However, in a number of cases, the scientific information is adequate. In these cases, the emergence of problems in response can frequently be attributed to the process of transforming data into a form that other disciplines (e.g., emergency managers, press, school systems) and the public can understand. Part of this translation problem has been linked to the assumptions commonly made by both the scientific community and response agencies (Dynes,1994). Dynes (1994) describes a range of consequences of the "dominant emergency planning model" that has existed since the "civil defence" era of the 1950's. It has the following characteristics:

- It assumed social chaos and dramatic disjuncture during the emergency;
- It assumed the reduced capacity of individual and social structures to cope;
- It created artificial social structures to deal with reduced capacity;
- It expressed at times a distrust of individuals and structures to make intelligent decision in emergencies;
- It placed responsibility in a top down authority structure to make the right decisions and to communicate those "right" decisions in official information to ensure actions;
- It created a closed system intended to deal with important emergencies.

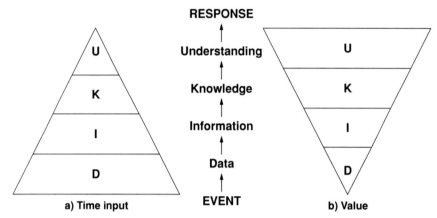

FIGURE 4.2. The information-knowledge transition showing the relationship between time input required and the value of each stage.

Unfortunately, elements of the old system still exist despite a move towards a more integrated, evidence-based emergency management model, emphasizing cooperative community-based problem-solving.

One consequence of the old model is that problems in coordination and a lack of pre-existing relationships can make linkages during a disaster problematic. As illustrated by Figure 4.2, considerable scientific effort and time is invested in producing data. In its raw form, it has little value for response agencies. Considerable effort is required in rendering data meaningful in the context of decision making, planning, and response by individuals and agencies with specific roles and responsibilities. There is often an inverse relationship between the amount of effort and cost required to move up the information value chain and the usefulness to society.

Despite the fact that this relationship has been documented (e.g. Saarinen & Sell, 1985; Paton el al., 1998), many continuing coordination problems have also been documented both prior to and following an event between scientific and response agencies across a variety of hazardous events. For example, keeping schools and other community settings closed for too long following a disaster may lead to a perception of continuing disruption. A number of reasons can lead to a delay—certainly, one of them can be a lack of linkage between response agencies and the school. In one recent example, schools remained closed after flooding owing to water availability being limited. However, the entire community was experiencing the same disruption. Water delivered to the community, along with portable toileting, might have seen schools re-opening in a more efficient manner. As described in earlier chapters (see also Chapter 7), returning communities to a sense of routine is recommended to assist the recovery process. With more understanding resulting from increased coordination between various disciplines and agencies, or perhaps simply a school's singular resolve to re-open, may serve as

FIGURE 4.3. Flood damage from the February 2004 floods in the central North Island, New Zealand. (photo D. Johnston)

an impetus in such a situation. In fact, we have suggestive evidence that resuming routine and normal operations in schools sooner after an event has a beneficial effect on youth (Ronan et al., 2005).

DEVELOPING CAPABILITY

A first step in developing a common understanding involves the networking between the scientific community, response agencies, schools, and communities. Response agencies and the public commonly presume that scientific providers will go beyond supplying scientific advice and provide information relevant for all their information and decision needs. This is usually the exception rather than the rule. Thus, while there is an equal onus on scientific response agencies to work with others to make data understandable, other organizations will do well to consider that this may not necessarily be the case.

To illustrate this using another volcano example and drawing from experience of recent events (e.g., Ruapehu eruptions in New Zealand in 1995–1996—Johnston et al., 2000 and Mt St Helens eruption in 1980—Saarinen & Sell, 1985), we can consider information needs during a hazardous event. Several agencies require data on ash distribution and composition. However, different agencies use this information to meet distinct needs: conservation (effects on flora and fauna), utility (effect on power/water supply), agriculture (effect on crops, livestock), civil aviation (effect on aircraft movement) and transit (effect on road/rail networks) agencies interpret this data to meet their specialized information and decision needs (Johnston et al., 2000). Geographical factors (e.g., changes in ash thickness as a function of distance from source, implications of ash-based interactions between ash and soils or water, or the built environment) and meteorological factors (e.g., ash threat will change depending on wind speed and direction, humidity) contribute added complexity to the decision environment. Scientific agencies often have neither the resources nor the expertise to respond to all the possible requests that could emerge within such a decision environment. Response agencies must acknowledge that they can receive data from scientific sources, but rendering it into a meaningful format, and one that is consistent with their decision needs, is a function of the quality of their prior dialogue (Paton et al., 1999).

Acknowledging the demands on scientific agencies during a crisis highlights the need to plan for and provide appropriate resources to deal with new and unanticipated requests for assistance and information. Demand for information can be intense and strain an organization's ability to respond (see Figure 4.4). This again was highlighted during the 1995-1996 Ruapehu eruptions (Johnston et al., 2000). However, once systems were in place, most media organisations reported a satisfactory information flow. For the first 10 days of the eruption in September-October 1995, the events received over 300 minutes of television evening news "air-time" making it the biggest story in the year in New Zealand. The eruption in 1996 also received considerable coverage in New Zealand and overseas. New Zealand's Ministry of Civil Defence (now, Ministry of Civil Defence and Emergency Management) provided a public information phone line and during the first week of its operation, over 19,000 calls had been received. By end of the year, over 34,000 calls had been logged. The tollfree phone information service was again provided in response to another series of eruptions in June-August 1996. The pattern of calls received was similar in both years with high initial demand, dropping after a week (Figure 4.5).

These eruptions again highlighted the need for improved liaison between monitoring agencies and response organisations. Paton et al. (1998) found of 30 organizations that had response roles during the event, only one had any formal link established prior to the eruption (see also Figure 4.4.).

NEED FOR A MULTIDISCIPLINARY EFFORT AND COMMUNITY PARTNERSHIPS

The diverse and complex nature of information and decision needs that emerge from managing disparate hazard consequences, coupled with the spatial and temporal changes in hazard impacts in different localities across the shorter- and

INFORMATION FLOW

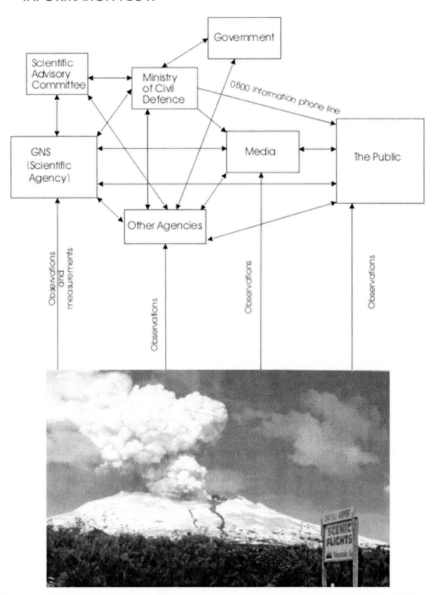

Figure 4.4. The flow of information during the 1995–1996 Ruapehu eruptions (from Johnston 1997).

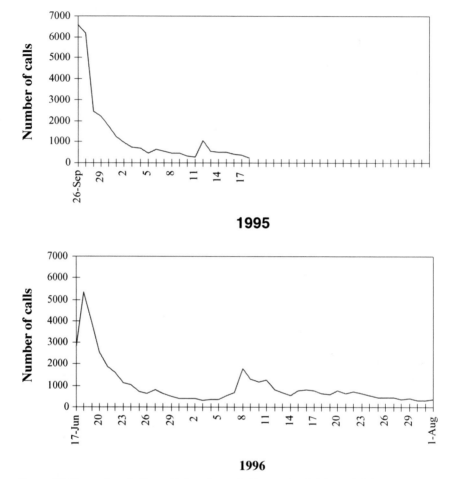

1995

1996

FIGURE 4.5. The number of calls received per day on the New Zealand Ministry of Civil Defence 0800 information line (tollfree) during the 1995–1996 Ruapehu eruption. The free information phone line was operational from 26 September to 4 December 1995 and 17 June to 6 August 1996. Unfortunately some of the daily call records were deleted, notably between 25 October and 4 December 1995 although the total number of calls received in 1995 is known (34,893). From Johnston et al., 2000.

longer term, increases the need for schools and agencies to have developed sound relationships with the emergency management and response community.

Often individual response agencies have neither the resources nor expertise to respond to all possible requests that could emerge within a complex decision environment. Response agencies will often be required to manage data delivered by scientific agencies and attempt to render that data into a meaningful format whilst acknowledging the uncertainties inherent in it. With sufficient planning and anticipation of information needs, schools and response agencies can develop dialogue with each other and with the scientific community. Response personnel in communities and schools should be encouraged, or even trained, to specify their information needs and develop networks with information providers (Paton et al., 1998).

Consequently, it is important for schools, and those who link to schools, including those more directly related to response generally, to have identified and developed their liaison, information management systems, and interpretative capability prior to an event. The emergency management community has a role to play in getting this message across to other agencies. Developing more systematic links between emergency response agencies and the community can reduce demands made on staff during an event, facilitate coordination and allow scientific and emergency management efforts to include activities likely to assist response management. Thus, schools developing a link with local emergency management is a first step.

Increasing the number of multidisciplinary relationships can have multiple benefits. For example, as described earlier, the initial response to the 1980 Mount St Helens eruption by response agencies was marked by a lack of coordination between organizations which prior to the eruption had little interaction (Saarinen & Sell, 1985). Since that event, the USGS's Volcano Program has radically changed the way in which it operates and has developed a more integrated response and outreach effort. A notable example has been the integrated approach taken to the assessment and management of the potential lahar risk from Mount Rainier, in Washington, USA. Since the early 1990s, the USGS has teamed up with other agencies and organizations, including school systems, through the Mount Rainier Volcano Hazard Work Group (National Research Council 1994; Pinsker, 2004). This example is described in more detail later in this chapter. The point for now is that relationship development can be initiated from a number of directions, and the more the better. This would include links to science and response agencies, but also with other organizations in a community including government, NGOs, business community groups, the media, and other community groups.

From this discussion emerges the clear need to develop multidisciplinary relationships and understanding of hazards and their consequences. In terms of research, traditional funding for studies have more often been directed into single disciplinary studies. However, over the last two decades the need for more interdisciplinary approaches has been much more clearly recognized. For example, the Natural Hazards Research and Applications Information Center (NHRAIC) in Boulder, Colorado, was set up in 1976 to served as a national and international clearinghouse of knowledge concerning the social science and policy aspects of disasters. It collects and shares research and experience concerning natural hazards and disasters. The key aim of the center is "*to strengthen communication among researchers and the individuals, organizations, and agencies concerned with reducing damages caused by disasters.*" (see: *www.colorado.edu/hazards/about_ us.html*). Other examples of interdisciplinary approaches are seen in the National

FIGURE 4.6. Evacuation signs in the town of Ilwaco, WA, USA. Photo by D. Johnston.

Science Foundation funding multi-university hazards research (Tierney, 2004) and our own Community Resilience to Hazards research and practice. Included in our team are physical and social scientists combining with practitioners, all of whom emphasize developing collaborative relationships with schools, organizations, emergency responders, and a variety of other groups (Ronan et al., 2000).

A further example of multi-organization and multidisciplinary hazard reductions efforts is illustrated by the US National Tsunami Program (Bernard, 2005). Beginning in the early 1990s, this State/Federal partnership brings together a range of agencies to share knowledge, support research and undertake a range of mitigation and outreach activities with the aim of creating tsunami-resilient communities in vulnerable areas (e.g., Hawaii, Washington) (Walsh et al., 2000).

JOINT TRAINING IN AN ALL-HAZARDS APPROACH

While the previous section alludes to the fact that certain areas can be vulnerable to specific hazards, we favor an all-hazards approach for several reasons. For example, using the example of Hawaii, while tsunamis certainly represent a potential hazard, the state overall is vulnerable to a wide range of hazards including volcanic eruptions, flooding, earthquakes, fires, and so forth. In addition, other events (e.g., technological, mass violence) happen in diverse localities. Given such possibilities, training is crucial to increase response effectiveness and should use an all-hazards approach to facilitate technical (e.g., information analysis, inter-agency communication, decision making, and managing uncertainty), physical and psychological preparedness, and the development of adaptive response capability (Paton et al., 1998; 1999). Training can afford opportunities to practice, using realistic simulations (e.g., scenarios) that can bring alive and better define the skills, roles, and functions that underpin effective emergency response. Managing these issues requires that training needs analysis (Paton, 1996; Paton et al., 1999) identifies the roles and responsibility of the various functions within an organization such as a school and develops appropriate training to build the capability to perform the required functions.

We recommend training and, in particular, simulation scenarios as useful and powerful tools. Scenarios provide a way of considering a range of events that are possible but have not yet occurred (Alexander, 2000). They do not attempt to test a specific hypothesis per se, but examine what would happen if a given hypothesis or set of hypotheses were to hold true under a set of variable conditions (Erickson, 1975). They attempt to set up a logical sequence of events from a given starting point and allow a range of possibilities to be considered. The utility of the scenario methodology is outlined by Erickson (1975) who highlights the following functions:

- As a tool for thinking about complex problems that have uncertain outcomes by linking individual elements in a dynamic system;
- Reducing random outcomes by producing results that help structure existing information into a coherent whole;
- Using scenarios as a preliminary sorting procedure for identifying a range of problems that may be subsequently examined by more quantitative analytical procedures;
- Providing a tool for decision makers; a scenario's function is to anticipate changes in the future which often depend on decisions made in the present;
- Providing value to educational and community end-users as scenarios are intentionally dramatic and literal in style.

Erickson (1975) defines two types of scenarios: exploratory and normative. Exploratory scenarios focus on the processes of change in a system whereas normative scenarios have a pre-determined outcome and explore alternative paths used to reach this outcome.

Simulations using scenarios afford opportunities for all organizations involved to review plans, develop technical and management skills, practice their use under realistic circumstances, receive feedback on their performance, increase awareness and facilitate rehearsal of strategies designed to minimize stress reactions while maximizing coping and effective response. Critical evaluation should follow all simulations and training exercises. This is where more learning and necessary adjustment occurs.

There are numerous examples of multi-organizational training exercises to test emergency plans. Every year, over 7000 residents around Sakurajima volcano, opposite the city of Kagoshima in Japan, practice a mass evacuation (Durand et al., 2001). The event is held on the anniversary (14 January) of a large eruption that occurred in 1914 and is an excellent example of an integrated initiative using the historic event as a focus to develop community capacity to respond to a specific peril. Similarly, in the United States, training simulations are used in a number of locations.

We turn to the Mount Rainier example that highlights the value of links between schools, community response agencies, and the scientific community in increasing preparedness and developing an overall sense of efficacy in the community about being able to respond effectively to a looming hazard.

REDUCING THE RISK FROM LAHARS AT MOUNT RAINIER: A CASE STUDY OF A COMMUNITY PARTNERSHIP

Mount Rainier is a 14,410 ft. active volcano in Washington, which poses a risk to residents of the increasingly developed valleys around its base. Lahars (volcanic mudflows) are the greatest current volcanic hazard in these valleys, with approximately 150,000 people at risk. These fast-flowing slurries of mud, boulders and water originate from eruption-produced melt water and occasionally from the collapse of weakened portions of the mountain. Lahars capable of reaching population centers have a recurrence interval of 100 to 500 years. Stumps excavated by builders and brought to the current land surface are a common sight in the Puyallup River valley and a constant reminder of a lahar that buried that area 500 years ago. This, the most recent major lahar, filled the valley with a wall to wall thickness of around twenty feet, including surrounding and killing trees. In addition, based on the historical record, future lahars will undoubtedly bring long-term disturbance of river systems, with subsequent flooding of sediment-clogged streams.

The USGS Geological Survey (USGS) has mapped lahar hazard zones (Scott & Vallance, 1995 and Hoblitt et al. 1998) and is now undertaking an effort to inform emergency managers in order to help them develop appropriate response measures. As part of this effort, the USGS, along with the Pierce County (Washington) Department of Emergency Management have installed a series of Acoustic Flow Monitors (AFMs) to provide effective warning of lahars in the Puyallup and Carbon River valleys. Alongside this effort, and based on the relationship developed between Pierce County and the USGS, emergency managers have produced an "Emergency Response Plan." This plan includes an evacuation plan, blueprint for agency and community co-ordination during crisis, and a plan for long-term public awareness of these hazards.

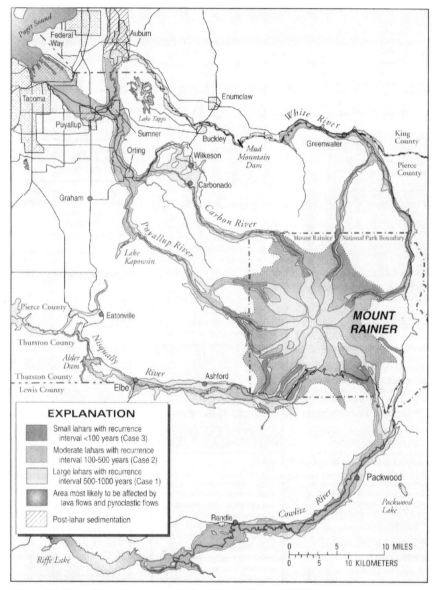

FIGURE 4.7. Map of hazard zones around Mount Ranier (Source: USGS).

We would add that this group has looked to the evidence to inform their efforts (Bailey, 2003). Currently the USGS, local schools and educators, and emergency managers are engaged in public education programs, with the intention of informing residents and visitors about volcano hazards, evacuation routes, and other appropriate response measures. Local school educators and their students here have played an

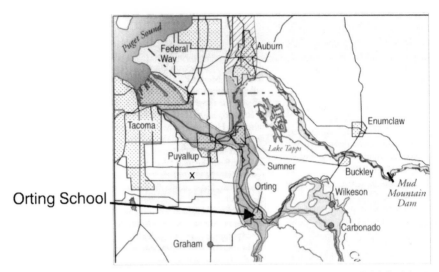

FIGURE 4.8. Location map of the four surveyed schools (darkened area at increased risk for lahars). Modified from Johnston et al. (2001a).

instrumental role by linking in with this effort. Schools have been useful in disseminating information about natural processes, hazards and recommended preparedness measures for lahars and other hazards. Our team is linked here and is able to provide technical advice, training and help with research, including in schools. Educators have incorporated geology and hazard and emergency management issues into their classrooms. The challenge here has been to increase the current understanding of the hazards and developing effective means for keeping alive the message of the mountain's potential in the long-term. The school-youth-family network has been a cornerstone of these public education efforts.

School-based activities were initially evaluated to determine the knowledge levels of students (aged between 13 and 18) in four middle and high schools (Johnston et al., 2001). The study also involved collaboration with the USGS, Washington State Emergency Management Division and the Pierce County Department of Emergency Management. Four schools (Orting High School and three others) agreed to take part in the survey. Orting High School and one of the other schools are located in high-risk zones; the other two, in lower risk zones.

While all schools have had hazard awareness programs, Orting has linked school programs with additional community initiatives. These initiatives have been the product of the linkages established between schools, emergency management, scientists, and others in government and in the community. These coordinated efforts have included practice and simulation (see also Chapter 6). The assessment itself measured students' level of awareness, perceptions of risk, factual knowledge, physical and psychological preparedness, related to hazards and mass emergencies. It also evaluated students' prior exposure to (a) hazards and (b) educational programs designed to increase awareness, knowledge, extent of preparedness as taught by Emergency Management or by school staff (primarily teachers). The results showed that students in all schools had good awareness of hazards that might affect them in their community. A range of hazards were reported as the most likely to occur in the future, with the majority reporting earthquakes, storms, and fires. The exception was in Orting High School where lahars were perceived as an additional likely hazard.

In terms of hazard awareness program involvement, students were encouraged to talk with their parents about hazards as part of their programs. However, not all reported this activity when asked. Of those who did go home and discuss with parents how to prepare for an emergency (from all schools), a significant majority reported willingness on the part of parents to discuss this with them. While the vast majority of students reported having practiced emergency preparation at school, far fewer reported having done this at home. However, given perhaps the value of initial hazards education programs stressing the local hazard, there was generally good knowledge of the correct procedures to respond to a volcanic threat in students at all schools.

The data from this assessment has provided a baseline in our current plans to help the community continue to evaluate the effectiveness of ongoing hazards education programs. Such data have also been used by local emergency management professionals to assess present community and preparedness-related educational needs, develop strategies and plan the allocation and use of resources for future events. To extend the baseline, another school assessment, linked in with a larger community assessment, would be useful to measure understanding, attitudes and levels of preparedness of other groups in the community. This includes plans for assisting teachers to deliver and assess hazards education in 2005. We will aim to update at our website (see Appendix 2) research and outcomes of this continuing school and community hazards education initiative.

Lastly, following initial initiatives in the community, a group of concerned citizens and parents formed a group called "A Bridge for Kids" to address the critical issue of school evacuation in the Orting School District, in the event of lahars (see www.bridge4kids.com). Its mission is "to support the Orting School District and the city of Orting in developing a pedestrian bridge/corridor linking the Orting Valley to the Cascadia Plateau, providing emergency evacuation". The group has been meeting weekly to find ways of gathering support and funding for a bridge across the Carbon River. In 2003, the group was able to commission a feasibility study and it has recommended a route and bridge design costing $US12 million. The group is continuing to push for congressional support for federal funds for the project (KPFF, 2003). This group has also taken it upon themselves to learn about hazards, expose themselves to the research evidence on preparedness and response, and take part and present at a recent multidisciplinary hazards conference (Smith & Smith, 2003).

TABLE 4.1. Ways of Getting Communities Engaged in Multidisciplinary
and Multi-agency Activities, Starting a Hazards Discussion

Schools	• Discuss with your staff and other members of the community what the emergency management issues are in your school and community, who is addressing them and the responsibilities and role of your school; develop momentum.
	• Link activities within your school with other activities outside the school.
	• Invite participation from outside individuals and community groups in school emergency management activities; start perhaps with a simple phone call for an initial chat.
	• Develop a culture of family and community involvement in your emergency planning and education programs.
Individuals and families	• Discuss with your family and other members of the community what the emergency management issues are in your community and who is addressing them.
	• Talk to your local school, council and other community groups about activities in which you could be involved.
	• Get involved in existing groups that may have a role to play in emergency management.
	• If you are already involved in a group explore what roles this group could play in planning for an emergency.
	• Look to start a new group (e.g., Bridge for Kids) if you feel things need to be done that no one is addressing.
Emergency management organisations	• Discuss with organizations and members of the community what the emergency management issues are in the community, who is addressing them.
	• Link organizational activities with all appropriate activities in the community.
	• Invite participation from outside individuals and community groups in your activities; offer your participation with schools.
	• Develop a culture of community involvement in your emergency planning and group activities programs.
Community groups	• Discuss with your group members and other members of the community what the emergency management issues are in your community, who is addressing them and the role of your group.
	• Link activities within your group with other activities outside the group.
	• Invite participation from outside individuals and community groups in your activities.
	• Develop a culture of community involvement in your emergency planning and group activities programs.

SUMMARY

Numerous other examples exist of community and school partnerships and initiatives (e.g., *http://www.fema.gov/pdf/mit/c_section08.pdf;*).

The main issue here is that the more that communities come together for a common cause, link to necessary expertise, and work together cooperatively, the more chance that a community has to be ready for a major disaster. In Chapter 8, we return to this topic and provide some more specific information related to developing school and community partnerships. Attention is now turned to the getting ready for a hazardous event. Related to the content of the current chapter, this includes a discussion of developing momentum within a school and community for incorporating a readiness and response ethos (see Table 4.1).

Chapter 5

Promoting Resilience
Readiness and Risk Reduction

A s outlined in the previous chapters and as a key theme of this book, we promote the need to address community resilience from a systemic perspective.
For the hazard management strategies described in this book to be effective, the
hazards posed by various natural, technology and other human activities must first
be understood. As explained in Chapter 4, this is best done from a multi-organizational and multidisciplinary perspective. A prior analysis of the local hazards
and their potential impacts provides vital information for the planning necessary
to minimize the unexpected. Understanding hazard agents has received the attention of physical and other scientists for a long time. Over the last few decades, our
understanding of the location, timing, scale, and nature of hazards has improved
considerably (Mileti, 1999; Cutter, 2001). We have seen this in the case study of
Orting and Mount Rainier, presented in Chapter 4, where two decades of detailed
scientific research has improved the communities' understanding of the lahar risk.
Many other cases illustrate how detailed scientific research has improved the
understanding of many of the other natural and technological perils (Cutter, 2001).

Despite this, impacts are still difficult to characterize precisely as hazard agents
can cause a range of threats and consequences (Lindell & Prater, 2003). Much of the
new focus of researchers in this field is directed towards a better understanding of
primary and secondary consequences and the inter-relationships (Petak & Atkisson,

---

Kirsten Finnis contributed to the authorship of this chapter.

89

TABLE 5.1. Possible Effects of Hazards

Hazards	Primary effects	Secondary effects	Higher order effects

Biological
  Introduced species/pests
  Animal disease/epidemic
  Human epidemic
Coastal
  Beach erosion and flooding
  Cliff erosion/Coastal instability
  Sea level rise
  Tsunami—distantly generated
  Tsunami—locally generated
Cyclone/ hurricane
Drought
  Agricultural drought
  Water supply drought
Earthquake
Fire
  Urban structure fire
  Catastrophic wildfire
Flooding
Land instability
Tornado
Volcanic
 	
Non-natural
Computer systems failure
Hazardous substances
Lifeline utility failure
Dam failure
Major passenger transport
Criminal acts/terrorism
	1. Death and injury to people and/or evacuation
	2. Psychological trauma and anxiety
	3. Death and injury to livestock and domestic animals and/or evacuation
	4. Implementation of mitigation measures (e.g. removal of assets, shut-down of services)
	5. Damage to structures and their contents
	6. Damage to utilities
	7. Damage to transport systems (e.g. road, vehicles, airports)
	8. Damage to crops, forests, etc
	9. Changes to the landscape, river flows, etc.
		1. Evacuation and/or homelessness
		2. Disruption to 'lifelines'
		3. Slowdowns or closure of business and industry
		4. Financial expenditure for mitigation measures, clean-up operations, repair and replacement of damaged utilities, buildings and contents, by central and local government, business, communities and individuals.
		5. Insurance payouts to policy holders.
		6. Secondary stress caused by disruptions
			1. Unemployment
			2. Loss of personal, business and industry income
			3. Depletion of personal and business savings and/or capital
			4. Diversion of investment capital into recovery
			5. Alteration of land and property values
			6. Alteration of population growth and migration
			7. Increased tax burdens to finance response and recovery
			8. Alteration in socio-economic viability

Source: Modified from Petak and Atkisson (1982).

90

1982; Mileti, 1999; Lindell & Prater, 2003). Table 5.1 outlines the nature of these consequences and a range of issues needing to be addressed. As highlighted in Chapter 2, there is a continuing need to improve the understanding of the links between physical perils and the social, economic, and political consequences at the individual, family, and community levels. More importantly from our perspective is the need to convert this understanding into strategies to plan for and manage these consequences. In this chapter, the current state of knowledge combined with the practices that can help schools and communities prepare for a disaster is presented.

As discussed in previous chapters, the management of disasters has traditionally been divided into four tasks: risk reduction, readiness, response and recovery. These terms capture the types of activities society must undertake if it is to coexist with a variety of natural and man-made hazards (Lindell & Perry, 1992). Of course, as stressed in the SS4R model in Chapter 3, prevention in the form of risk reduction and readiness activities is emphasized as setting the stage for effective response and recovery. There are a number of options available here: hazard mitigation and emergency preparedness approaches can take a number of forms. Physical protection works such as flood banks and sea walls may be used to prevent a hazard impacting directly on communities. However, such efforts are often expensive. In fact, funds spent on engineering solutions to control hazards may at times draw resources away from equally effective and less costly social solutions (Bates et al., 1990).

As a salient example of such a solution, land use planning can be used to avoid, control, or limit construction in hazardous locations. In a recent and comprehensive review of land use planning issues, Burby et al. (2000) highlight the importance of choices made in formulating planning processes, undertaking hazard assessments and the development of programs to manage urban design. Research over the last two decades has highlighted that disasters losses can be reduced in communities that use sound planning and decision-making (Lindell & Perry, 1992; Peek & Mileti, 2002). Tools available to communities include: 1) building codes and standards; 2) development regulations; 3) policy for critical and public facilities; 4) land use planning and property acquisitions; 5) taxation and fiscal policies and 6) information dissemination (Burby et al., 2000). The decision on which combination of tools to use remains a challenge to local governments and its citizens.

Even in circumstances when hazards cannot be avoided, their impacts can nevertheless be reduced at by adopting a range of readiness and risk reduction practices. The goal of such activities is to ensure that the appropriate physical and psychosocial resources are in place that are needed for an effective response or can be obtained when required (Johnston & Ronan, 2000). A goal of preparedness efforts is to educate all sectors of the community about risk and how to prepare and respond. This includes the creation of response plans, training (drills and simulation exercises), undertaking physical and other adjustments, including psychosocial ones, as necessary.

THE INFLUENCE OF RISK PERCEPTION
IN REDUCTION AND READINESS

Individuals' and communities' judgements about various mitigation options and estimates of risk are based on more than objective assessments of the likelihood of hazard activity and its consequences within a specific area. As reviewed in Chapter 2, a number of human beliefs and biases can have a major influence (e.g., normalization bias, unrealistic optimism, low level of perceived responsibility). Effective reduction and readiness planning for disasters requires an understanding of the way risk perceptions shape risk decision-making. As research has shown (see Chapter 2), risk and generalized notions of safety are social and psychological products, not simply objective absolutes. Thus, a clear distinction is drawn between objective measures of risk and perceptions of risk.

Perceived risk can be amplified or attenuated through the operation of personal, social, psychological, and community factors and ends up being interpreted in a manner that can differ substantially from the objective index of risk derived by scientists (Slovic et al., 1981). Risk management and education programs must consider the wide spectrum of psychosocial factors that determine levels of acceptable, and unacceptable, risk. As stressed in Chapter 4, it is important that risk and hazards management be seen as a multidisciplinary activity. Accordingly, developing models that reflect the dynamic and contingent nature of risk phenomena involve good communication between different professional groups including the scientific community, emergency planners, and those in a local community, including schools, who can then have a persuasive impact on others. Engaging the community to identify and take personal responsibility for local hazards and risks associated is an important part of any mitigation program and an element of the SS4R model proposed in this book.

As Mileti (1999) states:

> All stakeholders in a community need to be brought to the point of taking responsibility for recognizing their locale's environmental resources and the . . ., hazards to which it is prone. Stakeholders should use a consensus-building approach to determine community goals for the principles of sustainability: quality of life, disaster resilience, economic vitality, environmental quality, and inter- and intragenerational equity.

There are a number of issues that a community needs to consider when making risk decisions. Some of these include:

- what kind of lifestyle a community wants and needs;
- how should people live now, considering future generations;
- how many future generations should be taken into account;
- what is essential for a high quality of life;
- what point should growth be limited;

- what risks are people willing to take in their interactions with the environment;
- under what circumstances should prevention be chosen versus permissible
  hazard;
- what resources should be sustained and for whom;
- who will monitor and manage sustainability and in whose interest;
- the amount and kind of future losses that are tolerable.

Through this process, individuals and communities can come to realize that
they do have the potential to have increased control over the character and consequences of its future disasters. This can empower the local citizenry for hazard
mitigation in at least two ways:

1. Install a point of view that decisions made today determine what happens
   in the future in terms of reducing losses and strengthening communities.
2. Helps localities consider and become more concerned about (a) reducing
   long-term disaster losses and (b) be persuaded that *mitigation and preparedness can make a difference.*

To engage the community, long term community sustainability issues might
best be incorporated rather than simply having a hazard specific approach. However,
planning for hazards specifically is a worthwhile community endeavour. As related
to hazards, initial school and community actions here include increasing linkages
and engaging in multiple hazards "discussions":

- Having school and community forums and displays;
- Getting the school and community to have a more 'hands on' involvement
  with planning and preparedness;
- Use the school as a setting for community-based workshops;
- Involve a range of organizations with their long term plans and outlooks.

HAZARDS EDUCATION PROGRAMS

Dissemination of information about hazards is vital to efforts in encouraging an
appropriate public response and in reducing social and physical impacts. In many
countries, substantial funds are expended annually on risk communication programs to promote hazard preparedness. However, as elaborated in Chapter 2,
research over the past two decades has shown that the majority of the public do
not carry out the self-protective measures recommended by emergency management authorities during non-crisis times (Lindell, 2000; Lindell & Whitney, 2000;
Paton & Johnston, 2001). This finding may question the value of public education
activities. However, there is good evidence that hazard knowledge and understanding

is more likely to lead to preparation and to appropriate responding during an actual crisis (e.g., evacuation, warning compliance, Drabek, 1986; Perry & Lindell, 1990). In addition, research (e.g., Mileti & Fitzpatrick, 1992, 1993; Ward & Mileti,1993) has found that multiple messages, delivered by multiple agencies, through multiple channels, but carrying a consistent theme, along with other factors (see Chapter 2), can lead to increased preparedness activity that includes searching for more information from governmental, NGO, and informal sources. The actual nature of the message itself is important as is a consideration of the other factors that have been found to predict readiness. In fact, the effectiveness of many public education programs has been reduced by a failure to accommodate the risk and protective factors that link risk perception and risk reduction activities (Lindell, 2000; Lindell & Whitney, 2000; Paton, 2003).

An explanation for low preparedness has been presented using a process model of preparedness (Paton, 2003; Paton et al., 2003) that comprise distinct, but related, stages. According to the model, preparedness is motivated by a perception of hazard effects capable of posing a threat sufficient to cause "hazard concern" (see also Chapter 2 and 3). In the event of increased concern, the next link is then thought to be governed by a sense of personal responsibility, outcome expectancy (i.e., effectiveness of adjustments), and self-efficacy (i.e., ability to carry out adjustments). The main question here is "will actions that I take actually serve to prepare myself and my family for a future hazard that I am concerned enough about to consider taking some action?" Another important feature here is the time frame within which people anticipate the occurrence of the next hazard event (Paton, 2003), or as emphasized in Chapter 3, readiness to change related to an increased urgency about not putting off preparation efforts.

As stressed previously, a main issue in education is motivation and community engagement. To facilitate motivation, strategies are needed that first emphasize the salience of hazard issues for community members. As suggested by research, improved preparedness is also thought to accrue from enhancing community members' beliefs in the feasibility of mitigating hazard effects through personal actions (e.g., counter beliefs that hazards have totally catastrophic effects) and enhancing beliefs in personal competency to implement these activities. Changing these factors requires a mix of education, social policy, training, and empowerment strategies. As described in Chapter 3, part of the process here is to increase discrepancy between one's current status (unprepared) and a goal or value (e.g., protecting myself, my family, my school, my community from a future hazard).

The next stage, converting increased motivation and intentions into actual behavior, needs to be enhanced by focusing on encouraging acceptance of a 'sooner rather than later' message. It is also important to understand the belief and attitudes that underpin peoples' responses to risk communication messages. Consistent with our model, the design of hazard education programs should be integrated with community development initiatives and are likely to be more

TABLE 5.2. Main Features to Consider in Education Programs:
Willing, Able, and Ready

Change of process	Element	Basic questions
Willing	Hazard Concern Personal Responsibility	"Is there a hazard risk that causes me enough concern to consider doing something?"
Able	Self-efficacy Adjustment efficacy	"Are strategies going to be effective, do I have resources to carry them out, and can I carry them out effectively?"
Ready	Time	"Is it worth it to do something now rather than later?"

Note: See also Paton et al., 2003.

effective than stand alone, one off programs. Of course, as demonstrated in Orting, Washington, (see Chapter 4), school education programs can be one of the very centerpieces of a sustained, community-based effort. Table 5.2 shows the stages proposed in Chapter 3 that are necessary to increase intentions and actions. Highlighted are basic questions that the range of strategies used are designed to answer.

ROLE OF SCHOOLS

Hazards education in schools can play a vital role in increasing a community being ready, willing, and able to do what is necessary to prepare for and respond to a disaster. As initially introduced in Chapter 1, over two decades ago, Paul Slovic and colleagues (1981) reviewed psychological factors and social implications of perceived risk and concluded "that much of the responsibility (in the area of hazard education) lies with the school, whose curricula should include material designed to teach people that the world in which they live is probabilistic, not deterministic, and to help them learn judgement and decision strategies for dealing with that world." Given that hazards are a prominent risk in most communities, Alexander (1992) recommended integrating hazard teaching into school curricula: "[H]azards should be considered in an integrated way in terms of their . . . , impacts, their human repercussions and the opportunity for monitoring and mitigating them."

The school curriculum does afford opportunities to teach children about natural and man-made hazards. Of course, as we have stressed, the teaching of hazards can be either integrated into the existing core curriculum or as an additional activity. The integration of local hazard and risk information into the curriculum of science, geography, social studies, civics, and other disciplines increases the likelihood that it becomes part of the core education that children receive rather than an optional "add on". This integration also can start to assist youth to understand better the links involved in a local hazards sustainability model.

Research into the content of educational material aimed at increasing preparedness suggests that the following basic ingredients are important: personalized information, facts about the likelihood and severity of the hazards and the value of practical precautionary measures (Weinstein, 1989), along with a number of other evidence-based features (e.g., multiple programs, interactive features) identified earlier. When developing school hazard programs or material, planning and preparation should address the following:

- Identification of existing educational resources related to hazards and all current methods of disseminating public information on hazards in a specific community;
- Consideration of the appropriateness of current resources and methods of dissemination;
- Development of new resources and methods of dissemination where required;
- Identification of resources and training for staff and links with other disciplines including emergency management and others (see Chapter 4).

Although there are several studies that have looked at hazards education material (MCDEM, 2002) and many agencies list a range of educational resource materials available for schools (e.g., American Red Cross, USGS, FEMA), little research has explored the degree to which this material is actually used in schools, its effectiveness, and, importantly, from a teacher's perspective, barriers to its use.* In the course of undertaking our own research, we have heard from teachers that problems do exist here and some include:

- Too much material—there is much competition from other organizations wanting to push their message and producing 'information kits' for that purpose (road and rail safety, stranger danger, drug/alcohol/sex safety, caring for the environment, and so forth);
- Material out of date—material can either be factually out of date (through research, new technology, changes in the environment) or its presentation may be out of date. Even though information may still be relevant and correct, if it is not presented in a 'current style', it will not be appealing to the audience, including youth;
- Not appropriate to the curricula—teachers are limited to certain topics within the curricula and are also limited by time. Although there may be 6 weeks dedicated to looking at "natural (or other) disasters" (e.g., Ronan & Johnston, 2003; see Chapter 3), the curriculum at least initially may not be perceived as leaving time for discussion of the 4Rs;

* The second author is a former teacher.

- Changes in the curricula, making existing material obsolete—where education programs have been specifically designed to fit in with the curriculum, it only takes a change of government, or change in education strategy to have an impact on curricula content. This often renders the material produced for that particular program out of date;
- Teachers moving on and taking material with them—'established' teachers in a school may have a collection of resource material, or there may be only one teacher interested in teaching hazards education. When these teachers leave, the knowledge and information may go with them and may not be replaced.

Following the notion of local research and evidence-based planning, it is important that those involved in developing community and school-based hazard and emergency management education programs to be aware of the current status of hazards education in the schools and communities. A small scale survey of teachers and emergency managers can provide useful information to help overcome some of the barriers just identified.

Table 5.3 provides a range of questions that could be used. It is important that where possible as many teachers in a school be surveyed to identify the full range of issues limiting the development of education programs. Whether or not such a little survey is used, the point here is to identify barriers and facilitators to such programming. Consequently, the questions in Table 5.3 can be used as a guide for planning and discussions.

As reviewed in Chapter 3, empirical support has underscored the value of school programs in helping families and community members becoming better prepared for a range of hazardous events. Our studies have identified a number of specific factors can enhance the effectiveness of such programs (e.g., Ronan et al., 2001; Ronan & Johnston, 2001, 2003). These include: 1) the integration of school programs with wider community emergency management initiatives and focus; 2) programs that increase knowledge of hazards and specifics on what to do before and during events; 3) programs that include an interactive component where students are encouraged to share what they have learned at school with their parents or guardians; 4) interactive programs that encourage not only sharing and discussions, but also emphasize strongly the "doing" of preparedness; and 5) repeating programs over time. Additionally, invited talks by visiting specialists, local emergency managers, and others can be a useful addition to teacher-led activities.

Thankfully, disasters are mostly rare so in most cases people may not have personal experience of hazardous events. However, the media provides considerable information and news about natural hazards and other disasters. When disasters are reported in the media it provides an ideal opportunity for children (and families) to gain an understanding of an event. This includes what can be done to prepare, respond and recover. It can also be used to highlight the tendency of the media to provide images of destruction rather than, for example, examples of

TABLE 5.3. A List of Questions to Guide Planning

EMERGENCY MANAGEMENT AND SCHOOL SURVEY

Emergency management staff questions

1. How often do you visit schools?
    a. If never, why?
        i. Not your responsibility
        ii. Never asked
        iii. Costs too much (money/time)
2. Do schools/teachers invite Emergency Management out, or does Emergency Management approach the school?
3. When visiting schools:
    a. Do you target the whole school or particular year levels?
    b. What information/resources do you provide?
4. Do you liaise with teachers and other school staff before and/or after speaking to the students?
5. Do you provide follow up activities for the students/teachers?
6. What resource materials do you have for:
    a. primary students?
    b. intermediate students?
    c. high school students?
7. Do you have area specific information that is used (e.g., information on local hazards and a list of useful adjustments schools, youth, and families can undertake)?
8a. Do you ever evaluate
        i. How useful your materials are (for the teachers and students)?
        ii. The effectiveness of the information?
        iii. How often the material is used?
        iv. If the material needs updating?
8b. If so, how often?
9. Do you link school programs with other community initiatives?

School Staff Questions

1. Is Emergency Management part of your curriculum?
    a. If yes,
        i. What aspects/hazards do you cover?
        ii. What materials do you use (e.g. books, posters etc.)?
    b. If no, why not?
        i. Time
        ii. Relevance
        iii. Lack of resources   Other reason(s)_____
        iv. Lack of interest   _____
                                                       _____
2. What would encourage you to incorporate hazard education into what you teach?
3. What subjects do you incorporate EM education in?
4. Where do you get your resources/information from?
    a. Internet
    b. Textbooks   Other_____
    c. Emergency Management/Local Government   _____
5. Have you ever sought information from Emergency Management?
6. Do you feel the resources provided by Emergency Management are adequate?
7. Do you encourage parent/caregiver participation in your education programs?
8. Do you evaluate your programs?
9. Are your programs linked to other community initiatives?

good preparedness and response. When disasters actually do occur locally, schools can serve a vital role in responding as well as educating children about what has happened and helping with the coping process within a community. These issues are expanded on in Chapter 6 and 7.

EMERGENCY PLANNING

Any plan for dealing with a crisis requires a comprehensive emergency management approach, part of an "all hazards" strategy, linking mitigation, preparedness, response, and recovery (Wenger, 1988; Drabek & Hoetmer, 1991; Mileti, 1999). However, there needs to be sufficient flexibility to accommodate and target the different hazards and corresponding degrees of risk (May, 1997). A universal criteria of contingency plans is that they remain simple and flexible, and focus first on basic principles rather than complicated details. Their purpose is to facilitate an effective and appropriate response. The appropriateness of a simple response is preferred over a complex series of responses that cannot be recalled during a crisis. That is, in school and community education, the first principle is to get across the basic messages. Given this need to start simple, the planning process becomes a continuous and evolutionary one. It seeks to form and maintain a clear and accurate understanding of the roles and responsibilities of all involved in a community in the management of a disaster.

However, as introduced in earlier chapters, a number of researchers have documented that emergency planning is at times based on false assumptions and inappropriate analogues (e.g., Perry, 1985; Britton, 1986, 1995; Dynes, 1994). These may include misperceptions of human reactions and response (e.g. panic vs. effective coping), planning assumptions (e.g. specific hazard responses vs. general all-hazard response principles) and effectiveness assumptions (about safety devices, warnings, etc). Other obstacles to good planning practices include the lack of experience with past events (Kartez & Lindell, 1987). Perry (1985) notes: "Too often emergency plans which are administratively derived turn out to be based on misconceptions of how people react and therefore potentially create more problems than they solve" (p. 126). The alternative here is by looking to what the research tells us in terms of hazards education and planning such as that described thus far in earlier sections of this chapter and in Chapters 2–4.

Households

Household preparedness is routinely promoted by emergency management organizations due to the need for households to respond appropriately and have in place a number of protective measures to reduce impacts when disasters strike. Common activities suggested are storing food and water, obtaining emergency lighting, securing household fittings and preparing emergency plans (see also Table 2.2 in

Chapter 2 for a representative, but by no means exhaustive, list of preparedness activities; see later in this chapter for references to more exhaustive lists).

As discussed earlier, while household preparedness is routinely emphasized, preparedness in households almost universally falls below levels desired. However, as reviewed in Chapter 2, exceptions have been found that appear to be a function of a sustained education campaign over time that are accompanied first by basic messages and then by an increasing sophistication of educational delivery and content.

One basic measure is a household or family plan. The Federal Emergency Management Agency (FEMA) in their training program delivered through the Emergency Management Institute (FEMA, 1998) defines four steps to creating a family disaster plan. These steps are:

1. Find out what could happen to you.
2. Create a disaster plan.
2. Complete preparedness activities.
2. Practice and maintain your plan.

These steps are consistent with elements of our own model.

Step 1: Find Out What Could Happen to You

In the previous section, we have described a wide range of agencies involved in the assessment of hazards. Most of these organizations have material available as printed publications or on their web sites to help schools, individuals, families and communities better understand the hazards they face and how and when to respond. At a local level, many cities and counties also have hazard information in a form specific to their communities. Finding out more about the hazards in your neighborhood may be as simple as a phone call to a local emergency manager, a visit to the library, or a search on the web. We recommend as a first step in developing a hazards education program making that phone call to the local EM agency, or the EM agency calling the school, and begin to develop a relationship (see also Chapters 4 and 8).

As expanded on in the next chapter, local communities are usually connected into a variety of warning systems for different hazards. Part of finding out about hazards includes finding out what types of warnings that might be received for what types of hazards. As hazards can hit various locations such as home, school, or place of work, finding out the hazards these locations face is also recommended.

Step 2: Create a Disaster Plan

All members of a family need to know what to do in an emergency. As has been shown in earlier chapters, children who understand what hazards they face and have emergency management knowledge are more confident about their ability to cope and less fearful and are more likely to respond in an appropriate way.

Discussing what to do in an emergency and what steps to take to reduce the impacts before the event is an important step. When creating a disaster plan, there is a need to discuss a number of key issues that include the following:

- Pick a place (or two) to meet.
- Have an "out of town" contact.
- Discuss what to do in an evacuation.
- Draw a plan of the house.

Picking a Place (or Two) to Meet. If any one in the family has to leave the house or school in an emergency (e.g., fire), everyone in the family needs to know where they should meet. Choosing a familiar spot a safe distance from the house such as a neighbour's place, a street corner, or somewhere else is recommended. Having such a place will help family members or rescue workers avoid unnecessary worry and searching for missing people. It is also useful to select a second meeting place outside your neighbourhood if a family member can't return home. Make sure every one knows the location and contact details of this meeting place. We would add here that knowing the school's emergency plan and evacuation procedures should be part of this planning (see Chapter 6).

Have an "Out of Town" Contact. When a disaster strikes, it is often difficult and stressful to find out where family members are and to make contact with them. It is very useful to have a contact person "out of town" or out of the area where a family can leave messages and who can forward information to other members of the family who may be affected by the same disaster. Making sure every one knows who this contact is and how to reach them is important.

Discuss What to Do in an Evacuation. If the family has to leave the house or neighbourhood, again, making sure all members of the household know what to do is vital. Discussing and practicing the details beforehand so everyone knows what to do when a disaster strikes is recommended.

Draw a Plan of the House. One way to bring together all the planning steps is to draw a plan of the house and the various steps (as well as alternative plans) the family would take. It can also be used as part of the preparedness activities listed below on Step 3.

Step 3: Complete Preparedness Activities

During a disaster there is little time to learn new skills and undertake preparedness activities. Learning these beforehand make a tremendous difference, can save lives, and reduce the impacts of the disaster. Some of the basic activities for a family may be:

1. *Learn first aid:* basic first skills will make a difference. Ask your local Red Cross or emergency manager where to go for training.

2. *Learn how to shut off utilities:* In some events it may be necessary to shut off your power, gas and/or water. Know how to do this and have the tools to do it.

3. *Learn about storing water:* Water supplies can be disrupted for some time during a disaster. You need to store at least 3 gallons per person.

4. *Stock emergency supplies:* You need to store food for up to 3 days.

5. *Assess your insurance coverage:* Make sure your insurance covers you for what you think it does. Discuss exactly what you are covered for with you agent.

6. *Find the best ways out of your house:* You and your family should all know the easiest way out of each room. Children especially should know what to do if it dark and they have to leave the house and alternative escape routes.

7. *Plan to stay when required:* Several hazards require you to take shelter in or near your house. You need to know what to do and when.

8. *Conduct a hazard hunt:* You can bring a lot of the planning together and check you have done what you need to by having a "hazard hunt". If possible, involve the whole family. The checklist in Table 5.4 is a beginning guide to what can be looked for in the home.

9. *Consider other activities to include in a hazard and readiness hunt:* This can include a whole range of both general and more specific adjustments based on local hazards and includes items available in Table 2.2 in Chapter 2, at the FEMA website (*www.fema.gov*), and additional useful material available at the National Disaster Education Coalition website (*www.disastereducation.org*).

Step 4: Practice and Maintain Your Plan

Steps 1–3 need to be repeated regularly. Supplies will pass their "use by" dates, batteries will run low and children (and adults) will forget what to do. The child and family should check all steps every 6 months. Remember the purpose of the plan is to protect loved ones and lives could be saved by adequate preparations. We would add here that practicing the basics of the family emergency plan at regular intervals is recommended. We would also add that readiness activities, including practice, need not be time consuming or overly elaborate. Such activities are designed to prepare both physically as well as psychologically. One such advantage of these activities is instilling in youth, and parents, an increased sense of control that is vital to rapid decision-making under the duress of a crisis.

In addition to family emergency plans, and the range of specific activities recommended, specific localities may require additional adjustments. These are best determined in coordination with others, including a local EM professional.

TABLE 5.4. Hazard Hunt Checklist (Developed from FEMA, 1998)

Check for electrical hazards

- Replace frayed or cracked extension and appliance cords and loose prongs and plugs.
- Correct overloaded outlets and extension cords.
- Remove electrical cords that are run under rugs, over nails, heaters, pipes, or in high traffic areas.
- Cover exposed outlets and wiring.
- Repair or replace appliances that overheat, short out, smoke, or spark
- Provide overload protection by either circuit breakers or fuses.
- Have do-it-yourself wiring checked for safety by a professional.

Check for chemical hazards

- Move combustible liquids such as paint thinner, kerosene, charcoal lighter fluid, and turpentine away from heat sources. Store flammable liquids such as gasoline, acetone, benzene, and lacquer thinner in metal cans away from the home.
- If flammable materials must be stored in the home, use a storage can with an Underwriter's Laboratories (UL) or Factory Method (FM) approved label.
  - Move them away from heat sources, open flames, gas appliances, and children.
  - Place containers in a well ventilated area.
  - Close lids tightly.
  - Secure containers to prevent spills.
- Place oily polishing rags or waste in covered metal cans.
- Instruct family members that gasoline, benzene, and other flammable fluids should not be used for starting fires or cleaning indoors.

Check for other fire hazards

- Clear storage areas of old rags, papers, mattresses, broken furniture, and other flammable materials.
- Move clothes, curtains, rags, and paper goods away from electrical equipment, gas appliances, or flammable materials.
- Remove dried grass cuttings, tree trimmings, and weeds from the property.
- Clean and repair chimneys, flue pipes, vent connectors, and gas vents.
- Move heaters and candles away from curtains and furniture.
- Place portable heaters on a level surface, away from high traffic areas. *(Make sure that they are equipped with automatic shut-off switches and avoid the use of extension cords.)*

Check fire safety equipment

- Install at least one smoke detector on each level of the home, especially near bedrooms.
  - Test every month.
  - Change batteries at least once a year, or as directed by the manufacturer's instructions.

Acquire and learn to use a fire extinguisher (ABC type). Review the instructions provided with your fire extinguisher to learn its application (such as the type of fire that the extinguisher is designed to put out) and how it works. Be sure others in your household also understand how it works and where it is kept. This location should be easy to reach and near an exit. Maintain and recharge according to manufacturer's instructions.

Source: FEMA (1998).

Institutions

Emergency planning needs to cover a range of issues to ensure that institutions adequately prepare for disasters. Many of the steps outlined above for a family can be applied to other institutions, including schools. For most institutions, the planning needs to conform to the local, state, and federal statutory requirements for emergency management planning. This may differ in between jurisdictions, states, and countries. However, many authorities have guidelines to help institutions meet these requirements. In Chapter 6, a sample school emergency plan suggesting some key steps to be addressed in their planning is presented. One for educational institutions in the United States has also been developed by the United States Department of Education and FEMA. As there are a number of steps in the planning process, these are best coordinated by a designated plan coordinator within the school and drawn from interested staff and others (e.g., on local school boards, parent-teacher organizations). It is worth noting that the sample provided in the next chapter is not intended to be prescriptive. It is intended to provide a guide for the key issues to be included, not just within a written plan, but in an ongoing planning process. In other words, as described in Chapter 6, the written plan is far less important than the actual, ongoing process of planning, discussing, practicing, and doing.

SUMMARY

Although planning is done in some circumstances primarily to meet legal requirements, we have emphasized throughout this book that developing relationships and planning can serve a broader purpose that will provide wider benefits to the school and the community. These links and cooperative planning efforts can be used to help sell the need to prepare, obtain the resources needed, and achieve the readiness outcomes desired. With planning and preparation, response to the actual hazardous event can be made much more effective. In the next chapter, while attention is turned to response, the emphasis continues to be on *planning for response* rather than a manual to be picked up and used at the time of an actual hazardous event.

Chapter **6**

Promoting Resilience
Response

I n this chapter, the idea is promoted that planning for response is far more effective than a "spontaneous" response. Thus, this chapter extends into the response
phase while maintaining a focus on issues useful to consider in planning, education, and simulations. We first start with an overview of community level response
issues and then focus on the school setting.

PUBLIC EDUCATION AND RESPONSE DURING A CRISIS

During an emergency, demand for information is intense and this demand places a
strain on all responding agencies. When an emergency is in progress, emergency
management officials have to distinguish the function of sending messages
(warnings) which direct an emergency response from providing the public with
information about the emergency and its aftermath. Our experience during emergencies has shown that a crisis period is not the best time to prepare the content of
public information material nor devise response plans (e.g., Johnston et al., 2000;
Ronan et al., 2000). Public information and plans prepared in advance that can then
be reproduced or brought on-line (e.g., at a local website) during the crisis for rapid
dissemination is recommended. In the USA, the National Disaster Education
Coalition has produced "Talking About Disaster: Guide for Standard Messages" to

---

Kirsten Finnis contributed to the authorship of this chapter.

help produce consistent messages for public dissemination in an emergency. Since 2002, this review process has included extensive participation by more than 450 professionals, scientists, and researchers who have contributed to the material. Representatives from NDEC participating agencies have invested considerable time to refine and resolve content issues and questions, to ensure accuracy, consistency, and appropriateness of messages (see http://www.disastereducation.org/guide.html).

As lines of communication can be severely disrupted during an event, such information about what to expect and what to do must be able to be distributed early and preferably through multiple sources and media. It is important that responding agencies provide information to news services instead of waiting for the media to discover their own "news" (i.e., the need for a media response plan or plan component) (Vogt & Sorensen, 1994). Research has shown that the majority of people receive information through the media rather than from the response agencies which issued it. Since news media can have quite a pervasive influence on the public, direct and early attempts should be made to liaise and meet the needs of the media. This can often be helped by having established longer-standing links prior to emergency times. In fact, as discussed in earlier chapters, establishing links to assist community-readiness education campaigns can help to educate the media, get their support, and have them "on board" to promote useful, rather than alarmist or mass destruction messages, during a crisis.

During an emergency, systems may fail, information may be misinterpreted and conditions can rapidly change making previously released information 'out-of-date'. Incorrect or misleading information should be corrected by new information releases, accompanied by explanations as to why the earlier information may be "unreliable" (Perry & Lindell, 1990). When current information is full of uncertainty (a common situation immediately prior to and during a range of hazards), it is also important to avoid making or disseminating unrealistic forecasts. This can lessen concerns about the "cry wolf syndrome", a common concern for many public officials (Green et al., 1992). Controlling rumours is a critical function for agencies responsible for providing public information and these agencies should be proactive in identifying and correcting incorrect or misleading information. However, some caution and common sense is needed here. For example, immediate and harsh official denouncement of popular views may be counterproductive and treated with suspicion by the public. Research has demonstrated that the public often prefers to hear a range of opinions before drawing their own conclusions on a subject (Showalter, 1993). An example of a misinformed public response was to the Browning earthquake 'prediction' in the United States in 1989-1990 (Farley et al., 1993; Showalter, 1993; see also Chapter 2). Authorities in this case had only limited success in countering unsubstantiated public statements of an amateur scientist who forecast an imminent earthquake that ultimately did not occur. As the research showed, a significant portion of the community believed the forecast and some took on planned action to deal with the perceived eventuality (e.g., evacuation). Based on what we have learned since then, the situation possibly could have been dealt with more decisively and effectively.

THE ROLE FOR SCHOOLS

Schools play an important function during an actual emergency or disaster. The main function of course, as in all response plans, is ensuring safety. Functions to undertake include:

- Determining if an emergency is imminent or occurring.
- Identifying the type of emergency that is occurring and determine the appropriate response.
- Activating the incident management system (i.e., response plans).
- Ascertaining the form of immediate evacuation response (e.g., evacuation; lockdown; shelter-in-place).
- Maintaining communication among all relevant staff.
- Establishing what information needs to be communicated to staff, students, families, and the community.
- Monitoring needs for emergency first aid and attending to the injured.
- Deciding if more equipment, supplies, and personnel are needed.

To do that, as introduced in Chapter 5, having a good planning process is the foundation for a good response. As emphasized, the written plan is far less important than the planning process. Written plans themselves serve two primary functions (Tierney et al., 2001): (a) a written agreement that is signed off by respective organizations that documents roles and functions for promoting preparedness and activating response and recovery activities, and (b) a template for continuing education and training. The latter function can guard against the plan being written, "shelved", and forgotten. Of course, such a document (e.g., see Table 6.1) created between a school and community partners can then also better ensure an ongoing process of education, practice, simulations, linking school and family emergency plans, school and community emergency plans, evaluation, and other functions.

Picking up on the theme introduced in the previous section, media reporting can contribute to biased perceptions. The media frequently give uneven coverage focusing on high impact, low frequency events. There is commonly a bias towards reporting on areas of comprehensive damage and on the victims. As reviewed in Chapter 2, those where less damage occurs or those people who survive or who even cope well are focused on with lesser frequency. Wrathall (1992) also comments on a general lack of follow-up reporting when disaster-impacted communities successfully cope with their predicament. As a consequence of these tendencies, local school systems would do well to have their own relationships developed with local media to assist with school-based efforts. Additional links established within the community including with emergency management agencies can assist further with promoting useful public messages.

TABLE 6.1. Sample Outline of a Plan (Developed from Auckland City Website Plan Outline)

Introduction

- Purpose of Emergency Plan: (a) documentation of the plan; (b) template for ongoing education and training
- School mission statement and goals
- General information

Reduction

- Map of school and surroundings showing for example fire extinguishers, evacuation assembly point(s) and alternatives, first aid kit locations, main entrance and exits etc.
- Identification of hazards in the local community that have the potential to affect the school
- Identification of hazards within the school grounds and buildings
- Analysis of hazards to determine the possible consequences and effects on the school
- Steps to mitigate or reduce the effects of the identified hazards
- Curriculum-based interactive education programs that link with the home setting, in conjunction with local emergency management

Readiness

- Contact details of emergency services, local businesses, school neighbours, local government, and other agencies deemed relevant in the local area
- Responding to crisis and warnings including awareness of local warning systems and response to warnings including evacuation plan including signals for evacuation and assembly points, sheltering in place, reunification with families
- Procedures for care of the students within the school grounds or school buildings; staff training (e.g., first aid; CPR)
- Procedures for communicating the school's emergency plan to parents/caregivers, pupils (e.g., linking the family- and school-plans through curricula-based and interactive education programs) and the wider community (e.g., local emergency management liason; information in the local newspaper).
- Policy and procedure for communicating with the media in an emergency; establish early links with media (e.g., to publicize readiness education)
- List of school resources that can be used in an emergency (e.g., spades, first aid kits, blankets, etc)
- Places where additional resources can be sourced if required (e.g., local convenience store or supermarket)
- Practice and Simulations: response to warnings, evacuation, sheltering in place, communication and reunification with families, links with emergency services and emergency management
- Practical methods of evaluation for readiness education, interaction with home, simulations

Response

- Staff responsibilities—Principal's responsibilities, teaching staff, others including back-up plan
- Staff action plan—what to do in the initial stages
- Communication during an emergency both within the school (how will we keep everyone informed), with parents/caregivers, emergency services, and with the media
- First aid and procedures for an event where serious injury occurs
- Pupil release and pick-up procedures: activating the link between schools and families

Recovery

- Post emergency recovery procedures including information provision to youth and families, screening efforts, school-based education and intervention

TABLE 6.1. *(Continued)*

- Building/health and safety inspection of the school
- Re-occupation of the school including re-opening to promote return to routine
- Support for staff and students that promotes routine while educating about normal recovery and availability of additional help; do not ignore what has happened

Plan administration

- Update/review and maintenance of essential equipment cycle
- Location of plan and placement of emergency procedures notices around the school

Key information

- 2–5 page pullout section containing key response details (e.g., important contacts, staff action plan, who should do what etc)
- This section can be on a different coloured paper for easy recognition and should be removable
- Other handouts to be made available to students and families about readiness, response and recovery

As mentioned in the previous chapter, when disasters do occur, schools can and should play a pivotal role in first keeping children and staff safe. They then can serve a role in educating children about what has happened, help with the coping process, and participate in efforts to identify those youth and families in need of direct services. While promoting messages around the normal response and recovery cycle, such response- and early recovery-based programs can also screen for those in greater need (Ronan et al., 2004). We discuss these specific features more in depth in Chapter 7.

Prior to attending to psychosocial needs, the first principle in response is to help keep people safe. As seen in Table 6.1, this includes having a plan on how to respond effectively to the emergency. In the next few sections, a closer examination of main issues in response includes information about identification of local hazards, warning systems, response to warnings, evacuation, sheltering in place, and reunification with families.

WARNINGS

Warning messages are usually given to a specific community or communities when a direct response to a threat is required. The failure of warning systems to deliver timely or accurate warnings, or delivering ones that are responded to inappropriately, can obviously have tragic consequences. As a salient example here, the 1985 Nevado del Ruiz volcanic tragedy in which 21,000 people were killed in the Columbian town of Armero illustrates a worst case scenario. Voight (1990; 1996) in his review cited human error—misjudgement, indecision and bureaucratic short-sightedness—and not the magnitude of the eruption, lack of scientific warning or technological ineffectiveness as the cause of the tragedy. A main problem in this case was public officials' worry about "crying wolf". As a consequence, warnings from the scientific agency were not translated by emergency management into public warnings and mass evacuation. As a result, lahars were then responsible for burying the town. A less tragic example of the failure to transmit effective warnings includes the lack of warning given to residents of eastern Washington (U.S.A.) after the May 1980 eruption of Mount St. Helens of impending ash falls (Saarinen & Sell, 1985).

Warnings can be put out by a range of agencies or groups in a community, including the media, and can be both formal and informal. Over the last few decades, advances in the ability to predict and forecast impending perils has improved the quality of many of the formal warning systems (e.g., Sorenson, 2000). However, the links between formal warnings issued by agencies and community responses are still in need of improvement. In a review of flood warning systems in Europe, Handmer (2001) highlights a number of the shortcomings of existing systems and emphasizes them as being a function of agency-focused as opposed to community-focused needs. For example, flooding in the Midlands, England in 1998 resulted in five deaths and 4500 properties inundated. The majority of people reported receiving no direct warnings and there was a resultant public outcry (Bye & Horner, 1998).

There is considerable research pointing to the value of simple community-friendly alert schemes to assist responding to a developing crisis (Mileti, 1999, Sorensen, 2000, Handmer, 2002). In fact, a number of alert schemes have been developed in the US and other countries for a range of hazards, including drought, wildfires, tornadoes, hurricanes, volcanic hazards, and more recently, terrorism (e.g., see Figure 6.1). However, research has repeatedly shown that a single warning system or concept will not serve all hazards due to differing risks, temporal, and spatial impacts of different hazard types (Mileti & Sorensen, 1990). Thus, while simple warning systems have clear utility, they also have problems, including perceptions of overuse and being too emphatic (e.g., media reports of overuse of terrorist alert levels in the U.S.). Consequently, other mechanisms are necessary and research has identified a number of them.

As outlined in Chapter 2, a significant body of knowledge on organizational and individual response to warnings has been developed. Recapping this research, the response to warnings by individuals has been found to relate to i) individual perceptions (understanding, believing, and personalizing the warning); ii) the nature of the warning information (specificity, consistency, certainty, accuracy, clarity, media source and type, frequency); and iii) the personal characteristics of the recipient (demographics, knowledge, experience of the hazard, social network and others) (Mileti & O'Brien, 1993). The message should include specific guidance about what people should do to maximize their safety. The warning message must describe the exact location that is at risk and address the "when" aspect of the required response.

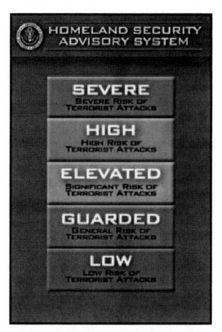

FIGURE 6.1 The recently developed Homeland
Security Advisory System for the United States.
(from Department of Homeland Security, http://
www.whitehouse.gov/news/releases/2002/03/
20020312-5.html).

An important dimension is the source of the information. Warnings are more
likely to be believed if they come from 'credible' sources. The public's perception
of credibility of information sources is a subjective judgement and has been shown
to be related to notions of expertise and trustworthiness. Perry and Lindell (1990)
have noted three general bases on which credibility can be judged: 1) the "creden-
tials" of the person or agency issuing the warning; 2) the relationship of the organizations to other "credible" organizations; and 3) the past history of job performance of that organization. Trust and credibility are valuable assets—difficult to
obtain and once lost, difficult to regain (Slovic, 1993; Vogt & Sorenson, 1994).
Prior to an event, agencies and organizations, including schools, which may have
to issue warnings or at least have a role in their dissemination can take a pro-active
step towards enhancing their credibility. Schools linking with credible agencies
and seen to be working in a coordinated and collaborative way with these agencies
can improve overall credibility. Having a senior or publicly recognized person with
good verbal skills issuing or associated with the issuing of a warning notice in association with other 'lead' agencies will also enhance credibility. A number of issues
need to be addressed when designing an effective system of warnings for vulnerable schools and communities and these are summarised in Table 6.2.

TABLE 6.2. Uncertainties of Warning Systems

Interpretation issues

- *Recognition of an event.* The variable abilities of people to recognise a threat may delay warnings and thus response time.
- *Recognition of hazard.*
- *Definition of magnitude.* Uncertainty of magnitude can lead to confusion over warning decisions and/or delayed (or premature) warnings and evacuation.
- *Self-definition of role.* Uncertainty on the part of those who play key parts in the chain of communication can slow activation of the system because key players who are uncertain of their role often do not convey risk in a timely manner. People are more likely to understand their role in a warning system if plans exist and training occurs.
- *Sorting of relevant information.* Sorting relevant from non-relevant information is necessary when there is too much or bad information facing the decision-maker.
- *Definition of authority.* Disputes may occur, information may not reach the right decision-maker, or decisions may be delayed or overlooked if no definition of authority has been decided prior to the event.

Communication issues

- *Whom to notify.* The communication process may not initiate, shut down or slow if it is not clear who to notify, delaying public response.
- *Ability to describe hazard.* If those who receive the warning cannot understand it, it compromises the usefulness of the message and the ability to warn.
- *Physical ability to communicate.* Loss of technical ability to communicate creates uncertainty (or fails to initiate notification).
- *Conflicting information.* Conflicting data or recommendations can lead to different conclusions about whether to issue a warning. Delays may occur in an attempt to clarify information or a bad decision may result if erroneous information is acted on.

Issues of perception

- *Adverse consequences.* Warning decisions are influenced by a decision-maker's perception of the adverse consequences of action.
- *Personal consequences.* Decision-makers may fear that transmitting risk information for a threat that might not materialise could lead to personal consequences such as loss of reputation, etc.
- *Costs of protective actions.* Decision makers may be influenced by their perceptions of the dollar costs or losses that may stem from warning.
- *Liability.* Warning decisions can be influenced by how organisations or the actors within them perceive liability.
- *Feasibility.* Feasibility refers to the potential success of a warning in regard to successful public protection.
- *Expectations.* Warning decisions can be influenced by the expectations or demands of persons outside the warning system environment.

Source: Modified from Mileti and Sorensen, 1990. Reprinted with permission of Dennis Mileti.

In terms of the planning for response to warnings, the first goal is to identify (a) local hazards, (b) local warning systems, and (c) how to translate warnings or crisis information into effective warnings and activation of the response plan in school that includes evacuation, sheltering in place, and linking with families.

EVACUATION

Evacuation is deemed necessary by authorities when a perceived risk to human life or property reaches unacceptable levels. As pointed out in Chapter 5, people living within high-risk areas who may need to evacuate should be made aware of this fact during preparedness campaigns and be willing to move away if advised. Defining such high risk areas in advance can assist any evacuation. However, this step is by no means universally undertaken. Notable examples of hazard zoning for a specific hazard type are the tsunami hazard maps in the Pacific Northwest, USA and lahar hazard maps around Mount Rainier (Hoblitt et al., 1998). Where areas of risk are defined, practical response exercises (i.e., simulations and practice) have proven invaluable in ensuring correct public actions when a crisis does occur. This was well illustrated by the successful evacuation of the town of Raubal during the 1994 eruption there. During a non-eruption unrest period in the 1980s and 1990s, the local community regularly rehearsed the evacuation of 20,000 residents (Blong, 1984). Similarly, as discussed in Chapter 4, schools in Orting, Washington regularly practice responding to eruption and lahar warnings including evacuation drills.

The principal function of evacuation is to ensure that people move from a place of relative danger to a place of relative safety via a route that is itself free from significant danger. The destination as well as the route must be considered in the plan, as well as other options such as sheltering in the place at risk. There needs to be careful coordination of the timing and conduct of an evacuation and this must be done in association with agencies who are assessing risk and ordering the evacuation, as well as those responsible for receiving evacuees or meeting evacuees at agreed upon locales.

Evacuation can be either pre-emptive or responsive. If evacuation of high-risk areas is deemed necessary to save lives, it must be done prior to the event reaching a critical or dangerous level. The higher the population density, the earlier an evacuation must begin, to cope with the logistics of a large number of people evacuating in a short period of time. Post event evacuation may also become necessary in areas where people have survived without difficulty, but in which the long term loss of water and food supply, electricity, waste disposal, and livelihood have made continued habitation untenable (e.g., Newhall & Punongbayan, 1996).

If the evacuation of a hazardous zone is to proceed in an orderly manner, it is essential that people know where to go, and what route to take. Unless the risk to life is immediate and obvious, people may be reluctant to leave their homes or other places, including schools. Assurance must be given that the evacuated area will be monitored and remain off limits to unauthorized people as well as information that untoward behavior (e.g., break-ins; looting) in evacuated areas is not common (Tierney et al., 2001).

In most communities, experience of large scale evacuations is minimal, and the logistical and social problems associated with such an action are substantial.

People forced to move are likely to feel demoralized and have other problems develop. Both physical and mental health problems may occur at a higher rate than normal as a consequence.

As stated in Chapter 5, evacuation planning is an essential part of emergency planning for a disaster. Although this section could be included in the previous chapter, we take the opportunity to review a number of key evacuation issues that need to be addressed. Evacuations usually involve four types of movement (Perry, 1985): 1) self-evacuation where people move out on their own or in their own vehicles or with friends/relatives; 2) movement of people through various means (e.g., pedestrian; for those who do not own or have access to private vehicles); 3) movement of people from institutions (e.g., jails, hospitals); 4) movement of people with handicaps who require specialized transport. Emergency planning must make provisions for the latter three types and provide recommendations for the first type. Evacuation planning must (Perry, 1985):

- Designate the lead agency who will issue the evacuation order;
- Designate the agencies who will play supporting and receiving roles;
- Outline the roles and responsibilities of all the agencies involved;
- Identify the potentially dangerous zones to which or through which the population might not be able to be evacuated;
- Identify the preferred evacuation routes and ways to keep them open under hazardous conditions;
- Identify assembly points for persons who require transport for evacuation and public information pertaining to these;
- Consider the means of movement, transport, traffic control, assistance and direction;
- Identify potential shelters and accommodation in safe zones;
- See also Table 6.3.

SHELTERING AND REUNIFICATION

In some emergencies, such as chemical release, terrorism and related (e.g., school shootings), tornado, and in some locations, evacuation may not be the best option. Instead, the appropriate response may be some form of sheltering-in-place. Appropriate planning, training, and exercises can prepare schools and households to know what and when to take certain actions. When and how to shelter-in-place depends on the type of emergency. During a tornado warning, people should go underground or into a "wind safe" room, whereas during a chemical release shelter might be better above ground. Remaining in a locked classroom may be the best option in some circumstances (e.g., mass violence). A key issue is to have a flexible response plan in place to respond to different situations.

Table 6.3. Evacuation Planning

School planning for evacuations

- Principal needs to communicate with all the staff, identifying specific needs and capabilities
- Principal lists interested staff or designates staff to particular roles covering these areas

  - Physical/medical needs
  - Emotional/mental health needs
  - Students with special needs
  - Staff with ability to convey information to the media
  - Staff with knowledge of transportation needs
  - Staff with knowledge of building/floor plan
  - Staff with knowledge of community resources
  - Staff with knowledge of parents (able to convey information to parents)

- Meetings with staff and students to explain roles and requirements in the event of an evacuation
- Designation/consideration of assembly areas and their contact details
- Consider utility problems (gas, sewer, power) and facilities (multiple story buildings, water towers, transformers, balconies)
- Designate areas in assembly area

  - Command post
  - Access for emergency vehicles
  - Student assembly areas
  - First aid area
  - Heliport landing area
  - Psychological first aid area
  - Student release
  - Media area
  - Alternative location—walking distance
  - Alternative location—requiring transport

- Determine student accounting, release and pick up procedures
- Communicate these procedures to parents
- Conduct training and drills for multiple scenarios (e.g. fire, earthquake, severe weather, bomb threats)
- Place copies of floor plans, evacuation routes and procedures throughout buildings
- If not already in existence, create and emergency/evacuation kit containing such items as

  - Staff list/plan/roster
  - Student roster/roll including contact information for parents
  - Maps (school and local area)
  - First aid kit(s)
  - Flashlights
  - Two-way radios and/or cell phones
  - Battery powered radios and batteries
  - Pens and paper
  - Name tag stickers and pens

- Local telephone directory
- Local responder personnel phone/fax/cell/pager numbers
- Other emergency numbers

Source: Adapted from the Emergency Management Guide Template developed by the Kentucky Center for School Safety. (http://www.kysafeschools.org/clear/issues/EMG.html).

Reunification with Families

Schools need to develop an effective student release system. During a disaster, the separation of children from the parents and caregivers is a cause of much anxiety and reuniting families is an important process. The earliest possible safe release of students should be aimed at but child safety is of course the paramount issue. Since reunification is not always possible for some time during a disaster owing to various reasons, the communication of accurate and appropriate information is essential (e.g., when parents call). Schools need to include a plan for communicating within the school, school community, and the wider community whereas parents and caregivers should know in advance what the release system is during an emergency and what their roles and responsibilities are as part of the system.

SUMMARY

Schools have a special need to protect children and there are a range of safety measures including responding to warnings and crises, evacuation, sheltering in place, and family reunification. We have summarized key issues needing to be considered before and during the response. In considering these measures, it is clear that the effectiveness of response is clearly influenced by the advanced planning, and practice, process.

In turn, the effectiveness of the response will almost undoubtedly influence recovery. For example, ensuring safety sets the stage for a quicker return to normalcy and routine in school, in families, and in communities. In addition, schools provide appropriate settings to assist with recovery as they provide a natural grouping of young people who share life experiences. Conducting discussions at school also can give youth the message that school life continues despite disruptions caused by the hazard event.

At a local level, Anderson (1987) suggests that

> most catastrophic events that strike communities should be given temporary precedence over the normal curriculum in order to help students understand the causes, consequences and recovery alternatives, as well as to allay whatever trauma, fear of recurrence, and general fear of isolation and helplessness that might accompany such an event (p. 230).

As expanded on in the next chapter, given a school's multiple roles in a disaster, it is important to plan for their reopening as soon as possible and develop appropriate programs during the initial recovery stages taking into account the admonition of Anderson (1987).

Chapter 7

Promoting Resilience
Recovery

RECOVERY PROGRAMS: FOCUS ON PHYSICAL AND SOCIAL FACTORS

As with readiness and response, a focus in planning should emphasize inter-related factors. For example, as we have discussed, when even a relatively benign hazard happens (e.g., Ronan et al., 1999), problems develop. In the case of volcanic eruptions, ash may be deposited in a community, people may have trouble with ash getting into machinery (Johnston et al, 2000); those with asthma may start to experience problems medically (e.g., Ronan, 1997a); people may be in future danger from other volcanic products (e.g., lahars, lava). When an earthquake hits, lives are sometimes lost, buildings are damaged, lifelines are disrupted, aftershocks occur, and so forth. In these and other hazards, it is almost invariably the case that physical disruption also carries with it social and psychological disruption. In terms of psychological effects, mass violence appears to be particularly pernicious. As additionally reviewed in Chapter 2, there is also the common sense notion—backed up by data (e.g., Norris et al., 2002; Ronan, 1997a, Ronan et al., 2000)—that a youth's social and emotional functioning is related to parents' functioning. When parents are not coping well, their children also tend to cope less effectively. It is also the case that when hazardous conditions are more extreme, so too are the social and emotional effects (Watson et al., 2003).

Social and emotional reactions include individual problems with increased distress, including diagnosable problems including Acute Stress Disorder (ASD) and Post-Traumatic Stress Disorder (PTSD) (American Psychiatric Association, 2000). Both of these conditions are the result of an extreme stressor that produces problems with (a) re-experiencing phenomena (e.g., intrusive memories, flashbacks, nightmares), (b) psychic numbing and avoidance of hazard-related stimuli, and (c) excess arousal (e.g., exaggerated startle response). In fact, research has indicated that hazardous events do not have to be catastrophic to produce symptoms of these disorders in either youth (Ronan, 1997b) or in their parents (Ronan et al., 2000). In addition, with time, while symptoms and problems start to reduce for many, some do not recover normally.

As reviewed in Chapter 2, apart from clinically significant problems such as ASD or PTSD, other problems develop. These include general distress, fears and generalized anxiety, grief and depression, and health-related difficulties. In the aftermath of a disaster, people may experience a loss of control and feel more uncertain about their current status as well as their future. The relationship between a loss of control and increased uncertainty has been established in psychological and related research (e.g., Ronan & Deane, 1998). One such consequence is emotional arousal that is of a form that does not prove adaptive. Whereas emotional arousal in the first instance is intended to help humans adapt to their surroundings, the form of arousal here can prevent, rather than facilitate, coping behaviour. Thus, as discussed in earlier chapters, there is a link between emotion- and problem-focused coping (Lazarus & Folkman, 1984; Lazarus, 1999). In other words, when emotions are working as they are intended, our ability to solve physical problems increases. The converse is also true. Successful problem-focused coping such as mastery at a task tends to increase positive emotions (e.g., Ben-Zur, 2002). In addition to internal coping resources, support from others is also obviously useful following a hazard. In fact, individual coping ability has been linked directly to the availability of more external sources of support (Huzziff & Ronan, 1999; NIMH, 2002; Norris et al., 2002). Further, as elaborated in one of the next sections of this chapter, help from naturally-occurring support systems appears to be highly beneficial and one of the most important features promoting increased coping and natural resolution of distress and related problems.

As a consequence, while people first need to deal with survival and other basic needs in the immediate aftermath of a disaster, the role of emotional and outside support is implicated in assisting people to carry out those activities. People who are experiencing shock, great distress, and so forth may not have the necessary psychological "fuel" to do what is necessary to meet physical needs. Consequently, to attend to basic needs, people do require both internal and external resources to help them approach, rather than avoid, necessary activities. In the sections that follow, these ideas are elaborated on starting with an overall framework that emphasizes maximizing the availability of resources available to a school and community following a hazard.

MULTIPLE GATING AND STEPPED CARE: A RESOURCE FRIENDLY PHILOSOPHY

As introduced in Chapter 3, the main idea here is to be able to do "more with less" (Davison, 2000). The two related notions of multiple gating and stepped care involve, respectively, parsimonious allocation of assessment (e.g., Hinshaw, March, & Abikoff, 1997) and intervention resources (e.g., Haaga, 2000). Given the fact that communities' resources are often stretched even during non-hazard times, a large scale event can make such resources scant (e.g., Tierney et al., 2001). The ability to access financial and other necessary resources represents an ongoing concern for those involved in various aspects of emergency management (e.g., Haddow & Bullock, 2003). Of course, this includes most aspects within a community: emergency management, government agencies, non-governmental agencies, search and rescue, fire, police, military, and other agencies and organizations including schools.

As introduced in Chapter 3, a multiple-gating, stepped care (MGSC) model of assessment and intervention is designed specifically to capitalize on those resources that are available to address needs within a community affected by problems including hazards (e.g., Johnston & Ronan, 2000; Ronan et al., 2005). The model itself involves the following components: (a) assessment using multiple gates, (b) forms of assistance that are sequenced and start at more basic and community, school, and large group-focused levels and move progressively to those that are more intensive and family-and individually-focused, and a (c) self-correcting feature designed to assist those not helped at earlier gates. This self-correcting idea is summarized by Davison (2000):

> [A]n inherent feature and advantage of (MGSC) is that it self-corrects; that is, it forces one to monitor constantly the effects of one's interventions and to adjust subsequent strategies based on what has just happened (p. 582).

The idea here of course is to assess whether basic forms of assistance, requiring relatively minimal resourcing, can help large groups of people. Examples here would include self-help information (e.g., emergency management guidelines; various forms of information to enhance physical and social recovery) provided through video forms (e.g., videotapes, television broadcasts), newspapers, radio, websites, computer programs, classrooms, books, and so forth. Another example, requiring more resourcing but still representing an early gate, would be larger group- or organizationally-based (e.g., school) interventions. In the school context, these might be carried out by trained teachers or perhaps others (e.g., emergency management professionals, school psychologists, scientists). At each successive step, or gate, the job is to be able to identify those who have not been assisted and to increase the resourcing necessary to provide adequate assistance to the majority of those people. This iterative, self-corrective process then is intended to continue until all in the targeted catchments have been provided adequate assistance.

Part of the idea in this model is not only to be able to use the least expensive intervention first but also that intervention which is least intrusive on people's lives (e.g., self-help information). However, a risk in using an inexpensive and least intrusive alternative is that it simply might not help or, perhaps in some cases, actually make matters worse (Wilson, Vitousek, & Loeb, 2000). Consequently, when planning on the various gates in an MGSC model, it is important that the planning is backed by sound decision-making that includes using those interventions that have been seen to help. Such models have been used in medicine (e.g., Smith et al., 2003) and in various areas of psychology (e.g., Haaga, 2000; McChargue, Gulliver, & Hitsman, 2003). However, while their promise has been discussed in the hazards and emergency management area (e.g., Ronan et al., 2005), they have not been as yet researched nor applied in any comprehensive sense. However, there are findings across different hazards and populations that do provide empirical support and can inform practice and research in this area. Those interventions that appear to have potential value at early and later gates are now reviewed. The first of course, as introduced in Chapter 5 and 6, is the value of readiness and response as early interventions that help people anticipate, prepare for, and respond to a disaster. In this way, well planned readiness and response efforts represent early forms of preventive interventions.

The Earliest Gate: Primary Prevention and Protective Factors

In psychological literature, there are three forms of prevention-based interventions. The first is primary: it represents those efforts that are carried out before a problem arises. For example, prenatal courses for prospective parents can be designed to include information on parenting strategies (e.g., value of warmth and affection, value of authoritative discipline environment). Such information might then be used by parents to prevent the occurrence of a range of childhood problems (e.g., disruptive behaviour; emotional problems).

Similarly in the hazards area, interventions carried out prior to the occurrence of any hazard are intended to assist people cope with both the immediate and longer term effects of a hazard—in such a way as to prevent major problems (physical or social) from occurring. Consequently, in designing educationally-based interventions in communities and schools during the readiness phase (see also Chapter 5 for more detail on the nature of the interventions), the aim is to assist people to prepare both physically and emotionally for the effects of a range of hazards. Thus, when we see that school-based interventions are seen to assist youth and families in these ways, we feel encouraged that this preparation will increase resilience when a hazardous event does eventuate (Ronan & Johnston, 2001, 2003).

The rationale here has to do with the idea of protective factors. When youth (and their families) have (a) more physical preparation and practice, (b) more confidence in their coping ability, (c) fewer hazards-related fears and (d) increased hazards discussions in school and at home, all of these may be seen to "protect" against the effects of a hazard both in the short- and longer-term (e.g., Huzziff & Ronan, 1999; LaGreca et al., 1996; Vernberg et al., 1996; see also Peek & Mileti, 2002). We discussed in earlier chapters a range of other protective factors identified in the literature and that are worth keeping in mind when designing early interventions.

Given the relationships between the 4Rs, we cannot stress enough the value of planning and primary prevention strategies. One issue worth repeating with respect to prevention is the value of repeated educational efforts across time and across agencies. The more that a community is exposed to specific, consistent messages by a variety of agencies that are trusted, and combined with motivational and other factors discussed earlier, the more potential value can be derived by the community when a disaster does strike.

The Next Gate: Response and Early Intervention

The next form of early prevention is often referred to as secondary prevention. This form of intervention is intended to be carried out when the first signs of problem begin to emerge. Consequently, when a hazard does occur, intervention efforts can be designed as a form of secondary prevention; mindful that some problems may begin to emerge early that can predict longer term disruption. For example, early levels of distress appear to predict later levels. Thus, while distress tends to decrease, those with initially high levels might be targeted for early intervention. Of course, some people may not be affected in the immediate aftermath of a hazard but begin to experience some delayed effect, though delayed effects have been found to happen relatively infrequently (Norris et al., 2002). However, as reviewed in Chapter 6, some response-based efforts (e.g., warnings, evacuations) may keep people safe and less exposed to harmful effects. In the case of schools and families, the more there is coordination between a school's response plan and families' emergency plans, the more that youth, and the families, should benefit. In addition to direct response-based activities, other forms of early intervention following a hazard are done quite often. However, research has not been particularly supportive of some forms of intervention in some circumstances.

Critical Incident Stress Debriefing (CISD): Proceed with Caution

CISD is a method developed during the 1970s by Jeffrey Mitchell from the University of Maryland (e.g., Mitchell, 1983; Mitchell & Everly, 1993). The basic procedure has a long history in the military (e.g., Salmon, 1919) and CISD was designed to be adapted for civilian populations. CISD is intended to be targeted to helping professionals (e.g., emergency service personnel, police, fire, health care) exposed to the effects of victims of disasters (Mitchell, 2003). However, it has also been applied to a variety of groups including victims directly exposed to a variety of traumatic experiences. Intended to be done in groups, the procedure involves certain stages of that are designed to prevent trauma amongst those exposed to hazards and disasters. These stages, or phases, done over 1-3 hours include the following:

- Introductory phase (establishing ground rules in the group such as confidentiality);
- Fact phase (what happened);
- Cognitive phase (thoughts that happened amongst group members);
- Reaction phase (emotions that occurred);
- Symptom phase (overview of signs and symptoms of normative reactions);
- Teaching phase (normative education and provision of coping strategies);
- Wind-down (summarizing aimed at "re-entry" to life outside).

The use of CISD and related models has been used worldwide including reportedly widespread use after the September 11th disaster in New York City (Kadet, 2002). However, despite widespread usage, there is no evidence that it assists above and beyond the normal process of resolution that appears to occur naturally over time for the majority of people exposed to a hazard (see also Chapter 2 and later sections of this chapter). In a recent meta-analysis, van Emmerik, Kamphuis, Hulsbosch, & Emmelkamp (2002) found that CISD did not improve symptoms of distress whereas non-CISD interventions and, indeed, no intervention were seen to improve functioning. These findings support other previous findings regarding the effectiveness of CISD (e.g., Rose, Bisson, Wessley, 2001).

Mitchell (2003) contends that studies included in the meta-analyses that have concluded negative outcomes for CISD such as the ones just cited are in fact not following CISD protocol. The primary problem with 17 studies identified as having negative outcomes according to Mitchell (2003) are the following (CISD protocol in parentheses):

- one-on-one interventions (homogenous groups);
- primary victims (secondary victims such as emergency personnel);
- exposure is direct (exposure is to another person's trauma);
- poorly defined protocols (well defined procedures);
- inadequate training of single providers (trained team including mental health professional);
- no planned follow-up (follow-up required);
- goals different from CISD (mitigate impact, enhance normal recovery, assess and refer those needing additional assistance).

Mitchell (2003) goes on to document a number of studies—both singular studies and statistical aggregations, including meta-analyses by CISD proponents (Everly, Boyle, & Lating, 1999; Everly, Flannery, & Eyler, 2002)—that have supported the effectiveness of the CISD approach when carried out in the intended manner.

It does appear obvious that the debate here at times has had a political edge to it. However, taken together, the findings overall suggest a number of implications. One of these is that data here, like that reviewed in Chapter 2, point to the idea that the process of normal reactions to a disaster follows a course of natural resolution for the majority of people. Once again, through a different line of research, we see the idea that "time heals" has evidence based support (e.g., Gist & Devilly, 2002).

However, as reviewed in Chapter 2, time simply is not healing for all (e.g., Amir & Lev-Wiesel, 2003). Thus, we agree with the balance of opinion in this area that early intervention is useful, and perhaps necessary, for some in the community (e.g., Gist, 2002; Cohen, Berliner, & Mannarino, 2003; Long, Ronan, & Perreira-Laird, 1998). However, we also agree with the idea that an early intervention needs not to be emphasizing "overhelping" (Gilbert & Silvera, 1996) or "overintervention" (Gist, 2002). In other words, most people will, through their own devices and social and community networks, be able to resolve the problems associated with a disaster without any formal, outside assistance.

In addition, the idea of "respecting the trauma membrane" (Lindy & Wilson, 2001) is relevant here. That is, if intervention approaches are prematurely trying to help people resolve feelings that actually may be adaptive and short-term responses (e.g., disbelief, denial), this may lead to problems (e.g., prevent release of "emergency" neurohormones, e.g, Raphael & Wilson, 2000). Thus, prior to entertaining the evidence-basis for formal efforts, we look at what the evidence has to say in terms of more natural courses of resolution and to translating that into helping efforts.

Promoting Natural Resolution of Disaster-Related Distress: The First Aim of Early Intervention

As reviewed in Chapter 2, the majority of people following a disaster recover from initial distress and related problems, including after a mass casualty event (e.g., 9/11). It was also pointed out that various factors can help, or get in the way of, what appears to be a natural recovery process. For youth, who represent a vulnerable population, what appears clear is that family factors are most important in this process. Further, those in families are more at risk for problems than those who do not have families currently (e.g., single persons, elderly).

Consequently, while it is the case that families can provide comfort, they can also be sources of stress and conflict. So, for youth, the idea that "as the family and parents go, so too the youth" has support. This is not to say that other factors (e.g., exposure, pre-existing problems, coping, other forms of social support) are not important. What is stressed here is that they appear to be secondary to factors such as parental level of hazard-related distress, conflict, and other forms of conflict- or distress-related communication. Thus, if parents are not able to manage their own arousal after a hazard, it is more likely that their children will be negatively affected.

What appears requisite here is that interventions aimed at assisting youth need to have a complementary focus on helping parents and family members. As in other areas of clinical psychology (e.g., juvenile delinquency; Curtis, Ronan, & Borduin, 2004), the evidence-based interventions found most useful are those that focus on how to help parents manage their child. We also know from areas of the literature other than hazards-based that while parents are the most important influence on youth, other adults also have an effect, including school personnel. In addition, from our readiness research, when teachers initiate conversations with youth about hazards, children can benefit in terms of both problem- and emotion-focused coping (Ronan et al, 2001).

Consequently, we first focus on how to help both adults and youth manage themselves, and then look more specifically at the special status of families.

Promoting Natural Recovery: A Community- and School-Based Focus

As concluded by a large National Institute of Mental Health conference of disaster researchers and professionals (National Institute of Mental Health, 2002): "A sensible working principle in the immediate postincident phase is to expect normal recovery . . ., except when there is a preexisting condition." (NIMH, 2002, p. 2)

Given such an organizing theme, the question is how best to promote natural recovery? Another related question is how best to identify those who actually do require formal assistance? The answer to the first is more straightforward. The second question is dealt with more specifically shortly. However, we feel that one solution to both lie in the application of a MGSC approach. *That is, provide those resources that can assist normal recovery while identifying and screening for those who need assistance is the theme.* The areas discussed in the next sections have been identified as part of the core of early intervention services (NIMH, 2002). We supplement that basic information with information more specifically targeted to youth and families. One area that has not received much attention is the role of schools in recovery efforts. Given that youth are at higher risk for disruptions to normal recovery, schools are a place where much work can be done to assist normal recovery, identify those youth at higher risk, and intervene with groups and individuals (Vernberg & Vogel, 1993). Additionally, features of the family context put both youth and adults in the home at higher risk (e.g., if adult and a survivor, the presence of youth in the home is a risk factor; if a youth, parental distress; the presence of distress in any family member; conflict, lack of support, distress-laden communication; see also Chapter 2). In fact, given the current evidence on risk and protective factors, interventions for youth distressed by hazards and disasters appear to require at least some focus on the family context. Given that the school is a centralized gathering place for most families in a community, it has potential as perhaps the main conduit for assessment and intervention efforts for both youth and families following an incident.

Basic Needs. In terms of providing support for the majority, at least two main sources of support have been implicated (see also Chapter 2). They are in order of importance (a) tangible support for basic needs and (b) informational support. Tangible and informational forms of support include addressing these areas:

- basic needs: survival and safety needs (food, shelter, clothing, health, communities; mitigating any ongoing risk);
- orientation to the disaster and local services;
- value of communication and support within family, friendship and community networks.

Psychological First Aid. The main idea here, like in physical first aid, is to (a) protect the victim(s) from additional harm and (b) attend to the most distressed and provide or mobilize tangible, informational, social, and emotional support. Some of the specifics of psychological first aid include support and soothing aimed at reducing arousal levels. Another hallmark is to keep families together to the extent possible including helping encourage reunions with family and friends. Another hallmark is to provide information: this certainly includes information and education that can help normalize initial reactions. For example, as introduced in the previous section, symptoms that occur in the immediate aftermath of a hazard (e.g., numbing, hyperarousal) are considered in the first instance to be "normal reactions to abnormal events." Another example here is providing parents with information and support around their role in the child's coping and recovery (i.e., expect normal recovery, role of parent's own coping and family environment factors in assisting youth). Another form of information normally provided concerns resources and supports available in the community and elsewhere (e.g., media, internet) that can assist short- and longer-term coping and resilience.

The main essence of psychological first aid as it has to do with youth and families emphasize physical safety, basic needs, and additional support as required. Children need to be able to feel safe, eat well, sleep well, know where there families are and be reconnected with them or with other supports (Gurwitch, Sitterle, Young, & Pfefferbaum, 2002). Another goal in psychological first aid— as in most early intervention—is to differentiate between the majority who appear to be having normal reactions and those at increased risk for longer term problems.

Needs Assessment. This includes screening for those at most risk for longer term problems. Needs assessment also implicates an overall evaluation about how ongoing needs are being met within the overall recovery environment. This of course includes what additional services are necessary for all affected (e.g., additional support, basic needs) as well as those most affected (i.e., any additional interventions).

Recovery Observation. Monitor the rescue and recovery environment for the following:

- stressors and toxins;
- ongoing threats;
- services that are, and are not, being provided;
- media coverage and rumors;
- those most affected.

Outreach. The goal here is providing outreach and information in the following modalities:

- "therapy by walking around" (NIMH, 2002)—offering support, information, and education;
- distribute information (e.g., printed information on supports, coping, family factors);
- provide web-based information;
- use the media: distribute press releases, engage in interviews and longer programs.

As seen in Figure 7.1, an example of a recent press release following some major flooding is provided. Also, as seen in Table 7.1, an information sheet made available through various means can be helpful. Other material available at the National Disaster Education Coalition website may also prove useful including their "Guide for Standard Messages" (see Appendix for website).

Organizational Outreach and Training. As in individual and family-based outreach, the goal here is to improve governmental and NGO capacity to assist in community recovery. One important example here is on the role of schools in helping communities recover. Schools can play a leading role by returning to normal activity as soon as possible following an incident. While we await more specific research support for this idea, data from our research program (e.g., Ronan & Johnston, 1999; Ronan, 1997a, b) has indicated some support for that idea. Following a volcanic eruption, the one primary school that reopened and returned to normal activities the soonest, while acknowledging the eruption with the children, was also seen to have children least affected overall. While there may have been other factors that played a role here (e.g., socioeconomic levels of the communities around the schools), it does support the overall idea in early intervention models around resuming normal routines. Schools are also a place where larger scale screening and some form of interventions are possible (e.g., Ronan & Johnston, 1999; Ronan et al., 2005).

Another area where schools can be of assistance is by training school personnel and those doing presentations in schools (e.g., on the physical science of a hazard, see Ronan & Johnston, 1999) how to talk with children and adolescents

News Release

Public Affairs

Telephone:
Mobile:
Fax:
Email:
Website:

TO: **PRESS OUTLETS HERE**   Total Pages: 2
FROM: **PUBLIC RELATIONS**

Anxiety and stress a natural reaction to flooding

People affected by flooding may experience symptoms of stress and other feelings. Such feelings are to be expected, may actually prove adaptive in the short term, and are likely to reduce once the situation begins to return to normal. Common reactions include different thoughts, concentration difficulties, recurring dreams, feeling numb or disconnected, on edge, angry, depressed, or even a sense of hopelessness about the future. Parents might feel overprotective. Sleep may be a problem for some; others may isolate themselves from natural support systems or have increased conflict with those close to them.

According to disaster psychology expert Dr. Kevin Ronan, "Take the example of feeling numb. It is not a dissimilar process physically when we go out into very cold weather. The body tries to adapt to that cold weather in various ways—one of them is to get physically numb, particularly in exposed places of the body. Similarly, when very stressful events happen, a common reaction for some can be a numbing feeling—an attempt psychologically to adapt to the situation in the short term."

Dr. Ronan says that people have such natural coping systems and, despite extreme stress and loss, most are able to adapt and heal with time. This is particularly so when certain factors are in place.

"The majority of people recover naturally. Interestingly, one thing that may help some is simply being reassured that they are likely to feel better over time. Part of helping along this natural process can come through trying to resume regular activities and routines to the extent possible, not to be shy in asking for support from and talking to families, friends, neighbours and other supports in the community, and of course to try to look after oneself and one's family, to sleep well, eat well, and, to the extent possible, re-establish work, school, and family routines."

Dr Ronan says this natural process means many people will not require direct assistance from health and counselling professionals. Citing the aftermath of September 11 in the USA, Dr Ronan says the number of people diagnosed with post-traumatic stress disorder was less than expected and that the majority (approximately two-thirds) who received an initial diagnosis of Post Traumatic Stress Disorder after the disaster were seen to be diagnosis free 4 months later.

"Feelings of stress, depression, numbness, of being disconnected are normal reactions to an abnormal event. In the first instance, survival is the most important issue of course, organising shelter, family, food, livelihoods. I would also add that when people are able to take care of physical needs and feel supported by others in a community that common sense, and research, would suggest that these activities themselves often have a useful effect on how people are feeling. It is when people begin to isolate and avoid taking care of needs that problems can start to develop.

While physical needs are most important initially, people may also start to think about or experience problems with their psychological well-being. However, it should also be stressed that a range of feelings are normal in events like this and some acceptance of those feelings in oneself and others as normal can quite often be helpful. By doing so, such acceptance can allow people to get on with helping themselves and their families.

By extension, while it can be difficult at times, patience can also help—patience with others and with oneself. In addition, not isolating oneself and maintaining connections with others, while not easy for some to do in these circumstances, can also be helpful."

He stresses however, the importance of seeking help for people who are struggling with stress and unhappiness in the aftermath, particularly if it begins to interfere with daily living in a significant way or things don't get better for a period of time once the external situation has returned to a more normal state. If people do seek assistance, approaches have been developed, some which are better supported by research evidence, that are aimed at assisting people cope with the stress of such an event.

Dr Ronan can be contacted: K. Ronan@cqu.edu.au

For more information please contact: Give a media relations contact here.

following an incident. This includes information on how school personnel can manage their own arousal. Information provided to staff following a hazard is a function of emergency management and mental health that can be done efficiently without too much unnecessary resource allocation. In addition to providing specifics about the content and tone of messages for children, this can also include information on how to screen and identify those youth and families at increased risk. We discuss these themes more in the following sections.

Screening, Promoting Resilience, Active Intervention. In line with what has been described in previous sections, the overall goal here is to foster recovery and resilience in those affected while keeping an eye out for those who need more

TABLE 7.1. Example of a Typical Information Sheet

INFORMATION SHEET ON STRESS RESPONSES TO FLOODING

What Reactions Are Normal?

People who experience a hazard such as a flood may also experience a range of normal stress reactions. These include:

- Feelings: numb; withdrawn; disconnected; fear; anger; guilt; grief; shame; feeling helpless; feeling empty; lack of interest or pleasure; tearful
- Thoughts: concentration, attention, and memory problems; memories and "flashbacks" of the event; disorientation or confusion; lack of decisiveness; blaming oneself
- Physical reactions: sleep problems (tension; fatigue; insomnia); stomach and appetite problems; other aches in the body; feeling on edge or startling easily; elevated heart rate, blood pressure, blood sugar
- Behavior: work, school, social, family problems and conflict; isolation and withdrawal from usual contacts; problems with trusting others; avoiding reminders of the event (e.g., places, people); keeping excessively busy; problems in close relationships (e.g., being overprotective or over-controlling, being more sensitive to others' comments); for youth, increased irritability, clinginess, tantrums, and disruptive behavior might occur.

What Can Help

A first principle in the event of a hazard such as a flood is that time helps and, with time, most people begin to recover. However, it is also the case that different people have different timelines to feeling better. Certain factors can assist the process of recovery. These include:

- do not isolate and withdraw; stay connected with others; talk to those whom you trust
- return to routines—these can help with returning a sense of order (e.g., meal times, family and daily routines)
- attend to basics: eat well, get enough sleep, reduce alcohol intake
- be patient with oneself and others; forgive yourself and others for any conflict during a high stress period
- remember that a range of feelings are normal during this time and that time and patience with oneself and support from others tends to help
- relationships (e.g., not being overprotective or over-controlling, awareness of potentially being more sensitive to others' comments; parents modelling coping behaviour for their children)

When to Seek More Direct Support

For some, reactions can become problematic to the point where direct assistance might be useful. These include:

- when reactions are more severe and do not get better with time
- when a person cannot begin to function more normally and start to resume normal activities like work, school, and within the family
- when a person herself or himself is concerned about his/her functioning

(Continued)

TABLE 7.1. (*Continued*)

Certain features of a hazardous event or the reactions to that event are may be more likely to lead to problems. The following factors have been found by research:

- Actual or perceived life or injury threat
- Witnessing extreme destruction; extreme property damage
- Loss of home and valued possessions; ongoing financial difficulties
- Loss of support from others (e.g., family, close friends)
- Intense demands during or after the event; additional stressors
- For children, parent's distress or family problems

Particular reactions that might lead to problems include:

- Dissociation or extreme numbing that lasts
- Intrusive and terrifying or extreme memories, nightmares, or flashbacks
- Continuing avoidance and withdrawal from others
- Intense arousal features (e.g., panic, rage)
- Extreme anxiety or depression (extreme agitation, worry, fears, hopelessness, loss of interest, thoughts of death)
- Extreme fatigue, hunger, sleep problems

If you would like more assistance, insert local referral sources here.

Sources: Adapted from the Disaster Mental Health Institute (DMHI, University of South Dakota) "Coping with the Aftermath of a Disaster" (Gerard Jacobs, Ph.D., DMHI); National Center for PTSD "Helping Survivors in the Wake of Disaster: A National Center for PTSD Factsheet."

direct forms of assistance. The first step is to do the following (NIMH, 2002; Ronan et al., 2005):

- provide education and information on normal responding: normal signs of stress (individual, family, community-based), subthreshold PTSD (and ASD) symptoms (re-experiencing, avoidance/numbing/ dissociative, hyperarousal features) that represent normal reactions to abnormal events, coping efforts (see also below), risk and protective factors, services available, normal versus abnormal reactions and where to seek help (see also Figure 7.1 and Table 7.1);
- promote social support and social interaction (but do not force it); foster natural social and community-based supports;
- provide information on useful coping skills (including use of approach-related versus avoidance-, withdrawal-, or blame-related coping; e.g., active outreach, informed pragmatism, efforts at reconciliation, North, Spitznagel, & Smith, 2001);
- train personnel on risk assessment and screening; conduct screening and assessment and identify those at high need;
- given that those of highest need may not seek services or identify themselves on screening instruments, provide for a mechanism for outreach (Ronan, et al., 2005);

- offer intervention for those who require it (e.g., for adults, for families, group-based); the aim is to reduce problems and increase skills and improve functioning; the level of intervention will be a function of need and resources available;
- deal with organizational factors (e.g., facilitating inter-agency coordination; educating and training relevant organizations and personnel).

Summary. As can be seen from the foregoing, the areas targeted in early intervention fit nicely within a MGSC philosophy. First, in anticipating normal recovery, the first efforts are directed towards facilitating supports to promote the natural recovery process. Second, while supporting recovery, there is also an obligation to locate those who are vulnerable to longer-term effects. Once identified, providing resources, training, or actual interventions is the next step to help vulnerable populations become more resilient. Information is now provided on how to carry out the basics at this gate of a MGSC approach, citing relevant research and case examples where available. We start with assessment and then follow on with intervention, including more specifics on promoting natural recovery.

School- and Community-Based Screening: How To, Problems, Solutions

This step is intended to identify all who might be at risk in any given community. However, while larger scale screenings have taken place after natural (e.g., Chemtob et al., 2002) and other disasters (e.g., 9/11; Applied Research and Consulting LLC, Health, and Institute, 2002), such an ideal has never to our knowledge been realized. For example, after the Oklahoma City Bombings, a citywide school screening program was attempted (Gurwitch & Pfefferbaum, 1999; see also Gurwitch et al., 2002). However, decisions to screen in individual schools, supported by the city superintendent, were ultimately left to principals as well as individual classroom teachers: "Several refused to participate, stating with assurance that all children at risk had already been identified by school personnel and school services." (Gurwitch et al., 2002, p. 346).

However, based on the incidence of PTSD symptoms prevalent and data on mental health care utilization, it was believed that many youth in need simply were never identified and offered assistance. They may indeed have suffered and perhaps continue to be affected.

Compounding this problem is the fact that some youth may minimize their reactions to events for various reasons, including the idea that such suffering in silence is protecting parents, teachers, and other adults (Gurwitch et al., 2002) or perhaps protecting the child him or herself (e.g., from not being teased by peers) (Ronan et al., 2005). With respect to the latter reason, there may be some aspects of good judgement here: research has shown that youth more prone to bullying are also those youth with more problems in living. For example, a recent study found those children with emotional problems and those who expressed emotion were more prone to being bullied (Johnson, Thompson, & Wilkinson, 2002). Further, a number of studies have found that both teachers and parents may minimize or not recognize distress reactions of youth (e.g., Almqvist & Brandell-Forsberg, 1997).

Thus, based on systems level, family-based, and child factors, those youth and their families most in need may be difficult to identify. This problem is of course not limited to children and families per se. It has also been found that adults in need of services may not identify themselves or ask for help, perhaps based on a perception that doing so might reflect a weakness of sorts (e.g., Sprang, 2000; see also Watson et al., 2003). There could also be other reasons including a lack of awareness as to the extent of problems, mistrust of social service professionals, or reflective of a pattern of avoidance coping and withdrawal. Consequently, early assistance should emphasize providing information about help available as well as attempts to identify those in need.

Steps in Early Screening: Potential Obstacles

The first step in screening within a community is to anticipate and assess for any potential obstacles to conducting such an effort. Certainly, one necessary step is to get key leaders support for such an effort (Gurwitch et al., 2002). As emphasized in our model and as discussed in Chapter 4, this includes multidisciplinary links with such groups as emergency management leadership, political and community leaders, school boards, superintendents, principals, and teachers. These links and related discussions might include a focus on the following topics to ease concerns:

- the role of early screening in overall help provision (including citing relevant research for adults, youth, families as well as describing the basics of the overall stepped care intervention program);
- that screening is brief and straightforward;
- that these efforts reflect well on a community looking after its own; and
- there is no evidence that screening efforts and participation in those efforts is harmful.

In fact, on this last point, recent research has demonstrated that victims of traumatic experiences (n = 430) not only tolerated "very well" an assessment experience (even when conducted during the acute phase following an event), but many of them also actually viewed that experience as "an interesting and valuable experience" (Griffin, Resick, Waldrop, & Mechanic, 2003, p. 221).

Parents themselves may or may not want to have their family or their child screened for problems. Recall the finding that at least some of those most likely to need direct support services after a hazard may actually be least likely to seek such services. Thus, based on such a finding, it might be assumed that those parents who are happy screening might also tend to be those parents who need less direct assistance. In addition, even if screening is possible, there is a likelihood that at least some children may minimize their own (e.g., Ronan & Deane, 1998) as well as parents' reactions (e.g., Cohen et al., 2000); parents and teachers may minimize or not recognize children's reactions (e.g., Almqvist & Brandell-Forsberg, 1997).

Given these potential problems, no consensus has yet been reached on the best means by which to engage in systematic screening of youth and families (Gurwitch et al., 2002). However, various guidelines have been proposed for the screening and treatment of trauma (AACAP, 1998; Cohen et al., 2000; March, 1999) as well as screening and assessment efforts after disasters and mass violence more specifically (e.g., AACAP, 2000; Gurwitch et al., 2002; LaGreca, Vernberg, Silverman, Vogel, & Prinstein, 1994; Saylor & DeRoma, 2002).

In drawing from recent literature (e.g., Griffin et al., 2003; Norris et al., 2002), one strategy is to use a screening model that coordinates community-wide screening with additional school-based efforts. To accomplish this, a first step is to begin linking in with local governmental and non-governmental agencies. That is, a linkage needs to be established between emergency management and school personnel and local, regional, and perhaps even national mental health agencies and resources. However, the first step is to start local and go from there. The more specific strategy is to make contacts and have face-to-face discussions with all parties that might be able to facilitate and support such an effort. Additionally, anticipation of obstacles and those who might oppose such efforts as described earlier is also important. Another salient consideration is to make the screening measures easy to administer and easy to fill out and return.

Initial Screening: How To

Here, the goal is simple. During the transition from response to recovery, and once some initial information (as described earlier) is disseminated within the community, this step might be undertaken. Keeping screening brief is likely to increase the return rate. Screening can include easy to fill out checklists, and more simply yet, whether people would like to be contacted for more information. Certainly, additional items or measures can be included but they are at the potential expense of a reduced return rate. Important to such an effort is to include information on direct services available that people can refer to if problems do arise, including any websites available.

For schools, the idea is the same. Brief screening instruments that are included in the classroom setting, perhaps combined with teacher or parent nomination, are recommended. Table 7.2 presents some representative measures compiled by the National Center for PTSD that have been used following disasters for screening with youth.

As has been discussed, while a range of problems can emerge, the main problematic themes in the more immediate aftermath of a disaster are (a) distress

TABLE 7.2. Child Self-Report Screening and Assessment Measures and Contact Information

Child measures	Domain assessed	Format	Target age group	Number of items/ratings per item	Time to administer (in minutes)	Allows multiple trauma	Corresponds to DSM diagnostic criteria	Published psychometrics
Childhood PTSD Interview	PTSD	Interview	Not specified	93/1	30–45	Yes	Yes	Yes
Children's Posttraumatic Stress Disorder Inventory	PTSD	Interview	7–18	43/1	15–20	No	Yes	Yes
Clinician-Administered PTSD Scale for Children and Adolescents	PTSD	Interview	7–18	33/2	30–120	Up to 3	Yes	Yes
Dimensions of Stressful Events	Traumatic events	Interview	Not specified	24/varies	15–30	Yes	Yes	Yes
Parent Report of Child's Reaction to Stress	PTSD	Self-report	Not specified	79/1	30–45	Yes	No	Yes
PTSD Reaction Index*	PTSD+	Interview	6–17	20/1	15–20	No	Part	Yes
Trauma Symptom Checklist for Children	Posttraumatic symptoms	Self-report	8–16	54/1	10–20	Yes	No	Yes

Traumatic Events Screening Inventory*	Traumatic events	Interview	4 and up	18/varies	10–30	Yes	Yes	Yes	Yes
When Bad Things Happen Scale	PTSD	Self-report	8–13	95/1	10–20	No	Yes	Yes	Yes

Childhood PTSD Interview (CPTSDI)

Fletcher, K. (1996). Psychometric review of the Childhood PTSD Interview. In B. H. Stamm (Ed.), *Measurement of stress, trauma, and adaptation* (pp. 87–89). Lutherville, MD: Sidran Press.

To obtain scale, contact:

Kenneth E. Fletcher, Ph.D., Department of Psychiatry, University of Massachusetts Medical Center, 55 Lake Avenue North, Worcester, MA 01655.

The Children's PTSD Inventory

Saigh, P.A., Yasik, A. E., Oberfield, R. A., et al. (2000). The Children's PTSD Inventory: Development and reliability. *Journal of Traumatic Stress, 13*, 369–380.

To obtain scale, contact:

Customer Care, The Psychological Corporation, 19500 Bulverde Rd., San Antonio, TX 78259-3701, Phone 1-800-872-1726, Fax 1-800-232-1223, *www.PsychCorp.com*

Clinician-Administered PTSD Scale for Children and Adolescents for DSM-IV (CAPS–CA)

Newman, E., & Ribbe, D. (1996). Psychometric review of the Clinician Administered PTSD Scale for Children [*sic*]. In B. H. Stamm (Ed.), *Measurement of stress, trauma, and adaptation* (pp. 106–114). Lutherville, MD: Sidran Press.

To obtain scale, contact:

National Center for PTSD (116D), VA Medical Center, 215 N. Main St., White River Junction, Vermont 05009, *ncptsd@ncptsd.org.*

(Continued)

TABLE 7.2. (*Continued*)

Dimensions of Stressful Events (DOSE)

Fletcher, K. (1996). Psychometric review of Dimensions of Stressful Events (DOSE) Ratings Scale. In B. H. Stamm (Ed.). *Measurement of stress, trauma, and adaptation* (pp. 144–151). Lutherville, MD: Sidran Press. (includes measure in its entirety)

To obtain scale, contact:

Kenneth E. Fletcher, Ph.D., Department of Psychiatry, University of Massachusetts Medical Center, 55 Lake Avenue North, Worcester, MA 01655.

Parent Report of Child's Reaction to Stress

Fletcher, K. (1996). Psychometric review of the Parent Report of Child's Reaction to Stress. In B. H. Stamm (Ed.). *Measurement of stress, trauma, and adaptation* (pp. 225–227). Lutherville, MD: Sidran Press.

To obtain scale, contact:

Kenneth E. Fletcher, Ph.D., Department of Psychiatry, University of Massachusetts Medical Center, 55 Lake Avenue North, Worcester, MA 01655.

PTSD Reaction Index

Nader, K. (1996). Assessing trauma in children. In J. Wilson & T. M. Keane (Eds.), *Assessing psychological trauma and PTSD*. New York: Guilford.

To obtain scale, contact:

Scale can be obtained from any of the authors. Scale and instruction manual can be obtained from Kathleen Nader, Ph.D., 2809 Rathlin Drive, Suite 102, Cedar Park, TX 78613, (512) 219-9446.

Trauma Symptom Checklist for Children (TSCC)

Briere, J. (1996). Trauma Symptom Checklist for Children professional manual. Odessa, FL: Psychological Assessment Resources.

To obtain scale, contact:

Psychological Assessment Resources, Box 998, Odessa, FL 33556, (800) 331-8378.

Traumatic Events Screening Inventory—Child Version (TESI-C)

Ribbe, D. (1996). Psychometric review of Traumatic Event Screening Instrument [*sic*] for Children (TESI-C). In B. H. Stamm (Ed.). *Measurement of stress, trauma, and adaptation* (pp. 386–387). Lutherville, MD: Sidran Press.

To obtain scale, contact:

National Center for PTSD (116D), VA Medical Center, 215 N. Main St., White River Junction, Vermont 05009, *ncptsd@ncptsd.org.*

When Bad Things Happen Scale (WBTH)

Fletcher, K. (1996). Psychometric review of the When Bad Things Happen Scale (WBTH). In B. H. Stamm (Ed.), *Measurement of stress, trauma, and adaptation* (pp. 435–437). Lutherville, MD: Sidran Press.

To obtain scale, contact:

Kenneth E. Fletcher, Ph.D., Department of Psychiatry, University of Massachusetts Medical Center, 55 Lake Avenue North, Worcester, MA 01655.

Source: Reproduced from National Center for PTSD (reprinted with permission—a public domain site).

and anxiety-related problems including ASD and PTSD, and (b) grief and depression (see Chapter 2 for a more detailed listing). However, it is also the case that while such problems tend to be reflected in relatively straightforward ways in adults, presentation in youth can be more variable. For example, anxiety and depression in some youth can appear as a form of irritability and some disruptive tendencies instead of the more prototypical forms. Thus, one issue particularly in early screening or nomination is to ask whether a child's functioning has shifted following the hazard in question.

Whatever the form that screening takes—direct screening, mail out surveys, or "indirect" forms (e.g., websites that have information and fact sheets that can assist people to ascertain whether direct services might be useful)—it is emphasized here that screening needs to conform to current ethical standards, including the idea of informed consent and voluntary participation (NIMH, 2002). Additionally, for those doing screening, the seeking approval of a sanctioned ethics panel can help ensure protection for the public as well as for the screening providers. It may also provide some additional reassurance for those in a community or school who might have concerns.

The Next Steps: Education and Direct Service Delivery in a MGSC Model

The next step is providing services to those that need them. Various modalities are available: education and information, large and small group interventions, peer and other support services, direct forms of family assistance, and individual interventions. It can also include providing assistance or training to individual help providers. For example, after recent floods, one group affected included farming and other families living in rural and flood affected areas. One source of request for assistance came through peer support and outreach networks: the resultant nature of our assistance was intended to arm those providers with information on how to identify those in need and how to provide direct support and referrals. Part of the assistance provided here was research on assisting the normal recovery process, risk and protective factors, who was at increased risk, what to look for, and direct services available.

For those requiring direct services, to supplement any brief initial screening, some additional assessment for ASD/PTSD, anxiety, depression, relationship difficulties, family functioning, coping strategies, level of support, and some of the main risk and protective factors is recommended. The purposes here are to assess the extent of the problem, to establish the presence of risk and protective factors, for treatment planning, and to establish a baseline against which progress can be measured. Owing to resource demands, another source available to assist with community-wide outreach is through a local community-based website (see next section for more detail).

Stepped Care Intervention: Web-Based Education and Information

In many cases, the first point of contact is through the provision of information and education materials such as that described earlier (i.e., expecting normal recovery, normalizing reactions, providing information on how to increase protective factors and reduce risk factors and what constitutes normal versus problematic reactions; see Figure 7.1 and Table 7.1 for information that can be included; also, see our website (Appendix 2) for any updated information).

Websites are ideal for such a purpose. While referral to relevant websites can work if no website development is available, the idea of a community or school developing their own purpose-built site that deals with that specific hazard and links physical recovery information with psychological recovery is preferred. It also is a forum for regular updates that can further promote recovery. This book's website intends to include information on what to include at such a hazard-specific site. If no such capacity is available, Appendix 2 includes some useful links and information. For local sites, in addition to educational information, referral information for those who may require direct services should also be included.

Stepped Care Intervention: More Direct Services

There are cases where initial screening and outreach indicates that more than educational materials and informal support from others may be required. Based on the screening profile or based on self- or other-referral, those needing further services can begin to be identified.

Services available then are offered and provided. For some, simply providing additional information and support may be sufficient. For others, more direct help may be required. Here, emphasizing any linkages with local mental health services, with schools, and with other supports in the community (e.g., emergency management, social services, peer assistance, phone lines) to have them be available for referral is recommended. At the same time, offering training to ensure they have at least some minimal training in evidence-based practice in this area is similarly recommended. The direct services with the most evidence to date are those from the cognitive-behavioral model (NIMH, 2002).

Cognitive Behavioral Intervention in MGSC. While more research is clearly necessary, the intervention model with the most support is that which incorporates cognitive-behavioral (CBT) principles, particularly exposure. This is true for both adults and for youth (NIMH, 2002). No research to date has looked at the effectiveness of any treatment approach for families. Our MGSC approach incorporates CBT principles and aims to assist both youth and adults to cope more effectively. However, addressing family factors to increase protective factors and resiliency is an important consideration. We now look at the support for CBT interventions as well as present their main ingredients in a stepped care model, beginning with large and small group-based interventions. Then, more intensive individual and family-based interventions are considered.

A CBT Approach: The Main Ingredients. The main ingredient in a CBT approach following a hazard or traumatic incident is exposure. The idea in exposure is similar to the idea offered by Confucius long ago: Go to the heart of the darkness for there you shall find safety. In other words, approaching a fearful stimulus and remaining there until fear, and related arousal, reduces is the idea. Helping children and adults "face their fears" is supplemented in the CBT model by a variety of other strategies including relaxation (e.g., deep breathing, muscle relaxation) and various other cognitive and self-talk (problem solving, cognitive restructuring) and behavioral (reinforcement, modelling, seeking support) methods. A hallmark of a CBT approach is providing information and education that is intended to (a) normalize reactions and (b) assist with symptom management and coping. More detail is provided now by way of example in the following sections as well as in more detail in the section on individualized and family-based approaches.

Group-Based CBT Intervention. When some direct intervention appears necessary, groups are a convenient way to deliver psychoeducational forms of treatment. Different formats are available ranging from large group, single session to small group, multiple session formats. Large group formats may be particularly suitable for single incident stressors where there is community-wide disruption (Yule, 2001) and as an initial step in terms of more formalized interventions. First provided is an example of a large group intervention with school-aged youth first reviewed in Chapter 3 but included here for reader convenience. This is followed up with a description of small group interventions.

Large Group Intervention. We carried out a large group intervention as part of a more comprehensive MGSC study following a volcanic eruption that lasted for several days (Ronan & Johnston, 1999). However, prior to simply going in and doing some intervention during the acute phase of the hazard, we first did screening and linked with others who were providing normative and other educational information to children and families in schools and the affected communities. Primary school aged youth (n = 113) between the ages of 7 and 13 were first screened approximately one month following the initial eruption and then again approximately 2 months later. The initial finding was that, like most other research in this area, the great majority of youth were seen to get better with time. This was particularly so for self-reported symptoms of acute stress and posttraumatic stress disorder (ASD and PTSD, respectively). Thus, while a number of youth reported prominent features of the disorder at the 1 month screening (e.g., Ronan, 1997a, b), there were significant reductions in these symptoms by the 3 month interval (Ronan & Johnston, 1999; see also Huzziff & Ronan, 1999). In fact, the change over that 2 month interval corresponded to an effect size of .80 (i.e., .8 of a pooled standard deviation; Cohen's d). In more practical terms, an effect size that is .80 or greater is considered to be a large effect and, here, reflected a 33% reduction.

Thus, the expectation for normal recovery discussed earlier in this chapter was certainly indicated for most youth. However, a proportion of youth still remained at least mildly symptomatic according to criteria established for the screening measure used, the PTSD Reaction Index (Frederick, Pynoos, & Nader, 1996). In addition, while PTSD-related distress was seen to reduce markedly for many, similar magnitude change in the ability to cope with eruption-related stimuli was not as great. In fact, in one school in particular, coping scores were seen to deteriorate across time. While not formally assessed, it is also the case that this school was in a community that appeared to have some risk factors (e.g., high unemployment and low socioeconomic status; not reopening as soon as some other schools). The overall change across time in coping in the whole sample corresponded to a smaller effect size (.21) compared to the change seen in PTSD-related distress (.80).

The upshot of these findings when taken together was that while most youth were seen to have reducing distress, an intervention program was considered to be suitable for those youth not showing desirable reductions in distress or increases in coping ability. At the two month interval, according to Frederick et al. (1992) criteria, just over half of the sample was still considered to be at least mildly symptomatic. Certainly, while many of these would be anticipated to continue seeing reduced distress scores over time, a small minority of youth had scores that were still at a level indicating potentially clinically significant problems.

Consequently, with the cooperation of the schools, we engaged in a large group- and CBT-based intervention with the youth in classroom and school settings with approximately 30 or so youth per group. The approximately one hour intervention itself was based on two main ideas from a CBT model: (a) exposure (video-based) and (b) providing normative (and other expert-based) information designed to assist coping. Given the large group nature of the intervention, it consisted primarily of a presentation by a volcanologist (second author), assisted by a clinical psychologist with expertise in working with youth and families (first author), and supplemented with questions from children and teachers.

The presentation itself included a 20-minute video of the eruptions accompanied by the science of eruptions. Such information was designed to give children an increased sense of control. Related, for this presentation, information was incorporated into the discussion that emphasized safety in relation to the science. Other information was presented to normalize reactions through the direct presentation of information (i.e., normal reactions to stressors) combined with the presenters modelling their own reactions to the eruptions. All children received this "exposure and normalizing" presentation: one group of youth (n = 69) were randomly assigned to a "CBT condition" that additionally included some other features of a CBT intervention. These included the modelling of how to re-shape distorted self-talk or misconceptions through a problem-solving approach. For example, a common misconception was that the water supply was poisoned with ash. The presenter modelled that initial self-talk and then took the children through the means necessary to locate information to confirm or dispel that notion. The culmination of this "cognitive restructuring" sequence was self-reinforcement (i.e., giving oneself a "pat on the back" for active attempts to cope and solve problems).

The overall finding was that intervention was successful in assisting youth to report significantly reduced distress and significantly increased coping ability. The more behaviorally oriented exposure and normalizing condition was seen to produce similar changes to the CBT approach. That is, while the addition of the CBT components did produce slightly larger magnitude change, overall the conditions were found to be not statistically different from each other. Thus, in this study, video-based exposure and information designed to increase a sense of control and safety were useful for youth.

Of note, given that all 113 youth who started the research were involved in the presentation, we also examined whether such a presentation would sensitize, or negatively impact, on those youth not reporting any problems. In fact, outcome data confirmed that non-symptomatic youth were not deleteriously affected by the presentation; in fact, overall, they too showed that they derived benefits (Ronan & Johnston, 1999). This provides some comfort for two reasons: the most apparent is that youth not reporting problems were not negatively sensitized. The less apparent issue is that some youth underreport problems and, if screening attempts rely on self-report, there will surely be some youth reporting low scores who are nevertheless distressed. Thus, this group of children may too derive benefit. Of course, as a relevant aside here, we advocate for the inclusion of methods other than just self-report to assist in identifying those in need as discussed earlier in this chapter.

Finally, in terms of this intervention study (Ronan & Johnston, 1999), at 4 month follow-up, changes were maintained for coping scores with continuing improvement seen for symptom scores. In addition, at this point, those children who were involved in the intervention showed significantly more adaptive scores on both measures compared to a group of children who did not attend the intervention.

A similar idea would hold for doing larger group presentations for parents and other adults involved in the lives of youth (e.g., other family members, school personnel). These would include additional information on the instrumental role of parents in helping youth cope effectively.

Small Group Intervention. Small groups are useful for doing more in the way of direct intervention, particularly for those who do not respond to more educational and informational forms of support.

A good example in the little research available is a study by March, Amaya and colleagues (March et al., 1998; see also Amaya et al., 2003) that used a group-based CBT intervention for PTSD-affected youth who had been exposed to single incident stressors (e.g., fires, motor vehicle accidents). The average duration of PTSD symptoms was around 2 years (c. 1.5 years for younger participants;

2.5 years for older). The intervention itself was manualized and administered over the course of 18 weeks. A number of elements of this approach are very similar to those from our own protocol for treatment of anxiety-related disorders including PTSD (Feather & Ronan, 2005; Girling-Butcher & Ronan, 2002; Huzziff & Ronan, 2005; Kendall et al., 1992; Ronan & Deane, 1998; Ronan, Johnston, & Finnis, 2005). For example, like our own protocol, elements including various cognitive and behavioural coping strategies combined with exposure are part of the March and Amaya and colleagues' protocol (Amaya et al., 2003). We describe our original CBT protocol, and current variations that can be used for recovery from hazards and trauma, in more detail in the next major section.

In the March et al. (1998) study, the most notable finding was that by the 6 month follow-up, 86% of the treated youth no longer met criteria for PTSD diagnosis. Another notable finding was that by follow-up, treated children had moved from an external locus of control to an internal focus. The significance of this shift is that an internal locus of control is associated with good mental health outcomes, positive forms of coping, and an overall sense of self-efficacy. That is, not only were symptoms of PTSD reduced, but the participants also reported an increased sense of being able to manage future events more productively.

A study using a combination of four group and two individual sessions was carried out by Goenjian and colleagues (Goenjian et al., 1997) with 64 adolescents following an earthquake in Armenia. The group-based component consisted of various anxiety management techniques combined with exposure (see next section for a full description of similar treatment components). The main finding of this study was that 1.5 and 3 years after the study, treated youth were seen to improve significantly in terms of self-reported PTSD symptoms whereas untreated youths' symptoms were seen to get worse. Additionally, while no significant change was seen in depression scores of treated youth, depression scores were seen to increase in the untreated group. Thus, treatment here was seen to improve PTSD symptoms while providing a protective function for depression. In fact, a relationship between anxiety and depression has been established in the mental health literature where increased anxiety, including PTSD, is a risk factor for depression (e.g., Goodwin, Fergusson, & Horwood, 2004; Miller, 2003). However, as seen below, findings based on our treatment protocol (e.g., Kendall et al., 1992; Ronan & Deane, 1998) have established that CBT interventions can reduce not only anxiety features but also have a direct ameliorative effect on other problems including depression, including following a natural disaster (e.g., Chemtob, Nakashima, & Carlson, 2002).

Individual and Family-Based CBT Interventions

A growing body of literature supports both individual and family-based CBT interventions for anxiety and related problems, including PTSD and depression, in youth. We now look at a well-researched program that was developed by a team including the senior author (Kendall et al., 1992; Ronan & Deane, 1998).

Focus on PTSD, Fears, and Anxieties: Exposure and CBT Interventions

Our original protocol for assisting youth and families with anxiety related problems is a 16 session intervention that includes various cognitive-behavioral strategies (Kendall et al., 1992; Ronan & Deane, 1998). These strategies are designed to help youth and families manage unwanted arousal effectively, reduce symptoms of anxiety and distress. Additionally, the precepts used in this youth and family-based program are those that are used in evidence-based adult-focused interventions for trauma and other anxiety problems (e.g., Watson et al., 2003) and emphasize the central role of exposure.

Our original protocol (Kendall et al., 1992), and more recent variations (e.g., group-and school-based, family-based, briefer forms), all emphasize exposure—looking directly back at the event itself and dealing with the symptoms associated. As an aside, interventions from other approaches (e.g., psychodynamic, emotion-focused) similarly stress the role of increased awareness of the impact of the event itself and its consequences and dealing with them directly. A main reason for this is that as has been stressed elsewhere in this book, a main feature of PTSD and other anxiety-related problems is the problem of avoidance. Exposure-related interventions aim to help gently "break through" avoidance and directly deal with the traumatic event. Exposure and the other elements of our CBT protocol are intended to help the person deal directly with anxiety-provoking situations both currently and in the past. One of the main ideas in exposure is "extinction" as well as "habituation". Here, as research has demonstrated, anxious arousal tends to peak and arousal begins to return to normal levels the longer one stays in the presence of a particular anxiety-provoking stimulus. Thus, part of the idea in exposure put more simply is helping people to "face their fears."

Our CBT program itself combines exposure with various coping strategies designed to help youth and family members manage anxious arousal. The first idea is to assist the child and family identify unwanted arousal and use that awareness as the trigger to apply coping strategies. The actual strategies themselves are taught in a sequential fashion and based on the FEAR acronym. This acronym, described in more detail later in this section, is designed as a "coping template" that is then applied in imaginal and real-life situations that provoke anxiety (i.e., exposure). Situations that can provoke anxiety following a disaster may be those that remind the child or family member of the features of the disaster that were anxiety-provoking or traumatic at the time of the event. The original treatment protocol emphasized intervening with youth and included a parent component to help with generalization of gains. More recent variations include the family more directly for the purposes of (a) helping better generalize skills and gains for the youth and (b) assisting family members themselves to manage anxiety effectively. Other recent variations of this protocol include group-based formats (Flannery-

Schroeder & Kendall, 2000) and trauma-focused formats (Feather & Ronan, 2005).

One advantage of this program is that it is well-structured and supported by research carried in out in a number of countries including the U.S. (e.g., Kendall, 1994; Kendall et al., 1997), Australia (e.g., Barrett et al., 1996), and New Zealand (e.g., Girling-Butcher & Ronan, 2005; Ronan & Johnston, 1999). Recent meta-analyses (Huzziff & Ronan, 2005a; McMurray & Ronan, 2005) have documented the effectiveness of this program and its variants over immediate and long-term follow-up as well as providing support for other behavioral and CBT interventions for anxiety and related problems in youth. In fact, as indicated earlier, this and similar programs have been seen to reduce not only anxiety, but it also has been found to have a significant impact on other forms of distress, most notably PTSD symptoms and depression. This is important as hazards and disasters can provoke not only anxiety-based reactions like PTSD but also depression and grief associated with loss. More recent research has provided additional support for shortened protocols, 8–10 sessions versus the original 16 (e.g., Girling-Butcher & Ronan, 2005; Huzziff & Ronan, 2005b). One reason this is important is that some other research has documented that those who seek services for distress and other problems are likely to have dropped out of treatment by the 10th session (Weisz & Weiss, 1989).

Given a systems and pragmatic focus, we emphasize a brief and more family-based intervention model. In fact, by making the original protocol (Kendall et al., 1992) briefer, it allows for the family to carry out some of the tasks that were initially intended to be done in session in the original program. However, here, the original protocol is described to allow the reader to see all of the main precepts of the most researched approach (Ronan & Deane, 1998). We describe some variation to this protocol based on more recent findings to include the family as well as shorten the treatment.

In the original program, the first half of treatment (first 8 sessions) involves helping children learn strategies underpinning the FEAR plan (Ronan & Deane, 1998): (a) cues to unwanted arousal, (b) relaxation strategies including progressive muscle relaxation and imagery, (c) management of self-talk, (d) using systematic problem-solving and coping procedures, and (e) self-evaluation skills to cope with both success (e.g., self-reinforcement) and failure (i.e., coping and learning from it). Thus, the coping template, or FEAR plan, incorporates the following elements:

F   Feeling Frightened? (identification of cues to anxious arousal and initial coping through relaxation strategies);

E   Expecting Bad Things to Happen? (managing anxious self-talk);

A   Attitudes and Actions that Help (problem-solving and coping strategies);

R   Results and Rewards (realistic self-evaluation and reinforcement/learning from failure).

The means by which these components are conveyed to the youth are through (a) direct teaching, (b) demonstrating (modelling), (c) role play and practice, (d) rewards (tangible, social, self), (e) out-of-session practice (homework), and, quite importantly, (f) a collaborative alliance between the service provider and the child and family. In terms of this latter point, the original program allowed for a parent session early to help convey these features to the parent to promote their helping the youth out of session. We now feel that more explicit inclusion of family members is a useful idea following a disaster and expand on this idea in the next section.

The second half of the original program relies on exposure, both imaginal and *in-vivo*. Sessions are arranged in such a way so as to expose the youth first to minimally anxiety-provoking material that is then graduated to exposure to increasingly anxiety-provoking, or traumatic, situations. The idea of course is to promote success and mastery at each successive level of exposure. In assisting those affected by a disaster, the main situations will of course be hazard-related. However, given the fact that those who are already anxious are more likely to be impacted by a hazard, keeping an eye open for other major anxiety provoking situations is also worthwhile. In other words, the hazard itself may be another anxiety-provoking stimulus to a person who has higher levels of "anxiety sensitivity". In such cases, the job is to help them manage the hazard and related distress specifically but also to help them develop the coping template to manage other current and future stressors.

The session structure across 16 sessions is now described. As described, various considerations (e.g., resourcing, individual needs, time limitations, research evidence) support a flexible application, including adding more of a family component and making the protocol briefer. However, it is useful for the practitioner to bear in mind the principles of the original program before considering more flexible applications (Ronan & Deane, 1998).

Treatment Sequence and Session Structure

The structure of individual sessions is the same across treatment. With the exception of the first session, each session begins with a review of homework (or STIC task, "Show That I Can"). The content of homework helps to practice and generalize skills learned in session. Depending on the age of the child, points or stickers are provided that can then be "banked" and turned in every 4th session for a reward.

Next is the introduction of the main topic for that session. In the learning phase (Sessions 1–8), it involves the following features:

- Session 1: Relationship-building and introduction to the main features;
- Session 2: Affective education: identifying emotions;
- Session 3: Bodily cues to anxious arousal (part of "F" in FEAR plan);
- Session 4: Progressive and cue controlled muscle relaxation (including audiotape for youth and family to practice and use at home; part of "F" in FEAR plan);

- Session 5: Identifying and modifying anxious self-talk ("E" in FEAR plan);
- Session 6: Problem-solving ("A" in FEAR plan);
- Session 7: Self-evaluation, self-reinforcement, coping with failure ("R" in FEAR plan);
- Session 8: Consolidation of skills using FEAR acronym:

> **F** = Feeling frightened?
> **E** = Expecting bad things to happen?
> **A** = Attitudes and actions that can help.
> **R** = Results and rewards.

Strategies that are used to help the child begin to learn and practice the individual skills include therapist explaining and modelling the skill. In the SS4R model, "coping" modelling is preferred over "mastery" modelling. In the former and as initially described in Chapter 3, modelling is carried out that demonstrates imperfect handling and that the initially imperfect coping is not only okay, but to be expected on some occasions. Further, this form of modelling goes on to cope with the initially imperfect attempt as well as convey the more general idea that failure can be planned for and, importantly, can be a "royal road" to true learning. Also valued is the idea in a coping modelling approach of demonstrating coping with success. Some anxious youth have difficulty dealing with success.

In addition to education and modelling, role-play and practice (rehearsal) are also used. Some youth enjoy role-play; however, others can be initially reluctant. Similarly, some therapists like role-play while others are more hesitant. For those youth who are hesitant, therapists can use coping modelling (particularly if they themselves have felt some reluctance in the past) as well as another procedure termed "tag along" (Ollendick, 1983). Here, the therapist takes the lead in the role play and the child follows or mimics the attempts. The therapist will not only demonstrate but will also talk aloud how they are thinking and feeling and ask the youth if he or she is thinking or feeling the same or differently (e.g., "are you feeling like that or differently"; "what is in your thought bubble?"). With such a procedure, children get gradually introduced to role play with the therapist. Making role play fun is also recommended. Additionally, switching roles can be both fun as well as instructive (e.g., the therapist plays the child; the child plays a parent, sibling, friend, teacher, etc.). Finally, as with all aspects of the program, planning for success in role-plays is crucial.

The end of the session is for going over the STIC (homework) task and for less structured time. The STIC task discussion (a) links the task with material from the session and (b) aims to ensure success in carrying out the task. The child writes down the task in a personal journal given to them in Session 1. Finally, less structured time at the end allows for a game to be played or some other pleasurable activity as reinforcement for the work put in during the session.

Second Half of Treatment: Exposure

The second half of treatment has the same structure as that of the first: review homework, session activity, provide homework, fun activity. However, here, the focus is on exposing the child to increasingly anxiety provoking situations. With the use of the FEAR plan, the child faces a hierarchy of stressful situations arranged from least to most anxiety provoking (and which are culled from initial assessment and over the first half of treatment). First, low anxiety producing situations are presenting imaginally (after some initial discussion, rehearsal, and role play as appropriate). However, with initial mastery, later sessions in this half of treatment are sometimes conducted out in the natural environment of the youth and family (*in vivo* exposure). Here, some of the discussion, rehearsal, and role play may need to be carried out in a previous session. A brief discussion or rehearsal might then be able to be done in the natural environment prior to the actual exposure attempt. Following each exposure, discussion and social reinforcement are used to help the child evaluate realistically, self-reinforce, and cope with less than total mastery. In terms of content, the focus here is on stimuli related to a hazard. This can include both imaginal exposure (e.g., imagining the situation and talking or writing about it) as well as other forms of exposure including some form of web- or media-based exposure (e.g., video exposure; Ronan & Johnston, 1999). Also, *in vivo* exposure to real life situations that continue to provoke anxiety is recommended when possible. This might include such situations as going back to the site where the hazard occurred or where the child (and family) was when the hazard occurred.

It cannot be stressed enough that planning is vital and that a main feature of planning is ensuring that exposure attempts are going to be a mastery experience for the child. We do not recommend rushing through exposure. That is, ensuring that each successive step of a hierarchy is mastered is more important than covering every single fear or anxiety. Another vital issue in exposure is making sure the exposure interval is long enough for the child's anxiety to be decreased. When in an anxiety-provoking situation, the natural tendency is for anxiety to increase first, peak, and then begin to reduce. Cutting short this process could inadvertently increase anxiety rather than decrease it. Consequently, depth is better than breadth and slow is better than fast: ensuring mastery at each step of the hierarchy is more important than covering the entire hierarchy. Finally, helping youth access and use the FEAR plan also involves their increasing ability to self-reinforce (e.g., give oneself a "pat on the back") for being brave and for facing their fears.

Homework tasks in this half of treatment tend to involve exposure to naturally occurring situations, particularly in the wake of initial session-based successes. Enlisting the help of parents and others (e.g., teachers) and thinking creatively here is recommended.

The program ends with a final session for summarizing successes and gains as well as the making of a videotaped "advertisement." This advertisement is intended to be a fun and creative way to help a child "advertise" their success in the program (Kendall et al., 1992; Ronan & Deane, 1998). Of course, the child and parents are made aware that booster sessions are available if necessary. Finally, a therapist follow-up phone call is recommended to ensure maintenance of gains.

Adaptations for Families and Real-Life Conditions

As discussed previously, we value the inclusion of families in the treatment of youth affected by a hazardous event. Given that parents and family factors appear to have a major influence on reactions of youth to a disaster, and that parents of distressed youth are more likely to be distressed themselves, including families more intimately from early in the intervention is recommended. This can include meeting with parents every session and having them become more involved with exposure. In a recent study (Girling-Butcher & Ronan, 2005), an 8–10 session protocol that included parents in every session and began exposure earlier was carried out (see Table 7.3).

Using a multiple baseline, single case methodology, we found this shortened protocol was successful in eliminating anxiety disorders in all participants. Additionally, coping and depression scores also improved from pre- to post-treatment. The youth, parents, and teachers all reported positive changes for the youth. Additionally, at 12 month follow-up, all youth continued to be diagnosis free.

In terms of using such an adaptation, the idea is to continue to see the child individually but also include bringing the parent in to have the child and therapist describe and demonstrate that session's activities and plan for the out-of-session activity (the STIC task). Finally, the therapist then meets briefly with the parent(s) along to discuss the child's progress and any problems encountered.

Following a hazard, we would recommend using this time to share information with parents about their vital role in helping children recover. This may include encouraging them to use strategies of the program for their own benefit, how to model coping with distress for their child (even if they are feeling distress), how to encourage approach- versus avoidance-coping, the value of returning to family and school-based routines, of seeking support from others, of providing support within the family, and so forth (see also earlier section for more information that can be conveyed here). We would add that if a parent were significantly distressed and in need of direct treatment, our preference, like other systemic interventions for youth (e.g., Hengeller et al., 1998), is to treat the parent directly rather than referring them for services. However, if direct treatment is not possible for the parent, referring them to services is recommended. However, it is worth noting that there is some evidence that parents derive benefit for their own anxiety and depression through a focus on the child's problems in this CBT program (e.g., Girling-Butcher & Ronan, 2005; Huzziff & Ronan, 2005; see also Cobham, Dadds, & Spence, 1998). Finally, even if a parent needs to be referred, it is important to keep them involved in the treatment for their child at a minimum to ensure

TABLE 7.3. A Reduced Protocol for Helping Youth and Families Manage Anxiety and Traumatic Reactions

---

Session 1

An overview of the concepts and strategies used in the treatment program.
The establishment of rapport, and an outline of the 4-step plan for coping with anxiety and trauma. The identification of anxious feelings, the normalisation of anxiety, and the introduction of relaxation training.

Session 2

A review of anxious feelings and the 4-step plan, and the identification of somatic responses to anxiety and trauma. The introduction with parents of contingency management strategies, planned ignoring, and differential reinforcement, to reduce anxious behaviours in their child.

Session 3

The role of anxious self-talk in anxiety, and the development of coping-based self-talk. The exploration of the relationship between feelings, thoughts and behavior, and the continuation of relaxation training.

Session 4

A review of the modification of anxious self-talk into coping self-talk, and the development of problem solving skills to help manage anxiety and trauma. Additionally, the session focuses on self evaluation and self reward for success in managing anxiety, as well as learning to cope with failure.

Session 5

Practice of the 4-step plan, in low to moderate anxiety provoking situations using imaginal and in-vivo exposure. The exploration of different elements of anxious experiences, and a review of the relaxation techniques taught.

Session 6

Application of the 4-step plan in in-vivo situations, producing moderate levels of anxiety.

Session 7

Practice of the 4-step plan in in-vivo situations that produce high levels of anxiety.

Sessions 8–10

Continued practice of the 4-step plan in a situation that produces a high level of anxiety, and the production of the child's videotaped commercial. A review of the treatment program, and saying goodbye to the child and their parents.

Source: Adapted from Girling-Butcher and Ronan (2002).

they are aware of their role in their child's coping efforts and involved in planning for the generalization of gains.

The Practitioner as Local Scientist: Evaluation of Helping Efforts

As initially indicated in Chapter 3, it is important here to emphasize again that we value the "local science" model of service delivery (Ronan, Johnston, & Finnis, 2005). In other words, it is vital to helping efforts that progress is actually measured. An MGSC model emphasizes the need for ongoing assessment to identify who is doing well, and who may need further assistance, at a particular step of the intervention continuum.

More detail is provided in Chapter 8 and 9 on ongoing, and pragmatic, evaluation within a stepped care program following a hazardous event. As stressed throughout this book, we strongly recommend this as part of usual practice. This includes evaluation as a reflection of our being willing to be accountable for practice, for providing feedback for clients and oneself, and as a feature of quality controlled service delivery.

Chapter **8**

Putting It All Together
*Evidence Based Guidelines
for Practice*

INTRODUCTION: THE MINDSET

Organizing a community or school to prepare for a hazard is not a simple task. Similarly, response and recovery from a disaster can be made complicated and chaotic without good planning, decision-making capability, and links established in the community. In terms of readiness through recovery efforts, as discussed in earlier chapters, there are also a number of levels of preparation: organizational (both within and across groups), household, and individual.

Given the complexities inherent in the response and recovery environment, planning for a disaster by detailing simplistic step-by-step tasks is not considered to be a fruitful approach. However, with that said, there are some logical steps or principles, that both research and common sense would suggest are fruitful to planning efforts. Prior to entertaining what to do and how to do it, developing a conceptual and evidence-based mindset is a useful first step. As with others, and as discussed at various points earlier, the SS4R model features collaborative networking and problem-solving within a community versus a top-down hierarchical structure. As discussed in earlier chapters, the features of a collaborative problem-solving model are compatible with our own ideas as well as those in local hazards sustainability models (Mileti, 1999).

153

TABLE 8.1. A Summary of the SS4R Mindset

Interactive community-based problem-solving approach
Commitment to evidence-based practice
Prevention as primary; planning for response and recovery
Linking physical and psychosocial factors in planning, response, recovery
Multiple Gating, Stepped Care model of education and intervention
Practitioner accountability
Motivate, Educate, Demonstrate, Discuss, and Do
Messenger and leadership attributes

Additionally, attention to some basic issues is vital. As seen in Table 8.1, the basic principles of the SS4R mindset are presented (see Chapter 3 for more comprehensive listing of information). In terms of a commitment to evidence-based practice, incorporating research findings into everyday practice, and the commitment to ongoing evaluation of one's own practice, is quite often easier said than done. Such practice requires effort to initiate and sustain. In fact, as discussed in earlier chapters, research indicates that an evidence-based practice approach is not the norm in some areas of emergency management (e.g., Perry & Lindell, 2003).

In terms of incorporating these principles into practice, attention is now turned to the basic tasks that bring this model to life. We start with readiness and risk reduction practice and emphasize this as a primary means to help the school and its youth and families cope with a hazardous event.

READINESS AND RISK REDUCTION PRACTICE: WHAT TO DO AND HOW TO DO IT

This section is intended to lay out tasks that are necessary to carrying out readiness activities. As seen in Table 8.2, an overview of those basic principles is provided. We do agree with the bulk of opinion in this area that a simplistic step-by-step approach will simply not be adequate. Consequently, these basic tasks are considered to be just that: fundamental principles of "what to do" and "how to do it" that are going to require flexibility and sustained effort to carry out. As indicated in this book, a focus on general principles while maintaining flexibility are attributes that have been shown to be useful in responding to a disaster (e.g., Quarantelli, 1988). In other words, the best laid plans may provide some initial direction but flexibility and sound, ongoing monitoring and decision-making is fundamental to practice in all areas including readiness and risk reduction. Consequently, some of the basic tasks are provided mindful that they are a template and not a cookbook.

Table 8.2. The Basic Principles for Readiness, Risk Reduction, and Planning for Response and Recovery

Principle I: Developing Momentum: Linkages and Relationships

    I. Ensuring Commitment of School Community: Anticipating Obstacles and Providing Leadership
    II. Emergency Management Links
        A. Establishing Relationship and Cooperation
        B. Establishing the Level of Hazard in the Community
        C. Local
        D. Statewide/Regional
        E. National
    III. Community Groups and Organizations
        A. First Responders
            1. Fire, Police, Emergency Services
            2. Victim Support Agencies (including supportive phonelines and direct support services)
        B. Other Government Organizations
        C. Non-Government Organizations
            1. Public
            2. Private
        D. Scientific and Academic Groups
        E. Media
        F. Community Groups, Businesses, Individuals
        G. Households and Families
        H. Youth

Principle II: Planning the Effort

    I. Hazards Education Programs in the School Setting
    II. Hazards Education Programs in the Family Setting
    III. Coordinating with Hazards Education in Community and Organizational Settings
    IV. First Step
        A. Gather Resources
        B. Joint Workshops and Planning Meetings
            1. Invite Groups including Experts for Presentations
                a. Physical Scientists (geologists, meteorologists, etc)
                b. Social Scientists (e.g., sociologists, psychologists)
                c. Hazard and Disaster Practitioners
            2. Focus on the Evidence
                d. Evidence-based Practice
                e. The Role for Local Science
            3. Plan for Workshop Follow-up: Initial Conceptual and Concrete Planning; Not Leaving a Workshop Behind
    V. Converting Planning to Doing: The Role of the Written Plan

Principle III: Establishing a Practical Assessment Methodology: Baseline and Ongoing Evaluation

    I. School-Based
    II. Family- and Household-Based
    III. Community-Based

Table 8.2. *(continued)*

Principle IV: Education/Intervention

    I. The Primacy of Motivation and Engagement
       A. Developing Discrepancy: Linking Concern with Efficacy
          1. Willingness to Change
          2. Ability to Change
          3. Readiness to Change
       B. Promoting Concern- and Change-Talk; Promoting Interaction and Search for Information
          I. Prior to, During, and Following Education Efforts
          II. Multiple Messages
          III. Multiple Media
          IV. Multiple, Linked, Trusted Sources
          V. Consistency of Messages
          VI. Incorporating the Evidence
       C. Thinking Creatively
          1. Competitions
             A. School-based
             B. Neighborhood-based
             C. Community-based
          2. School and Community Reminders
             D. Preparedness Thermometer
             E. Press Releases
             F. Web-based
             G. Flyers
             H. Ongoing Presentations
    II. Means of Delivery of Education Programs: The Messengers
    III. Types and Content
       A. School- and Evidence-Based Hazards Education Programs for Youth
          1. Didactic Information
             a. Preparedness Information: What to Do and How to Do It
                i. problem-focused coping, physical prep
                ii. psychosocial prep
             b. Response and Recovery Planning
                i. include building in flexibility and decision-making capacity
          2. Promoting Hazards Discussions
          3. Demonstrations and Modelling
          4. Practice and Simulations
          5. Interactive Components
             a. Links between Other Curricula and Preparedness: Integrated Curricula
             b. The Spreading Activation Network
                i. Links between school education and home (e.g., preparedness and planning homework)
                ii. Links between school education and community settings and initiatives
       B. The Role of Education, Modeling, and Practice: First Learn and Discuss, Then See, Then Practice and Do
       C. Integrated programs
          1. School-based
          2. Community-based

The Tasks of Readiness and Risk Reduction: Planning and Preparing for Response and Recovery

Developing Linkages and Relationships

As discussed in Chapter 4, linking with the rest of the community is important. An initial relationship that can be developed is between the school and local emergency management. Additionally, linking to emergency management (EM) at the state and national levels can be useful. For example, national emergency management agencies (e.g., FEMA in the U.S.; Ministry of Civil Defence and Emergency Management (MCDEM) in NZ) often have school- or child- and family-based materials, along with more community-focused resources. In fact, we have included some of those resources in this book. More than just web-, pamphlet-, or other informational-based material, such linkages with local through national levels may be able to provide direct consultation, additional educational material, presentations, and other resources that can assist with planning and delivering an educational program in schools and community settings. In terms of local emergency management, it has been our experience that local emergency managers are ready, willing, and able to assist schools and link them into other resources. In fact, this relationship can of course be initiated from either side—by the school or by emergency management or, in fact, by some other interested group or individual.

Some of the other fundamental linkages as discussed in earlier chapters are obvious: school-youth, youth-family, school-family. While the standard linkage here is at least initially in a sequential order starting with an education program (i.e., school-youth-family), it is useful to think about each individual link so as to promote creative thinking about increased possibilities. It may also be useful for individual schools to link with each other through whatever local means are available. This might include through the community superintendent or school board or through local EM and government. It might also include links with local, regional, or national education boards or departments, who may have materials and initiatives useful for the local school. For example, the U.S. Department of Education has initiatives and resources related to assisting schools plan, prepare for, and respond to disasters some of which have been included in this book.

In between the emergency management and the school, youth, and household links, there are a number of other links that may prove fruitful. These include with first responders (fire, police, emergency services), government (e.g., education departments; politicians) and non-governmental agencies (e.g., Red Cross/Red Crescent; various help providers), private and service and volunteer organizations and individuals (e.g., local business, insurance, neighborhood and community groups; enthusiastic parents, citizens), scientific groups (e.g., universities and educational institutions; physical and social science groups) and others (e.g., health care providers, faith-based organizations, senior citizen organizations). As stressed in a number of places in this book, an important link can be with the media. With a relationship developed, they can become more willing to deliver useful messages within the larger community. We expand on these ideas below.

Developing Community Partnerships: Emergent Groups, Value, and Obstacles. Disasters have been shown to bring out the best in people (Beggs, Haines, & Hurlbert, 1996). In addition, as in Orting, Washington, community groups have been shown to develop not only during and following disasters, but also in advance of a hazardous event. In the latter case, these "emergent citizen groups" (ECGs) (Quarantelli, 1985) have tended to be related to community concerns including the threat of local hazards.

Another line of educational research appears to indicate that schools and the community benefit from collaborative partnerships of many types. In studies looking at schools developing community partnerships generally, Epstein and colleagues have produced resources (e.g., Epstein et al., 1997; 2002) that can be useful including developing the National Network of Partnership Schools (NNPS) (e.g., Sanders, 2001). They have also developed a website based at Johns Hopkins University (http://www.csos.jhu.edu/p2000/default.htm). Based on their research, Epstein has identified six types of involvement that are suggested as useful conduits to developing community partnerships: (a) parenting (b) communicating, (c) learning at home, (d) volunteering, (e) decision making, and (f) collaborating with the community.

In some recent NNPS research (Sanders, 2001) looking into 355 schools linked to the NNPS, 88% reported having one or more community partnerships developed. Over 45% of these reported (i.e., 40% overall) having 4 or more partnerships developed. When asked about quality of partnerships, only 13% said they were not satisfied. In addition, while 57% of schools in this study were happy with the number of partnerships, 43% were not. In other words, while most schools were happy with the partnerships they had, many wanted to have more.

Importantly, as concluded by Sanders (2001):

> schools with widespread support for school, family, and community partnerships were more likely than those without such support to have satisfactory school-community collaborations. (p. 31)

In addition to the relationship between support and satisfaction, it was also the case that those schools with more active partnerships also reported being more satisfied with partnerships in general.

Thus, once schools enter into partnerships, those involved appear to derive benefits. However, the first issue to address is to develop momentum within a school community and to anticipate obstacles to creating partnerships. For those schools in the Sander's study (2001) that did not develop partnerships, obstacles identified included difficulties identifying community partners, time constraints, and a lack of leadership to help facilitate partnerships. Other obstacles that have been identified include territorialism or "turf" problems (Mawhinney, 1994), staff burnout, school staff perceiving the community to be uncaring or without proper partnership resources, and fear of public scrutiny (Cushing & Kohl, 1997). In terms of public scrutiny, this apparently is related to the fear of a community partnership receiving negative media scrutiny. As we have emphasized in this book, the media can prove to be an ally rather than otherwise in school efforts (see also Ronan et al., 2000).

As a consequence, and in following up the initial discussion on this issue from Chapter 5, it is essential that momentum in a school is created and that potential obstacles including time constraints, staff workloads, and curricula constraints are taken into account. Additionally, the more that those involved in a school community can initiate and sustain first the idea of creating partnerships, the greater likelihood that momentum can begin to build. We agree with Mawhinney (1994) here that dialogue and planning can overcome potential obstacles.

In terms of addressing some of the obstacles, part of the value of creating these partnership relationships is that it has the potential to disperse workload. In having an initial chat between school and local emergency management people, both can describe what ideas they have, find common ground, and then agree on an initial action plan. This process repeated over time between these and other organizations and groups may actually prove a timesaver rather than produce yet another additional workload burden. For example, emergency management will have available a useful conduit into the majority, or near majority, of households in a school district. School officials may likewise find that EM officials can help them shape an education program that is able to take account of local conditions, including the natural and technological hazards that are most prominent in that area. They are also likely to be aware of the range of adjustments available to prepare for those hazardous conditions. As another example, in our practice and research efforts in schools, we provide materials and resources to the schools that include evidence-based information and resources (e.g., teacher training), presentations to students, and evaluation and feedback related to current hazards education programs. Finally, any number of groups are linked in with, or can be linked in with, a school community. These include parents, parent groups, parent-teacher groups, service and volunteer groups and individuals (e.g., enthusiastic local senior citizens), and many others (Sanders, 2001).

As these examples illustrate, and as also discussed in Chapters 3 and 4, such relationship development is designed to serve a variety of functional purposes. However, in the first instance, these relationships can begin to build momentum in the school and local community for creating a discrepancy between the current status of the community (low preparedness in the face of a potential hazard) and an emergent value or goal (e.g., help keep kids and family safe; help my organization's profile by linking in with such an effort; see an avenue for useful research). As the "hazard discussions" continue, more people become exposed to and aware of a potential motivationally-based discrepancy. In addition, as links begin to accrue, confidence can also start to build around being able to reduce this discrepancy: that preparation may be valuable, worth the time and effort, and be able to be carried out. Thus, developing discrepancy and then starting to resolve that discrepancy is part of the motivational undertow in the building of these relationships (see Chapter 3 and later section here for a more full description of the motivation and change process).

The steps involved particularly in the initial phases of relationship development need not be made overly complicated. Once others in the school have agreed to explore the idea of a partnership, and without any commitment necessary in the first instance, someone designated from the school community (e.g., principal; enthusiastic teacher, parent, others) can simply make a phone call or send an email to initiate a "hazards" discussion or get together.

Planning the Effort

Once discussions are established and common ground is found, planning for the program itself is next. Here, there are two main pieces around planning: the program itself (the what to do) and the delivery of the program (the how to do it). Also included in these two aspects are keeping in mind characteristics of the people who are delivering the program as well as the recipients of the program. The basic program that we discuss in the following section is a graduated school- and community-based program that is intended in the first instance to have a direct link to the home and family setting. Through the partnerships established, the integration of these programs with larger community programs can also take place. First, features of the planning process are considered.

Planning the Program

Here, the main issues revolves around choosing and planning the school- and community-programs and answering questions related to where to obtain resources, how best to sequence, link, and deliver the programs, and whether to promote standalone hazards education programs or to promote more integrated efforts, and curricula (e.g., tying readiness and risk mitigation into other subject areas). Part of the emphasis in planning will be on coordinating an integrated effort in the school and in the community. In addition, the other main issue here is planning for organizational level response. As with others (e.g., Clarke, 1999), we see these tasks as part of the same overall process.

As pointed out by Kreps (1991; see also Haddow & Bullock, 2003; Tierney et al., 2001), planning for response to disasters, while improved in the past 25 years, continues to have problems. Amongst a number of problems, these include planning in isolation and not working collaboratively with others in a local community. To ensure the success of planning, Quarantelli as well as Lindell and colleagues have identified features of the planning process that appear to be important. In terms of planning the process, Quarantelli has documented what he

TABLE 8.3. Planning for Response and Readiness Education

Continuous and integrated process
Based on anticipated physical and psychosocial effects (i.e., evidence-based)
Help gain sense of control
Focus on general principles
Includes educational activities
Needs to anticipate and overcome obstacles and resistance
Needs to be evaluated
Includes the idea of remaining flexible during planning and during disaster
    response, as every possible effect cannot be anticipated
Focus on planning ingredients shown to work:

- Multiple organizational involvement
- Gathering resources to assist planning (e.g., from federal agencies; neighboring emergency management agencies or schools)
- Specialized subcommittee that includes high levels of effort and attendance and low turnover
- Organizational climate including leadership emphasis on goals, support, promoting cooperation and team pride.

---

considers to be the important features of that process (e.g., Quarantelli, 1982, 1988, 1993). Lindell and colleagues have identified additional features of planning through their research efforts. First, as introduced at the beginning of this chapter, the use of a collaborative problem-solving approach is recommended. In this model, disasters are seen not as chaotic situations that need to be directed from some command structure but rather problems that are within the realm of a community working together to identify and bring to bear its inherent capabilities, while developing those capabilities deemed necessary. As seen in Table 8.3, principles generated by hazards and disasters researchers include features compatible with our own approach (e.g., Lindell & Perry, 1992; Lindell, 1995; Quarantelli, 1983, 1988; Whitney & Lindell, 2000).

A main finding from the hazards research literature is that leadership qualities appear vital to people's commitment to the process: the ability to structure tasks, communicate clearly, and to demonstrate sensitivity to team member's needs (Whitney & Lindell, 2000). Another issue identified is that creating opportunity for recognition and personal skill development appears to increase commitment to the planning and organizational process.

A Written Plan: Perhaps Useful, but Definitely Not Sufficient

To buttress the overall idea of collaborative and supported problem-solving, a first tenet is that written plans are sometimes not worth the paper on which they are printed. In other words, planning is better thought of as an ongoing process rather than simply the creation of a written document. In line with this idea, as introduced in Chapter 6, a written plan should perform two major functions (Tierney et al., 2001): (a) a written agreement that is signed off by respective organizations that documents roles and functions for promoting education, pre-paredness, and activating response and recovery activities, and (b) a template for continuing education and training. The latter function can ensure that the plan is not written, "shelved," and forgotten. Of course, any such document created between a school and community partners can then also document the response plan combined with the ongoing process of education, practice, simulations, linking school and family emergency plans, school and community emergency plans, evaluation benchmarks, and other functions.

Establishing a Baseline: Ongoing, Pragmatic Evaluation of the Program

As emphasized from Chapter 1, part of good practice is reflected in the evaluation of its effectiveness. The main components of an assessment approach for a school-based program would include:

- *Multiple intervals* including pre-post measurement (before and after the program) and ongoing assessment (done during the carrying out of the program);
- *Multiple sources* including from the child, additionally from the household and family, from school sources including assessment of simulations;
- *Multiple methods* including knowledge-based, activity- or behavior-based; paper and pencil assessment, simulation- or practice-based assessment;
- *Multiple programs* done across school years in a graduated sequence; those linked with community initiatives.

Pre-Post Assessment. Certainly, the assessment of increased knowledge and related features should be included. Schools will have many resources available for assessing knowledge. We would add that the inclusion of emergency management focused factors should be included. This includes assessment of the following factors:

- Hazards risk awareness (i.e., level of awareness of local hazards);
- Hazards concern (i.e., level of concern about local hazards);
- Knowledge of emergency preparedness including protective actions (e.g., duck, cover, and hold during an earthquake; see Chapter 5);
- Level of child and family motivation to engage in readiness and risk mitigation;
- Level of interaction between child and others about hazards (e.g., discussions with parents about hazards learning);
- Emergency preparedness and mitigation activities undertaken by the child and family including adjustments at home, family emergency plans, and practice and simulations at home and school (including between home and school)

At our website we will be including a measure that we have used in various forms in our own research in New Zealand and the United States (e.g., Finnis et al., 2004; Gregg et al., 2004; Johnston et al., 2001; Ronan & Johnston, 2001, 2003; Ronan, Johnston, Daly, & Fairley, 2001). This particular measure takes no more than a half hour to complete and might be best used before and after a program to assess gains.

The assessment of practice and simulations at school is also useful. We are mindful that such an activity can involve quite a bit of effort. However, we are also aware that such an effort is likely to be fruitful for a number of reasons (e.g., recognition that community is motivated to keep youth and families safe) and can include a cooperative effort by schools, households, local emergency management and others combining with each other.

Ongoing Assessment. At a minimum, some ongoing assessment of child- and family-based adjustment, planning, and practice and simulation activities is worthwhile. Combined with this assessment, ongoing assessment of children's knowledge can be done through brief paper and pencil exercises as well as through classroom-practice discussion and "quizzes." That is, the teacher can say "okay class, let's pretend that an earthquake/storm with high winds/flood/ fire/local hazard, etc. is happening (or about to happen via a warning). What should we do here at school? Do you know what your family plan would say to do?"

In terms of home-based assessment, this can be combined with homework activities that can include the child and parents discussing selected topics, making public statements of commitment about undertaking some activities, undertaking initially simple adjustments (e.g., food and water, flashlights, radios) and moving to those that require more effort (e.g., family emergency plan and practice; structural adjustments at home; getting ready for a school-home-community simulation) (e.g., Ronan & Johnston, 2003). We return to the topic of evaluation again in Chapter 9.

The Hazards Education Program in the School and Community: Summary of Main Features

Here, we summarize information that is available in more detail in earlier chapters. The basics to consider in planning and carrying out hazards and disaster education programs include:

1. Graduated sequence across school years: start with basic messages. Our research has found that some education is better than no education and that more education is better than some; older children are also more likely to be able to retain and convey more information (Ronan et al., 2001; Ronan & Johnston, 2001); integrate this education with other learning in school (e.g., environmental education and sustainability; other curricula including science, social studies, civics, geography, and so forth).

2. Combine the raising of concern about local hazards with a confident, coping model ("hazards are a concern here that we need to plan and prepare for AND we have the means and the ability to carry out planning and preparation"); promote messages that increase a sense of control (e.g., "what children and families do to plan and prepare can make a tremendous difference and can be done, some quite easily")—this can include presenting realistic information about risks—combining such messages with information and learning and doing activities that foster a greater sense of control and coping confidence appears to be useful for youth (Ronan et al., 2001); stay away from messages that reduce a sense of control or efficacy (e.g., promoting overwhelming fear messages, presenting mass destruction images and messages that might convey a sense of helplessness or fatalism).

   a. Promote attributions of damage preventability, adjustment effectiveness for things that matter (e.g., to protect persons (children, spouses, family), households, and property; for other non-hazard- specific uses) (Lopes, 1992; Lindell & Whitney, 2000; McClure et al., 2001);
   b. Promote increased concern (Kunreuther et al., 2001; Rustelmi & Karanci, 1999; Dooley et al., 1992) that is not overwhelming (e.g., Weinstein et al., 2000) and is combined with a sense of control (see next point);
   c. Promote self-efficacy/personal and family control that emphasizes "what we do can make a significant difference, that we can do them, and that we can and should do them now" (Dooley et al., 1992; Lindell & Whitney, 2000; McClure et al., 2001; Paton & Johnston, 2001; Rustelmi & Karanci, 1999);

3. Interactive features (i.e., with family first, with others in the community) (Ronan & Johnston, 2003) include home-based discussion, learning, and doing activities for children and parents; graduated sequence of specified home-based activities that starts at simple, easy to do activities and progresses to other tasks (e.g., developing a family emergency plan, more effort-based adjustments at home); and links with others in the community (e.g., other classrooms, schools, community education and organizations).

4. Incorporating an emergency management perspective that focuses on readiness, response guidance, and planning for recovery (Ronan & Johnston, 2001, 2003); being mindful of the evidence-based means by which to convey messages (see earlier chapters).

5. Using natural opportunities to learn (e.g., media coverage of a hazard); using materials in the public domain that include what actually to do to be better prepared to respond to and recover from a hazard (e.g., using checklists from this book, from FEMA, from other websites—see Appendix 2).

6. Demonstrations and adult modeling and participation to supplement learning; use of interactive (e.g., computer, web-based) and visual aids (e.g., videos or slides of people engaging in specific preparations, e.g., Lopes, 1992); learning about

and seeing other preparation efforts that are ongoing—and perhaps linked to the school program itself—in the larger community (e.g., Mileti & Darlington, 1997; Ronan, Johnston, & Hull, 1998); inviting guest speakers to present and demonstrate (as well as inviting them in advance to help with planning and research); linking in with enthusiastic parents and others in local area to assist.

7. In- and out-of-class practice and simulations; again, we want to emphasize the critical value of combining the learning of preparedness activities and response planning with *DOING AND PRACTICE, PRACTICE, PRACTICE; practice is vital to help youth and adults be able to override excess arousal and other factors to have responses immediately available during a crisis situation.*

8. Promoting the program in the community (e.g., through partnerships) to increase community-based "hazards discussions" and "hazards doing"; being creative with outreach and links including liaising with media, parent-teacher groups, emergency management agencies, community and neighborhood groups, local businesses (e.g., local stores promoting "hazards awareness and preparation month"); promoting school or community preparedness competitions; placing and updating a preparedness "thermometer" in front of classrooms, schools or in visible public settings; links with other readiness-based efforts.

9. Related to the last point, and to summarize, integrating the school efforts with other community-based programs; emphasizing consistent, evidence-based messages that are designed to increase concern about hazards, promote the value and effectiveness of preparation, that basic preparation is within the realm of the community and that this basic preparation can make a difference; give specific guidance on basic preparation first; promote basic emergency plans and practice; evaluate the effectiveness of the program; adjust the program based on evaluation findings.

RESPONSE AND RECOVERY: THE PRIMACY OF PLANNING

The first task in planning for response and recovery again lies in relationship development and partnerships. This can allow for the coordinated planning of school and community education programs as just discussed. It can also be the forum for the second major part of an emerging partnership—planning for coordinated response and recovery, first within the school community and then linked to the larger community. In this section, we review the basic principles of the planning process to supplement the material located in Chapters 6 and 7.

Planning for Response and Recovery

As discussed previously, planning for a disaster aids in response and recovery. The research that is available has demonstrated that response is more effective in the face of good planning and preparedness at the household and organizational levels (e.g., Kartez & Lindell, 1990; Mileti, Drabek, & Haas, 1975; Peek & Mileti, 2002; Perry & Green, 1983). Thus, in terms of the discussion in earlier chapters and the previous section, it is far better to plan in advance than have to have to be reactive in the face of a disaster.

A main issue here in planning and engaging in the tasks of response and recovery is the link between physical and psychosocial recovery, between problem- and emotion-focused coping. Initial efforts at helping a community, schools, and families cope with a disaster should start during the response phase and continue on into recovery. Once a hazardous event is probable or is actually in progress, the first issue of course is physical response. As documented in earlier chapters, there is no substitute for motivating people to prepare and practice in advance of a hazardous event.

In fact, the primary theme of this book is that the planning for response and recovery during quiescent times portends adaptive response and more efficient recovery during and following hazardous times (e.g., Peek & Mileti, 2002). It involves helping a school and community "prepare to respond and recover" using the idea that to be "forearmed is to be forewarned." Thus, motivating people to prepare and practice in advance of a hazardous event allows them to have critical responses primed and at the ready (e.g., evacuation routes, school and family emergency plans) as well as establish a greater sense of control.

Similarly, in the wake of an event, and even in the absence of families having emergency plans available, the more that a school—in cooperation with other agencies, community groups, and indeed families—can respond well, the more likely that the children and families are going to benefit. As discussed in Chapter 6, there are a number of features of a school response plan that can be useful. The first issue is around response to warnings, assessment of safety, and protective response (e.g., evacuation, sheltering in or out of school, reunification with families—see Chapter 6). Ensuring that school personnel and the youth are all well versed in the *very basics* of the response plan is vital here. Even if families are themselves not prepared, school and student preparation and effective response is likely in a number of instances to be able to override that problem.

Once safety and reunion have been established, physical needs looked after and assurance that the hazardous event has run its course, it is at this point that various forms of assistance to promote psychosocial recovery are activated: attention to basic needs, psychological first aid, and so forth (see Chapter 7). Non-intrusive forms of helping people early include providing them with information, calming strategies, and linking them in with various forms of support (tangible, informational, social) is a first line form of assistance. In addition, the value of support through listening is sometimes underestimated. We do not recommend in early response-phase interventions being too direct with interventions (e.g., we do not recommend critical incident stress debriefing in school and family settings—see Chapter 7). Attention to the basics as documented in Chapter 7 is likely to be more helpful first.

In addition to providing basic forms of assistance through "therapy by walking around" (NIMH, 2002), we value larger scale forms of informational assistance designed to promote both psychosocial and physical recovery. Chapter 7 provides guidance and examples of how that form of assistance might look. This includes the idea of "normal reactions to abnormal events" (normalizing reactions) as well as normalizing the recovery process (i.e., time helps and most people generally recover from the effects of a hazard).

We also stressed in that chapter that there are various factors that can get in the way of this recovery process (risk factors) and those that can help promote, or perhaps hasten, recovery (protective factors). In addition to a number of factors highlighted in Chapters 2 and 7, we have stressed throughout the vital role that adults, and, in particular, parents, play in helping children to respond and recover. Consequently, in any form of informational assistance, stressing that children look to adults as models for reaction and coping is vital. Consequently, returning to routines in the family, in school, and in the community, give both children and adults the message of a community moving back to a sense of normalcy—that bad things can happen but this community can carry on with its day to day activities. In addition, parents managing their own distress and presenting a "coping modeling" approach for their children is most definitely recommended. Parents too can model for their children that hazardous events can be scary, even quite scary, but that they can also be coped with and recovered from based on a commitment to seek support and to solve, rather than avoid, problems or reactions.

Another feature of the recovery environment that can maximize resources available involves the MGSC model elaborated on in Chapter 7. School- and community-based outreach and screening efforts are means for identifying those who are not recovering normally. While more information is available in that chapter, we would emphasize here that ensuring the active support of administrative and other officials in school and community settings is essential. Additionally, making screening an easy-to-do process will ensure more of a likelihood of "buy in" from schools and the community and make it easier on those filling out any forms.

Finally, here, this process of screening-basic intervention-screening is intended to carry on until all of those involved have been provided with an adequate level of assistance (see Figure 8.1). In Chapter 7, we provided information on screening and the forms of both basic assistance that may be adequate for the majority as well as more intensive forms that may be necessary for some who are more affected. Chapter 9 provides additional information on researching the effectiveness of programs.

Finally, we emphasize again that planning and community collaborations are essential here: they allow for activation and consistency in help provision and better ensure that a community is working together on getting back on its feet. We know that every contingency cannot be planned for when disaster does strike: continuing relationships and open communication lines are the major conduits to (a) activating the basic principles of the response and recovery plan while (b) remaining flexible to unanticipated developments.

WHO IS RESPONSIBLE: THE ROLE OF LEADERSHIP, RELATIONSHIPS, AND ACCOUNTABILITY

We end this chapter with a consideration of the issue of leadership and accountability. As reviewed in this book, individuals, households, and organizations are not all that motivated to prepare for a hazardous event. Whether from lack of awareness, lack of concern, a sense of fatalism, a sense that responsibility for preparation and response is someone else's business (e.g., government agencies),

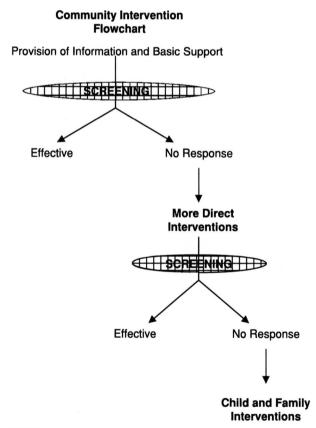

FIGURE 8.1. MGSC Flowchart.

TABLE 8.4. The Basic Principles and Tasks of Response and Recovery

RESPONSE TASKS AND PRINCIPLES

Principle I: Developing Emergency and Disaster Plans

    A. School-based
    B. Household-based
    C. Links between School and Home Plans
    D. Links between School and Community Planning

Principle II: Disseminating the Plan

Principle III: Practicing and Evaluating the Plan

Principle IV: Activating Emergency Plans and Attending to the Basics First

    A. Assessing and Ensuring Safety
       1. Evacuation
       2. Emergency Shelter
       3. Physical and Basic Needs
       4. Monitoring the Environment for Any Other Risks
    B. Family Linkages, Communication, and Reunion
    C. Psychosocial Response

Principle V: Continuing Coordination and Communication between Schools, Families,
    and Response and Recovery Organizations

Principle VI: Remaining Flexible and Problem-Solving Unanticipated Developments

RECOVERY TASKS AND PRINCIPLES

Principle I: The Role of Primary Prevention

Principle II: Activating/Establishing/Maintaining School, Home, and Community Linkages and
    Open Communication

Principle III: The Overall MGSC Flowchart (see Figure 8.1)

Principle IV: Support during the Impact and Early Recovery Phase

    A. Ensuring Safety and Basic Needs
    B. Informational, Tangible, and Psychosocial Support
    C. Activate Approach Coping and Utility of Social Support
    D. Reestablish Routines ("we can carry on with life")
    E. Helping Parents Understand Their Vital Role and How to Support Children
    F. Focus on Other Risk and Protective Factors (see Chapter 2 and 7)

Principle V: Screening at the First Gate; More Basic Intervention at the First Step

Principle VI: Screening at Later Gates; Interventions at Later, More Intensive Steps

planning and preparation efforts in households and communities is generally given low priority.

Consider then other findings related to readiness and response based organizational networks that have indicated generally poor cohesiveness, communication and ongoing relationship problems, poor use of resources, and, importantly, responsibility and leadership ambiguity (e.g., Drabek, 1985; Nigg, 1997). It then comes as no surprise to learn that response to many disasters is not coordinated, does not access needed resources, and resultant levels of conflict can emerge at various levels in a community.

On the other side, and in looking at those factors that do promote organizational effectiveness in readiness and response, a number of studies converge to suggest the following common sense factors are important (e.g., Bolin, 1998; Clarke, 1989; Drabek, 1985; Nigg, 1997; Sorenson, Mileti, & Copenhaver, 1985):

- clear understanding and shared knowledge and agreement of the purpose and goals of the network or partnership;
- frequent communication, interaction, and relationships developed (including informal) prior to a hazard;
- cohesiveness and pre-disaster cooperation across organizations;
- clear lines of authority and responsibility including good planning;
- leadership.

Following such findings, it is our most definite opinion that the first steps in helping a community become more aware and one that takes more responsibility for preparing themselves involves perhaps even one person or small group who can champion and move forward the idea within a school and within the community. Whether that person or group is an emergency manager, a principal, teacher, school psychologist, a family, a parent, a local community group or individual, someone from the media, a scientist, an emergency services provider does not matter. What does matter is that person or group having the enthusiasm and energy to start developing relationships and promoting the ideas included in this book.

As seen in the Orting, Washington example in Chapter 4, part of the very impetus of that program has in our estimation been provided through particular individuals—professionals along with community groups composed of parents, community members, and local educators—who have championed and worked to promote preparation for hazardous events, have developed relationships with each other, linked with supportive scientific and emergency management expertise, have become media savvy, and have become highly knowledgeable themselves— even in the face of many frustrations and obstacles (e.g., Bailey & Woodcock, 2003; Smith & Smith, 2003). Such initial leadership, dogged determination, and continuing persistence may very well be part of the characteristics of the person who is now reading these words. This determination combined with a sense of personal responsibility are the very qualities that we believe, and research underscores, are highly useful in a community becoming more educated, more prepared, and more responsive in ways that save lives and help people get on their feet when a hazardous event does strike.

Chapter 9

The Research-Practice Interface and Recommendations

L inking to the previous chapter, another essential part of accountability has to do with the practice-research link. Practitioners who are willing to "stick their necks out" and take the responsibility of evaluating their own practice are also those practitioners who are more likely to succeed. Of course, such accountability will no doubt assist those whom we are intending to reach with our messages.

In their assessment of the number of people dedicated to blending hazards and disaster research with practice in the United States, Dennis Mileti and many expert colleagues (Mileti, 1999) have noted that people of this sort exist but that numbers need to increase. Movement forward in this area is predicated on an increased conversation between researchers and practitioners: "Knowledge transfer . . . requires extraordinary researchers and extraordinary practitioners who are able to step out of their paradigms and effectively communicate with each other." (pp. 331–332)

However, with that said, it is clear that the past 30 years has seen an increase in increased research-practice collaborations. As emphasized from Chapter 1, part of the very essence of this book has been devoted to trying to continue bridging the gap between pure research and pure practice. Similar to training in a number of professional areas, we believe that movement forward in assisting communities, schools, and families to become more resilient to the effects of hazards

173

and disasters lies in an increased focus on a scientist-practitioner model. Chapters 1–8 have focused more on reviewing the research evidence with an eye to incorporating what findings are currently available into day-to-day practice efforts.

In this chapter, we look at what research is necessary to increase knowledge but, more importantly, to inform current and future practice. The focus here is on research first within the school-youth-family network within local community settings. Consistent with the emphasis on establishing links between this network and others to promote the larger community resilience effort, we discuss future research in this area here as well. However, the focus here is not going to be exhaustive. Other resources here that focus on future research in related areas would include Mileti (1999), Tierney et al. (2001), Norris et al. (2002).

METHODOLOGIES WITH AN EMPHASIS ON PRACTICAL PROGRAM EVALUATION

The areas of research that are available are quite numerous indeed. Before addressing content areas, a few words are necessary on the form of research. Research in this area can be quantitative or qualitative, group- or case-based, cross-sectional or longitudinal, correlational or experimental. The methodology that has been the mainstay across readiness through recovery research has been quantitative, group-based, and primarily cross-sectional and correlational (i.e., based primarily on mail-out surveys in readiness and response research; based primarily on self-report measures in recovery research). Additionally, as reviewed in Chapter 2, measures used for research have varied between those better constructed (i.e., reliable, valid, normed, comprehensive) to measures of lesser utility (i.e., single item measures, no reliability and validity data, no norms). Thus, the first call here is when doing correlational research to use measures that are defined and for which at least minimal psychometric data are reported (e.g., internal consistency estimates, criterion-related validity data). The second call is to include other forms of school- and community-based correlational research (e.g., Ronan et al., 2001; Ronan & Johnston, 2001) to supplement the more often used mail-out survey methodology. This includes moving the field forward from a simple reliance on self-report to the use of other methodologies (e.g., reports from significant others, direct observation). It also includes moving from cross-sectional research to longitudinal designs (e.g., Ronan & Johnston, 1999, 2003; see also Norris et al., 2002).

Related to research done across time are the additional benefits of experimental, or quasi-experimental, methodologies. For example, in some of our research that has used quasi-experimental methodologies prior to a hazard (Ronan & Johnston, 2003) and in the aftermath (Ronan & Johnston, 1999), we have been better able to make less tentative statements about causal inference.

Given that our first focus is on what we have referred to as *local science* research, recommended first is the use of longitudinal or experimental designs that are able to assess the fruits of everyday practice in this area. Additionally, while it is clear that researchers need to "up the ante" with respect to the use of better measure and methodology development and selection, we are also mindful, and have emphasized, the merits of using straightforward measurement of practice efforts. One of the possible reasons that some practitioners do not engage in evaluating their practice in this way is perhaps related to admonitions from the research community to use better and more sophisticated methodologies. Such admonitions may create tension between wanting to do quality-improvement research and feeling it is too difficult. It is our experience that people who do practice in relation to education and hazards management areas are very busy already.

Thus, for those in the research community, particularly those of us who value the research-practice interface, we will do well to keep in mind trying to balance our own values of using sophisticated methodologies with the obvious value of more pragmatic efforts, particularly for the everyday practitioner.

Thus, in terms of recommendations, doing longitudinal or experimental forms of program evaluation is likely to have two primary typologies—both having their place in moving knowledge and practice forward. The first is of the sort more traditionally carried out in research settings with the gold standard here for some being the randomized, controlled trial (e.g., Kazantzis, Ronan, & Deane, 2001): random assignment (e.g., by individual, by classroom, or by school) to well defined control and experimental conditions, the use of more sophisticated assessment measures, and the use of more sophisticated data analytic techniques. Mindful of increased threats to internal validity (Cook & Campbell, 1979), we would also include one group only pretest—posttest (and follow-up) designs here. Related to one group designs, we would also include here the continuing use of correlational designs but with added sophistication. Finally, there is also a place for single case methodologies, particularly those that use some identified design (e.g., Kazdin, 1998). In all of these methodologies, there is more control over certain design features to increase internal validity (i.e., to make more definite statements about relationships between variables).

Pragmatic Program Evaluation

The second type of research is of the more everyday type. For example, such research is designed to answer questions such as "does the program developed in this school and community setting work as intended?" Of course, practitioners developing links with researchers in this area is a valuable first step: getting information and resources, and perhaps even the research work done for them, can have benefits. However, some practitioners may prefer to evaluate their own efforts. Here, fairly simple, straightforward measures are available. As with any kind of research, this practical form will benefit from some advanced planning and by considering the "who, what, when, where, how" factors:

- What will constitute success of the program (i.e., what specifically needs change to consider the program to be effective)?;
- How best to assess those features that define the success of the program (i.e., what specifically has to be measured and how to do it)?;
- When to do the measurement during the program (including before the program, at intervals during the program, and following the program)?;
- Who is best to include in evaluation (e.g., who are going to be included here; students, parents, teachers, others in the community)?;
- Where to do evaluation (e.g., in school, at home, other settings)?

As indicated earlier in this book (e.g., see Chapter 8), our assisting schools to evaluate readiness-based hazards education programs has emphasized measures that are straightforward and easy to fill out by both students and parents. We will be including at our website measures used in correlational and experimental research and which can be used for assessment of educational efforts. Of course, we would ask that anyone who chooses to use such measures be qualified to administer them (e.g., trained school and emergency management personnel). Some aspects of our child-focused measure may be deemed not applicable to a particular educational effort, it may be deemed to be too long, and so forth. However, as a minimum, we would recommend evaluating a few basic areas in line with our emphasis on learning, discussing, demonstrating, practicing, and doing (see Chapter 8 for a listing of those areas; see also our website listed in Appendix 2).

We also include contact information at our website if a particular school or community is interested in getting some assistance with the program they are planning and with the research they would like to see accompany that program.

As for response and recovery, and in the first instance, simple is likely to be better, particularly when working with large groups. For example, in group-based intervention research, we have used a parsimonious battery that has included the PTSD Reaction Index (PTSD-RI; Nader, 1996) and a measure developed for use in our anxiety treatment research (e.g., Ronan & Deane, 1998), the Coping Questionnaire (CQ; Kendall et al., 1992). The PTSD-RI is a 20 item measure that is designed to reflect a specific hazardous event (e.g., do you get scared, afraid, or upset when you think about the (hazardous event)). The items are rated on a 5 point scale anchored none, little, some, much, most. The measure has adequate reliability and validity as well as treatment sensitivity (e.g., Ronan & Johnston, 1999). The CQ consists of 3 items that state "When you _____. Are you able to help yourself feel less upset?" Given this structure, it can be individualized in two ways. The first is for larger group interventions and can be hazard specific (e.g., When you are thinking about the (hazardous event). Are you able to help yourself feel less upset?). The second is using it for more intensive interventions and individualizing it based on an individual child's specific fears and anxieties or situations related to the hazardous or traumatic event. There is also an accompanying parent form for parents to rate the same items as the child (i.e., When your child _____. How well is he/she able to help himself/herself feel less upset?). Items on both child-reported and parent-reported measures are rated on a 7 point scale (1 = not at all able to help myself; 7 = completely able to help myself feel comfortable). The measure has been used in many studies looking at the effectiveness of anxiety- and disaster-based treatments for youth and families (see Chapter 7), has adequate reliability and validity, and is sensitive to the effects of treatment.

In the case of the CQ, it was designed based on other measures used to assess the specific features related to a person's distress, including target complaints measures and global ratings, the latter sometimes also referred to as SUDS scales (subjective units of distress). SUDS scales are a bit of a misnomer—they do not have to rate only distress, they are designed to rate specifics related to the subject of interest. They are often rated on a 5, 10, or, in some cases, 100 point scale. A related measure, a visual analogue scale (VAS), can present graphically the SUDS anchor points and have the person indicated where on that continuum they might fall (e.g., 0 (distressed) _____ 10 (calm). The point here is that ratings such as the CQ, SUDS, and VAS scales are quite practical, easy to use, and can help those evaluating programs track change across time on indices of interest.

Of course, forms of global assessment can also be used to assess readiness factors, response factors, individual factors, organizational features, and so forth. In terms of organizational features, it is the case that community partnerships created for educational purposes generally and for readiness and response purposes more specifically can experience problems (see Chapter 8). First, with respect to schools initiating the idea of promoting hazards education and developing community partnerships, a first line issue is ensuring support within the school community. In Chapter 5, we provided an example of a little questionnaire that can be used to gauge interest as well as potential obstacles. In addition, the use of global measures to assess various aspects of support within the school community, important features of community partnerships (e.g., shared agreement on purpose and goals; relationships developed; clear communication) can be also assessed via global measures.

Again, it is our contention that those who engage in various aspects of local science from the inter- and intra-organizational levels down to the child and family level are those programs that are more accountable for their practice. Importantly, there can be no doubt that such accountability through ongoing evaluation increases the chance of success through a continued monitoring program. When ratings on various instruments are not as intended, consultation and programmatic adjustment as necessary can proceed. When ratings are at a target level, there can then be recognition, including public recognition, of the successes that can serve as further momentum for future efforts.

FUTURE RESEARCH NEEDS

This section is intended for larger research efforts to be carried out by those who have the resources available (e.g., scientists, researchers, practitioners with available resources). For findings to date and for research necessary in terms of readiness through response, the reader is referred to some comprehensive reviews (e.g., Mileti, 1999; Tierney et al., 2001); and for recovery (Norris et al., 2002). It is not our intention here to be exhaustive but to focus on the main topic of this book. First, we do feel that linking in youth-family-schools research with community level research is a "royal road" to knowledge gathering and application. Second, we recommend strongly research that is about "doing": in particular, evaluation of interactive programs designed to assist a community become more resilient to the effects of a hazardous event—before, during, and after an event. While school-based programs have been found to help both before and after a hazardous event, there are many things as discussed in this book that we do not know in relation to these programs (e.g., Ronan et al., 2001; Ronan & Johnston, 2001, 2003), including the specific role of preparation and response promoting recovery. Second, school-community partnerships can produce benefits during readiness and recovery (e.g., Johnston et al., 2001; Ronan & Johnston, 1999). However, what is not known is the extent to which schools linking in with community initiatives helps more specifically. Here, as with schools-based research (e.g., Ronan & Johnston, 1999, 2003), the use of experimental or quasi-experimental designs that use comparison groups and random assignment are useful for considering the value of school-community linkages and programs.

In addition to assessing the overall effectiveness of school programs and school-community partnerships, the continuing assessment of what constitute the "active ingredients" is also a useful pursuit. For example, Ronan and Johnston (2001) found that an emergency management perspective, multiple programs, and promoting interactions between children and parents appear to be useful features in hazards education programs for youth. However, here, as supplementary to pre-post group comparison designs, the assessment of factors that correlate with outcome (e.g., preparation efforts linked to recovery factors) will certainly move the field forward and findings will certainly assist with program planning. The main question here in identifying predictors of change is "do these programs work and, if so, what specific features of the program, of the messenger, and of the receiver make this program more or less effective?"

For example, in readiness efforts, we have initial evidence from different lines of research that keeping away from fatalistic and mass destruction messages (e.g., McClure, Allen, & Walkey, 2001) while emphasizing the efficacy and specific "how to" of adjustments (e.g., Lindell & Whitney, 2000; Lopes, 1992) are worth continuing to explore. In addition to specific features of hazards education or intervention programs, assessing messenger characteristics is worthwhile. For example, is it the case that the manner in which a program is delivered within a school- or community-context is important? If the program deliverer conveys enthusiasm, the expectation of success, encourages higher levels of activity and interaction, and has other features identified in our model as well as other literatures as predictors of change (e.g., Lambert, 2004; Miller & Rollnick, 2002), does this program produce more effective outcomes than the very same program delivered in a simply more didactic fashion. Similarly, if the receivers of the program have higher expectations and are more actively involved, does this matter? Finally, what are the community- and school-level factors that facilitate and get in the way of developing partnerships, promoting readiness and recovery campaigns, and so forth? Does leadership matter here as preliminary evidence has indicated; what about getting initial support within the school community? Such research across these various levels will assist in developing our knowledge base about how to get programs initiated and developed, what programs should look like to produce the most effective outcomes, and how best to deliver the program to ensure that the recipients are more actively engaged.

While there is certainly value for cross-sectional research, that which focuses solely on selective topics may not be so worthwhile. Thus, a more singular focus on issues like hazard awareness, or perhaps levels of preparation in a few basic areas, might not be as worthwhile as a focus on a fuller range of variables that the literature has identified as worth studying. The availability of more user friendly and sophisticated analytic packages including structural equation modelling (SEM) and hierarchical linear modelling (HLM) (e.g., Paton et al., 2001) allows for looking at the simultaneous and collective impact that various variables have on each other. We do have a fair amount of knowledge on a range of individual factors; it will help the field to have increased testing of models of preparation, response, and recovery than to look at variables in isolation. Included here is addressing more in depth the role of psychosocial factors, including emotional and social cognitive features, and their links with physical preparation and response (see also Chapters 2 and 3 for additional lines of investigation worth pursuing).

Related to this issue, there is now a need to present enough data in studies that will allow for statistical aggregation (e.g., power and meta-analysis) both in the readiness, response, and recovery areas (see also Lindell & Perry, 2000; Norris et al., 2002). Sample sizes, means, standard deviations, and specifics of statistical tests will assist here.

Promoting Research Partnerships

In addition, at our website, we are developing a research link that can allow for resources to assist with a school or community engaging in various forms of research. One of them that we envisage is having the facility to collaborate with communities and assist them directly with data collection and data analysis, along with feedback that would be designed to assist with continuing improvements. At the website, we are also aiming to include literature updates as they become available.

RESEARCH-PRACTICE INTERFACE: A COMMENT ON TRAINING PROGRAMS AND RESOURCES

Various training programs have as a focus the work described in this book. The most obvious are those with a specific emergency management focus. In the United States, such programs have been on the increase. The Federal Emergency Management Agency has a number of training opportunities available, including independent study courses (*http://training.fema.gov/*). Courses available for emergency managers are also available on a state-by-state basis (*http://www.training.fema.gov/emiweb/*). In terms of university and college level training, there are over 200 separate programs across most states as listed at the FEMA website (*http://www.training.fema.gov/emiweb/cgi-shl/college/User.cfm*). However, not included on this list are a number of other university level programs that focus on hazards and disasters in some form (e.g., Hazards Reduction and Recovery Center at Texas A&M University; Natural Hazards Center at University of Colorado; Disaster Mental Health Institute at University of South Dakota). These include training programs in diverse areas including education, physical science, social science, the helping professions, and others. Internationally, training in these diverse areas, all with at least some focus on disaster readiness, response, and recovery research and practice, appears also to be on the increase. Our team has been involved in a university level emergency management training course as well as providing workshops and multi-day training for emergency managers, teachers, and others in a community who are interested in helping a community prepare and respond to disasters. In the U.S. as well as in other countries, many agencies, national, statewide, and local have additional emergency and disaster training opportunities.

While not focused on training per se, many countries have school-focused preparedness information including FEMA (e.g., www.fema.gov/kids/) and the U.S. Department of Education *http://www.ed.gov/admins/lead/safety/emergencyplan/index.html?exp=0*) in the U.S.; the Ministry of Civil Defence and Emergency Management in New Zealand (*www.minedu.govt.nz*); and Emergency Management Australia (*http://www.ema.gov.au/ema/emaSchools.nsf*). FEMA does offer some teacher training opportunities (*www.fema.gov/kids/schdizr.htm*).

If interested in any training program, we would say *caveat emptor* (let the buyer beware). Because inconsistent or less than formalized standards of training may be in place for some programs (Alexander, 2003), it is important to look into what that program has to offer. Alexander (2003) has offered a set of criteria against which to compare training programs. Like us, Alexander emphasizes the development of research competencies as part of a training course in the form of a supervised research project. However, here, we would go further and also advocate for the integration of a scientist-practitioner perspective that permeates all levels of training and eventual practice. Such a perspective would emphasize critical analysis skills that allow for assessing the empirical literature and being able to draw on that literature to inform day-to-day practice. Similarly, with respect to practice, developing a sense of accountability for practice through ongoing research will allow increased confidence that efforts are effective, provide feedback to improve practice, reassure communities that we are ready to "put our money where our mouth is" by doing and reporting on research, and by publicizing findings to generate continuing momentum in a community to motivate additional change.

Planning for a Crisis in a School: Checklist of Actions

☑ ACTION CHECKLIST

Reduction

Connect with community emergency responders to identify local hazards. ☐

Review the last safety audit to examine school buildings and grounds. ☐

Determine who is responsible for overseeing violence prevention
and risk reduction strategies in your school. ☐

Encourage staff and parents to provide input and feedback into the crisis
planning process. ☐

Review incident data. ☐

Determine the major problems in your school with regard to student
crime and violence. ☐

Assess how the school addresses these problems. ☐

Conduct an assessment to determine how these problems—as well as
others—may impact your vulnerability to certain crises. ☐

Readiness

Determine what crisis plans exist in the district, school, and community.   ☐

Identify all stakeholders involved in crisis planning.   ☐

Develop procedures for educating and communicating with staff, students, families, the community, and the media.   ☐

Establish procedures to account for students during a crisis.   ☐

Gather information that exists about the school facility, such as maps and the location of utility shutoffs.   ☐

Identify the necessary equipment that needs to be assembled to assist staff in a crisis.   ☐

Response

Determine if a crisis is occurring.   ☐

Identify the type of crisis that is occurring and determine the appropriate response.   ☐

Activate the incident management system.   ☐

Ascertain whether an evacuation; reverse evacuation; lockdown; or shelter-in-place needs to be implemented.   ☐

Maintain communication among all relevant staff at officially designated locations.   ☐

Establish what information needs to be communicated to staff, students, families, and the community.   ☐

Monitor how emergency first aid is being administered to the injured.   ☐

Decide if more equipment and supplies are needed.   ☐

Recovery

Consider safety and physical needs as the first principle.   ☐

Strive to return to learning as quickly as possible.   ☐

Provide information to facilitate recovery.   ☐

Restore the physical plant, as well as the school community.   ☐

Monitor how staff are assessing students for the social and emotional impact of the crisis.   ☐

Identify what follow up interventions are available to students, staff,
and first responders.   ❐

Conduct operational debriefings with staff and first responders.   ❐

Assess curricular activities that address the crisis.   ❐

Allocate appropriate time for recovery.   ❐

Plan how anniversaries of events will be commemorated.   ❐

Capture "lessons learned" and incorporate them into revisions
and trainings.   ❐

Source: Modified from U.S. Department of Education, Office of Safe and Drug-Free Schools, Practical Information on Crisis Planning: A Guide for Schools and Communities, Washington, D.C., 2003.

Appendix 2

Web Resources

OUR BOOK WEBSITE
(www.hazardseducation.org)

FEDERAL EMERGENCY MANAGEMENT AGENCY (FEMA)
Ready.gov—From the U.S. Department of Homeland Security (www.ready.gov)
FEMA: Talking About Disasters (www.fema.gov/rrr/talkdiz)
FEMA for KIDS Homepage: Education, Schools, Disasters, Games, Teachers,
Art, Hurricane (http://www.fema.gov/kids/)
USFA Training and Education (www.training.fema.gov)
Emergency Management Institute—Federal Emergency Management Agency
(www.training.fema.gov/emiweb/)
FEMA Higher ED—College List (http://www.training.fema.gov/emiweb/
cgi-shl/college/User.cfm)

U.S. DEPARTMENT OF EDUCATION
Emergency Planning—Office of Safe and Drug-Free Schools
(http://www.ed.gov/admins/lead/safety/emergencyplan/index.html?exp=0)

SCHOOL PARTNERSHIP INFORMATION
National Network of Partnership Schools: Homepage
(http://www.csos.jhu.edu/p2000/default.htm)

SCHOOL-BASED AND RELATED WEB-BASED RESOURCES
NCEF Resource List: Disaster Preparedness and Response for Schools

(http://www.edfacilities.org/rl/disaster.cfm)
National Disaster Education Coalition (http://www.disastereducation.org/
guide.html)
American Red Cross (http://www.redcross.org)

References

Adams, J. (1995). *Risk*. London: UCL press.

Aldwin, C. M. (1994). *Stress, coping, and development: An integrative perspective*. New York: Guilford.

Alexander, D. (1992). Natural disasters: a framework for research and teaching. *Disasters, 15*, 209–224.

Alexander, D. (2000). Scenario methodology for teaching principles of emergency management. *Disaster Prevention and Management, 9*, 89–97.

Allen, R. D., & Rosse, W. (1998). *Children's response to exposure to traumatic events*. Quick Response Report No. 103. Boulder, CO: Natural Hazards Center.

Almqvist, K., & Brandell-Forsberg, M. (1997). Refugee children in sweden: Post-traumatic stress disorder in Iranian children exposed to organised violence. *Child Abuse and Neglect, 21*, 351–366.

Amaya-Jackson, L., Reynolds, V., Murray, M. C., McCarthy, G., Nelson, A., & Cherney, M. S., et al. (2003). Cognitive-behavioral treatment for pediatric posttraumatic stress disorder: Protocol and application in school and community settings. *Cognitive & Behavioral Practice, 10*, 204–213.

American Academy of Child and Adolescent Psychiatry. (1998). Practice parameters for the assessment and treatment of children with posttraumatic stress disorder. *Journal of the American Academy of Child and Adolescent Psychiatry, 37*(10 Suppl.), 4S–26S.

American Academy of Child and Adolescent Psychiatry. (2000). *Helping children after a disaster* (Facts for Families: Number 36). *http://www.aacap.org/publications/factsfam/disaster.htm*

American Psychiatric Association (1994). *Diagnostic and statistical manual of mental disorders*. (4th ed.). Washington, DC: Author.

American Psychiatric Association (2000). *Diagnostic and statistical manual of mental disorders*, Fourth edition (DSM-IV-TR). Washington, DC: Author.

Amir, M., & Lev-Wiesel, R. (2003). Time does not heal all wounds: Quality of life and psychological distress of people who survived the holocaust as children 55 years later. *Journal of Traumatic Stress, 16*, 295–299.

Anderson, J. (1987). Learning from Mount St Helens: catastrophic events as education opportunities. *Journal of Geography*, 229–233.

Applied Research and Consulting LLC, Columbia University Mailman School of Public Health, & New York State Psychiatric Institute. (2002). *Effects of the World Trade Center attacks on New York City public school children: Initial report to the New York City Board of Education.* New York: Authors.

Bailey, S., & Woodcock, J. (2003). Mt Rainier - a small event equals a public relations nightmare. Abstract, Cities on Volcanoes 3 conference, Hilo, Hawaii, July 14–18, 2003.

Ballantyne, M., Paton, D., Johnston, D., Kozuch, M., & Daly, M. (2000). *Information on volcanic and earthquake hazards: The impact on awareness and preparation.* (Science Report No. 2000/2). Wellington: Institute of Geological and Nuclear Sciences.

Bandura, A. (1986). *Social foundations of thought and action: A social cognitive.* Englewood Cliffs, NJ: Prentice Hall.

Baron, J., Hershey, J. C., & Kunreuther, H. (2000). Determinants of priority for risk reduction: The role of worry. *Risk Analysis, 20,* 413–427.

Barrett, P. M., Dadds, M. R., & Rapee, R. M. (1996). Family treatment of childhood anxiety: A controlled trial. *Journal of Consulting and Clinical Psychology, 64,* 333–342.

Barton, A. H. (1969). *Communities in disaster: A sociological analysis of collective stress situations.* Garden City, NY: Doubleday & Co.

Bates, F. L., Dynes R., & Quarantelli, E. L. (1990). The importance of the social sciences to the International Decade for Natural Disaster Reduction. *Disasters, 15,* 288–289.

Beggs, J. J., Haines, V. A., & Hurlbert, J. S. (1996). Situational contingencies surrounding the receipt of informal support. *Social Forces, 75,* 201–222.

Beggs, J. Haines, V., & Hurlbert, J. (1996). The effects of personal network and local community contacts on the receipt of formal aid during disaster recovery. *International Journal of Mass Emergencies and Disasters, 7,* 57–78.

Ben-Zur, H. (2002). Coping, affect and aging: The roles of mastery and self-esteem. *Personality & Individual Differences, 32,* 357–372.

Bernard, E. (2005). The U.S. National Tsunami Hazard Mitigation Program: a successful state_federal partnership. *Natural Hazards, 35,* 1–4.

Blong, R. J. 1984. Volcanic Hazards: A sourcebook on the effects of eruptions. Academic Press, Australia.

Bolin, R. C. (1998). *The Northridge earthquake: Vulnerability and disaster.* London: Routledge.

Bourque, L. B., Shoaf, K. I., & Nguyen, L. H. (1997). Survey research. *International Journal of Mass Emergencies and Disasters, 15,* 71–101.

Braswell, L., Kendall, P. C., Braith, J., Carey, M. P., & Vye, C. S. (1985). "Involvement" in cognitive-behavioral therapy with children: Process and its relationship to outcome. *Cognitive Therapy and Research, 9,* 611–630.

Britton, N. R. (1986). Developing an understanding of disasters. *Australian and New Zealand Journal of Sociology, 22,* 254–271.

Britton, N. R., & Lindsay, J. (1995). Integrating city planning and emergency preparedness: some of the reasons why. *International Journal of Mass Emergencies and Disasters 13,* 93–106.

Burby, R. J., & French, S. P. (1980). The U.S. Experience in Managing Flood Plain Land Use. *Disasters: The International Journal of Disaster Studies and Practice, 4,* 451–457.

Burby, R. J., Deyle, R. E., Godschalk, D. R., & Olshansky, R. B. (2000). Creating hazard resilient communities through land-use planning. *Natural Hazards Review, 1,* 99–106.

Burns, W. J., Slovic, P., Kasperson, R. E., Kasperson, J. X., Renn, O., & Emani, S. (1993). Incorporating structural models into research on social amplification of risk: implications for theory construction and decision making. *Risk Analysis, 13,* 611–623.

Burton, I., Kates, R. W., & White, G. F. (1978). *The Environment as hazard.* New York: Oxford University Press.

Bye, P., & Horner, M. (1998). *Easter 1998 floods: Report by the independent review team to the board of the Environment Agency.* Bristol: Environment Agency.

Cas, R.A.F., & Wright, J. V. (1987). *Volcanic successions: modern and ancient.* Chapman and Hall, London.

Chemtob, C. M, Nakashima, J., & Carlson, J. G. (2002). Brief treatment for elementary school children with disaster-related posttraumatic stress disorder: A field study. *Journal of Clinical Psychology, 58,* 99–112.

Chemtob, C. M., Nakashima, J. P., & Hamada, R. S. (2002). Psychosocial intervention for postdisaster trauma symptoms in elementary school children: A controlled community field study. *Archives of Pediatrics and Adolescent Medicine, 156*(3), 211–217.

Chu, B., & Kendall, P. C. (in press). Positive association of child involvement and treatment outcome within a manual-based cognitive-behavioral treatment for anxious youth. *Journal of Consulting and Clinical Psychology.*

Clarke, L. B. (1989). *Acceptable risk? Making decisions in a toxic environment.* Berkeley: University of California Press.

Clarke, L. B. (1999). *Mission improbable: Using fantasy documents to tame disaster.* Chicago: University of Chicago Press.

Clarkin, J. F. & Levy, K. N. (2004). The influence of client variables on psychotherapy. In M. J. Lambert (Ed.), *Bergin and Garfield's handbook of psychotherapy and behavior change* (5th ed). New York: Wiley.

Cobham, V. E., Dadds, M. R., & Spence, S. H., (1998). The role of parental anxiety in the treatment of childhood anxiety. *Journal of Consulting & Clinical Psychology, 66,* 893–905.

Cohen, J. A., Berliner, L., & Mannarino, A. P. (2000). Treating traumatized children: A research review and synthesis. *Trauma, Violence, and Abuse: A Review Journal, 1,* 29–46.

Cohen, J. A., Berliner, L., & Mannarino, A. P. (2003). Psychosocial and pharmacological interventions for child crime victims. *Journal of Traumatic Stress, 16,* 175–186.

Cohen, J. A., Berliner, L., & March, J. S. (2000). Treatment of children and adolescents. In E. B. Foa & T. M. Keane (Eds.), *Effective treatments for PTSD: Practice guidelines from the International Society for Traumatic Stress Studies.* New York: Guilford Press.

Cook, J. D., & Bickman, L. (1990). Social support and psychological symptomatology following a natural disaster. *Journal of Traumatic Stress, 3,* 541–556.

Cook, T. D., & Campbell, D. T. (1979). *Quasi-experimentation: Design & analysis issues for field settings.* Boston, MA: Houghton Mifflin Co.

Crandell, D. R., & Mullineaux, D. R. (1978). *Potential hazards from future eruptions of Mount St. Helens volcano, Washington.* U.S. Geological Survey Bulletin 1383-C.

Cuny, F. C. (1983). *Disasters and development.* Oxford: Oxford University Press.

Curtis, N. M., Ronan, K. R., & Borduin, C. (2004). Multisystemic Treatment: A meta-analysis of outcome studies. *Journal of Family Psychology, 18,* 411–419.

Cushing, E., & Kohl, E. (1997). *Allies for education - Community involvement in school change: A two year exploration.* San Francisco: San Francisco School Volunteers and the William and Flora Hewlett Foundation.

Cutter, S. L. (Ed.) (2001). *American hazardscapes: the regionalization of hazards and disasters.* Joseph Henry Press: Washington, DC.

Dadds, M. R. (2002). Learning and intimacy in the families of anxious children. In R. J. McMahon & R. DeV. Peters (Eds.), *Effects of parental dysfunction on children.* New York: Kluwer Academic/Plenum Publishers.

Dadds, M. R., Barrett, P. M., Rapee, R. M., & Ryan, S. (1996). Family process and child anxiety and aggression: An observational analysis. *Journal of Abnormal Child Psychology, 24,* 715–734.

Davis, M. S. (1989). Living along the fault line: An update on earthquake awareness and preparedness in Southern California. *Urban Resources, 5,* 8–14.

Davison, G. (2000). Stepped care: Doing more with less? *Journal of Consulting and Clinical Psychology, 68,* 580–585.

De Man, A., & Simpson-Housley, P. (1987). Factors in perception of earthquake hazard. *Perceptual and Motor Skills, 64*, 815–820.

Dooley, D., Catalano, R., Mishra, S., & Serxner, S. (1992). Earthquake preparedness: Predictors in a community survey. *Journal of Applied Social Psychology, 22*, 451–470.

Drabek, T. E. (1985). Managing the emergency response. *Public Administration Review, 45*, 85–92.

Drabek, T. E. (1986). Hazard perceptions. In *Human System Responses to Disaster: An Inventory of Sociological Findings*. New York: Springer-Verlag.

Drabek, T. E. (1986). *Human system responses to disasters: An inventory of sociological findings*. New York: Springer-Verlag.

Drabek, T. E., & Hoetmer, G. J. (Eds.) (1991). *Emergency Management: principles and practice for local government*. Municipal Management Series, International City Management Association, 368.

Drabek, T. E., & Key, W. H. (1984). *Conquering disaster: Family recovery and long-term consequences*. New York: Irvington Publishers.

Durand, M., Gordon, K., Johnston, D., Lorden, R., Poirot, T., & Scott, J., et al. (2001). *Impacts of, and responses to ashfall in Kagoshima from Sakurajima Volcano: Lessons for New Zealand*. Lower Hutt, N.Z.: Institute of Geological & Nuclear Sciences Limited (Science Report No. 2001/30).

Dynes, R. R. (1994). Community emergency planning: false assumptions and inappropriate analogies. *International Journal of Mass Emergencies and Disasters 12*, 141–158.

Endo, R., & Neilsen, J. (1979). Social responses to natural hazard predictions. *Western Sociological Review, 10*, 59–69.

Epstein, J. L., Coates, L., Salinas, K. C., Sanders, M. G., & Simon, B. (1997). *School, family, community partnerships: Your handbook for action*. Thousand Oaks, CA: Corwin.

Epstein, J. L., Sanders, M. G., Simon, B. S., Salinas, K. C., Jansorn, N. R., & Van Voorhis, F. L. (2002). *School, family, and community partnerships: Your handbook for action*. Thousand Oaks, CA: Corwin.

Erickson, N. J. (1975). *Scenario methodology in natural hazards research*. Program on Technology, Environment and Man Monograph 34. University of Colorado: Institute of Behavioral Science.

Everly, G. S., Boyle, S. H., & Lating, J. M. (1999). The effectiveness of psychological debriefing with vicarious trauma: A meta-analysis. *Stress Medicine, 15*, 229–233.

Everly, G. S., Flannery, R. B., & Eyler, V. A. (2002). Critical Incident Stress Management (CISM): A statistical review of the literature. *Psychiatric Quarterly, 73*, 171–182.

Farley, J. E. (1998). *Earthquake fears, predictions, and preparations in mid-America*. Carbondale (IL): Southern Illinois University.

Farley, J. E., Barlow, H. D., Finkelstein, M. S., & Riley, L. (1993). Earthquake hysteria, before and after: a survey and follow-up on public response to the Browning Forecast. *International Journal of Mass Emergencies and Disasters, 11*, 305–321.

Faupel, C. E., & Styles, S. P. (1993). Disaster education, household preparedness and stress responses following Hurricane Hugo. *Environment and Behavior, 25*, 228–249.

Feather, J., & Ronan, K. R. (2005). *Cognitive behavioral intervention for PTSD in youth: A series of multiple baseline evaluations*. Manuscript in preparation.

FEMA (Federal Emergency Management Agency) (2002, September). *Are you ready?: A guide to citizen preparedness*. Washington DC: FEMA (Publication H-34).

FEMA (1998). *Emergency preparedness USA*. Federal Emergency Management Agency and Emergency Management Institute IS-2, June 1998.

Finnis, K., Standring, S., Johnston, D., & Ronan, K. (2004). Children's understanding of natural hazards in Christchurch, New Zealand. *Australian Journal of Emergency Management, 19*, 11–20.

Fisher, R. V., & Schmincke, H.V. (1984). *Pyroclastic rocks*. Heidelberg: Springer-Verlag.

Flannery-Schroeder, E. C., & Kendall, P. C. (2000). Group and individual cognitive-behavioral treatments for youth with anxiety disorders: A randomized clinical trial. *Cognitive Therapy & Research, 24*, 251–278.

Flin, R. (1996). *Sitting in the hot seat: Leaders and teams for critical incident management.* Chichester: John Wiley and Sons.

Frederick, C., Pynoos, R., & Nader, K. (1992). *Childhood Post-Traumatic Stress Reaction Index.* Unpublished copyrighted instrument for measuring childhood trauma levels. Authors.

Gaddy, G. D., & Tanjong, E. (1987). Earthquake coverage by the Western press. *Journal of Communication, 36,* 105–112.

Galea, S., Boscarino, J., Resnick, H., & Vlahov, D. (2002). Mental health in New York City after the September 11 terrorist attacks: Results from two population surveys. In R. W. Manderscheid & M. J. Henderson (Eds.), *Mental Health, United States, 2002.* Washington, DC: U.S. Government Print Office.

Galley, I., Balm, R., Paton, D., & Johnston, D. (2004). The Ruapehu Lahar Emergency Development Plan process: an analysis. *Australasian Journal of Disaster and Trauma Studies.* Online Journal *(http://www.massey.ac.nz/~trauma/)*

Garcia, E. M. (1989). Earthquake preparedness in California: A survey of Irvine residents. *Urban Resources, 5,* 15–19.

Gilbert, D. T., & Silvera, D. H. (1996). Overhelping. *Journal of Personality and Social Psychology, 70,* 678–690.

Girling-Butcher, R., & Ronan, K. R. (2002). *The Coping Kiwi treatment manual.* Massey University: Authors.

Girling-Butcher, R., & Ronan, K. R. (2005). & Ronan, K. R. (2004). *Effectiveness of brief CBT intervention for youth and parents: A multiple baseline study.* Manuscript in preparation.

Gist, R. (2002). What have they done to my song? Social science, social movements, and the debriefing debates. *Cognitive & Behavioral Practice, 9,* 273–279.

Gist, R., & Devilly, G. J. (2002). Post-trauma debriefing: the road too frequently travelled. *Lancet, 360,* 741–742.

Goenjian, A. K., Karayan, I., Pynoos, R. S., Minassian, D., Najarian, L. M., & Steinberg, A. M., et al. (1997). Outcome of psychotherapy among early adolescents after trauma. *American Journal of Psychiatry, 154,* 536–542.

Goodwin, R. D., Fergusson, D. M., & Horwood, L. J. (2004). Panic attacks and the risk of depression among young adults in the community. *Psychotherapy & Psychosomatics, 73,* 158–165.

Gori, P. L. (1993). The social dynamics of a false earthquake prediction and the response by the public sector. *Bulletin of the Seismological Society of America, 83,* 963–980.

Green, C. H., Tunstall, S. M., & Fordham, M. H. (1992). The risk from flooding: which risks and whose perception? *Disasters, 15,* 227–236.

Gregg, C. E., Houghton, B. F., Johnston, D. M., Paton, D., & Swanson, D. A. (2004). The perception of volcanic risk in Kona Communities from Mauna Loa and Hualâlai volcanoes, Hawai'i. *Journal of Volcanology and Geothermal Research, 130,* 179–196.

Gregg, C. E., Houghton, B. F., Johnston, D. M., Paton, D., & Swanson, D. A. (2005). Community preparedness for lava flows from Mauna Loa and Hualâlai volcanoes, Kona, Hawai'i. *Bulletin of Volcanology, 66, 531–540.*

Griffin, M. G., Resick, P. A., Waldrop, A. E., & Mechanic, M. B. (2003). Participation in trauma research: Is there evidence of harm? *Journal of Traumatic Stress, 16,* 221–227.

Gurwitch, R. H., Sitterle, K. A., Young, B. H., & Pfefferbaum, B. (2002). The aftermath of terrorism. In A. M. LaGreca, W. K. Silverman, E. M. Vernberg, & M. C. Roberts (Eds.), *Helping children cope with disasters and terrorism.* Washington, DC: American Psychological Association.

Haaga, D. A. F. (2000). Introduction to the special section on stepped care models in psychotherapy. *Journal of Consulting and Clinical Psychology, 68,* 547–548.

Haddow, G. D., & Bullock, J. A. (2003). *Introduction to emergency management.* New York: Butterworth Heinemann (Elsevier).

Handmer, J. (2001). Improved flood warnings in Europe: a research and policy agendas. *Environmental Hazards, 3,* 19–28.

Handmer, J. (2002). Flood warning reviews in North America and Europe: statements and silence. *The Australian Journal of Emergency Management, 17(3)*, 17–24.

Hengeller, S. W., Schoenwald, S. K., Borduin, C. M., Rowland, M. D., & Cunningham, P. B. (1998). *Multisystemic treatment of antisocial behavior in children and adolescents*. New York: Guilford Press.

Hinshaw, S. P., March, J. S., & Abikoff, H. (1997). Comprehensive assessment of childhood attention-deficit hyperactivity disorder in the context of a multisite, multimodal clinical trial. *Journal of Attention Disorders, 1*, 217–234.

Hiroi, O., Mikami, S., & Miyata, K. (1985). A study of mass media reporting in emergencies. *International Journal of Mass Emergencies, 3*, 21–49.

Hoblitt, R. P., Walder, J. S., Driedger, C. L., Scott, K. M., Pringle, P. T., & Vallance, J. W. (1998). Volcano hazards from Mount Rainier, Washington, Revised 1998. *U.S. Geological Survey, Open-File Report* (98–428).

Hock, E., Hart, M., Kang, M. J., & Lutz, W.J. (2004). Predicting children's reactions to terrorist attacks: the importance of self-reports and preexisting characteristics. *American Journal of Orthopsychiatry, 74*, 253–262.

Huzziff, C. A., & Ronan, K. R. (1999). Prediction of children's coping following a natural disaster—the Mount Ruapehu eruptions: A prospective study. *Australasian Journal of Disaster & Trauma Studies, 3*(1) (http://www.massey.ac.nz/~trauma/).

Huzziff, C. A., & Ronan, K. R. (2005). *Meta-analysis of CBT intervention for childhood anxiety*. Massey University: Unpublished manuscript.

Huzziff, C. A., & Ronan, K. R. (2005). *Brief exposure based treatment of anxiety in youth: A series of single case studies*. Manuscript submitted for publication.

Jackson, E. L. (1977). Public response to earthquake hazard. *California Geology, 30*, 278–280.

Jackson, E. L. (1981). Response to earthquake hazard: The West Coast of North America. *Environment and Behavior, 13*, 387–416.

Jackson, E. L., & Mukerjee, T. (1974). Human adjustment to the earthquake hazard of San Francisco, CA. In G. F. White (Ed.), *Natural Hazards: Local, National, Global*. New York: Oxford University Press.

Johnson, H. R., Thompson, M. J. J., & Wilkinson, S. (2002). Vulnerability to bullying: Teacher-reported conduct and emotional problems, hyperactivity, peer relationship difficulties, and prosocial behaviour in primary school children. *Educational Psychology, 22*, 553–556.

Johnston, D., Driedger, C., Houghton, B., Ronan, K., & Paton, D. (2001). *Children's risk perceptions and preparedness: a hazard assessment in four communities around Mount Rainier, USA—preliminary results*. Lower Hutt, N.Z.: Institute of Geological and Nuclear Sciences. (Science Report No. 2001/02).

Johnston, D., Paton, D., Crawford, G., Ronan, K., Houghton, B., & Büergelt, P. (2005). Measuring tsunami preparedness in coastal Washington, United States. *Natural Hazards, 35*, 173–184.

Johnston, D., Paton, D., Driedger, C., Houghton, B., & Ronan, K., (2001). Student perceptions of hazards at four schools near Mount Rainier, Washington, USA. *Journal of the American Society of Professional Emergency Planners, 8*, 41–51.

Johnston, D., & Ronan, K. (2000). Risk education and intervention. In H. Sigurdsson, B. Houghton, S. R. McNutt, H. Rymer & J. Stix (Eds.), *Encyclopedia of volcanoes*. San Diego, CA: Academic Press.

Johnston, D. M. (1997). *The impact of recent falls of volcanic ash on public utilities in two communities in the United States of America*. Lower Hutt, N.Z.: Institute of Geological and Nuclear Sciences (Science Report, No. 1997/5).

Johnston, D. M., Houghton, B. F., Neall, V. E., Ronan, K. R., & Paton, D. (2000). Impacts of the 1945 and 1995-1996 Ruapehu eruptions, New Zealand: an example of increasing societal vulnerability. *Geological Society of America Bulletin, 112*, 720–726.

Johnston, D. M., Paton, D., & Houghton, B. (1999). Volcanic hazard management: Promoting integration and communication. In J. Ingleton, (Ed.), *Natural Disaster Management*. Leicester, England: Tudor Rose.

Kadet, A. (2002). Good grief! *Smart Money, 11*, 109–114.

Kartez, J. D., & Lindell, M. K. (1987). Planning for uncertainty: The case of local disaster planning. *American Planning Association Journal, 53*, 487–498.

Kartez, J. D., & Lindell, M. K. (1990). Adaptive planning for community disaster response. In R. T. Sylves, & W. L. Waugh, (Eds.) *Cities and Disaster: North American Studies in Emergancy Management.* Springfield, IL: Charles C Thomas.

Kasperson, R. E., Renn, O., Slovic, P., Brown, H. S., Emel, J., & Goble, R., et al. (1988). The social amplification of risk: A conceptual framework. *Risk Analysis, 8*, 177–187.

Kazantzis, N., Deane, F. P., & Ronan, K. R. (2000). Homework assignments in cognitive and behavioral therapy: A meta-analysis. *Clinical Psychology-Science and Practice, 7*, 189–202.

Kazantzis, N., Ronan, K. R., & Deane, F. P. (2001). Concluding causation from correlation: Comment on Burns and Spangler (2000). *Journal of Consulting and Clinical Psychology, 69*, 1079–1083.

Kazdin, A. E. (1998). *Research design in clinical psychology* (3rd edition). Boston: Allyn & Bacon.

Kazdin, A. E. (2004). Psychotherapy for children and adolescents. In M. J. Lambert (Ed.), *Bergin and Garfield's handbook of psychotherapy and behaviour change* (5th edition). New York: Wiley.

Kendall, P. C. (1994). Treating anxiety disorders in children - Results of a randomized clinical-trial. *Journal of Consulting and Clinical Psychology, 62*, 100–110.

Kendall, P. C., Chansky, T. E., Kane, M. T., Kim R., Korlander, E., & Ronan, K. R., et al. (1992). *Anxiety disorders in youth: Cognitive-behavioral interventions.* Needham Heights, MA: Allyn & Bacon.

Kendall, P. C., Flannery-Schroeder, E., Panichelli-Mindel, S. M., Southam-Gerow, M., Henin, A., & Warman, M. (1997). Therapy for youths with anxiety disorders: A second randomized clinical trial. *Journal of Consulting and Clinical Psychology, 65*, 366–380.

KPFF (2003). *Orting Bridge for Kids Executive Summary: To the type, size, and location feasibility study.* Report prepared for Pierce County Department of Public Works and Utilities and State of Washington, Military Department Emergency Management Division. KPFF Project No. 103273. 10, December 5.

Kreps, G. A. (1991). Organizing for emergency management. In T. E. Drabek, & G. J., Hoetmer, (Eds.) *Emergency management: Principles and practice for local government.* Washington, DC: International City Management Association.

Kumpfer, K. L. (1999). Factors and processes contributing to resilience: The resilience framework. In M. D. Glantz, & J. L. Johnson, (Eds.), *Resilience and development: Positive life adaptations longitudinal research in the social and behavioral sciences.* Dordfecht: Kluwer.

Kunreuther, H. (1993). Earthquake insurance as a hazard reduction strategy: The case of the homeowner. In Committee on Socioeconomic Impacts (Ed.), *1993 National earthquake conference: Socioeconomic impacts.* Memphis: Central United States Earthquake Consortium.

Kunreuther, H., Ginsburg, R., Miller, L., Sagi, P., Slovic, P., & Borkan, B., et al. (1978). *Disaster insurance protection: Public policy lessons.* New York: John Wiley and Sons.

Kunreuther, H., Novemsky, N., & Kahneman, D. (2001). Making low probabilities useful. *Journal of Risk and Uncertainty, 23*, 103–120.

La Greca, A. M., Silverman, W. K., Vernberg, E. M., & Prinstein, M. J. (1996). Symptoms of post-traumatic stress in children after Hurricane Andrew: A prospective study. *Journal of Consulting and Clinical Psychology, 64*, 712–723.

La Greca, A. M., Vernberg, E. M., Silverman, W. K., Vogel, A. L., & Prinstein, M. J. (1994). *Helping children prepare for and cope with natural disasters: A manual for professionals working with elementary school children.* Miami, FL: The BellSouth Foundation & The University of Miami.

Lambert, M. J. (2004). *Bergin and Garfield's handbook of psychotherapy and behaviour change* (5th edition). New York: Wiley.

Lazarus, R. S. (1999). *Stress and emotion: A new synthesis.* London: Free Association Books.

Lazarus, R. S., & Folkman, S. (1984). *Stress, appraisal, and coping.* New York: Springer Publishing.

Lindell, M. K. (1994). Perceived characteristics of environmental hazards. *International Journal of Mass Emergencies and Disasters, 12,* 303–326.

Lindell, M. K. (1995). Assessing emergency preparedness in support of hazardous facility risk analyses: An application at a U.S. hazardous waste incinerator. *Journal of Hazardous Materials, 40,* 297–193.

Lindell, M. K. (2000). An overview of protective action decision-making for a nuclear power plant emergency. *Journal of Hazardous Materials, 75,* 113–129.

Lindell, M. K., & Perry, R. W. (1992). *Behavioral foundations of community emergency planning.* Washington, DC: Hemisphere Publishing Company.

Lindell, M. K., & Perry, R. W. (2000). Household adjustment to earthquake hazard: A review of research. *Environment & Behavior, 32,* 461–501.

Lindell, M. K., & Prater, C. S. (2000). Household adoption of seismic hazard adjustments: A comparison in two states. *International Journal of Mass Emergencies and Disasters, 14,* 317–338.

Lindell, M. K., & Prater, C. S. (2003). Assessing community impacts of natural disasters. *Natural Hazards Review 4,* 176–185.

Lindell, M. K., & Whitney, D. J. (2000). Correlates of household seismic hazard adjustment adoption. *Risk Analysis, 20,* 13–25.

Lindy, J. D., & Wilson, J. P. (2001). Respecting the trauma membrane: Above all, do no harm. In J. P. Wilson, J. P. & M. J. Friedman (Eds.), *Treating psychological trauma and PTSD.* New York: Guilford Press.

Lipman, P. W., & Mullineaux, D. R. (Eds.) (1981). *The 1980 eruptions of Mount St. Helens, Washington.* U.S. Geological Survey Professional Paper 1250.

Long, N. R., Ronan, K. R., & Perreira-Laird, J. (1998). Victims of disaster. In N. N. Singh (Ed.), *Comprehensive clinical psychology: Applications in diverse populations.* New York: Pergamon Press.

Lopes, R. (1992). *Public perception of disaster preparedness presentations using disaster images.* Washington, DC.: The American National Red Cross.

Mader, G. G., Spangle, W. E., Blair, M. L., Meehan, R. L., Bilodeau, S. W., Degen Kolb, H. J., Duggar, G. S., & Williams, N., Jr. (1980). *Land use planning after earthquakes.* Portola Valley, CA: William Sprangle.

March, J. (1999). Assessment of pediatric posttraumatic stress disorder. In P. A. Saigh & J. D. Bremner (Eds.), *Posttraumatic stress disorder: A comprehensive text.* Needham Heights, MA: Allyn & Bacon.

March, J. S., Amaya-Jackson, L., & Murray, M. C. (1998). Cognitive-behavioral psychotherapy for children and adolescents with posttraumatic stress disorder after a single-incident stressor. *Journal of the American Academy of Child & Adolescent Psychiatry, 37,* 585–593.

Mawhinney, H. B. (1994). *The policy and practice of community enrichment of schools.* Paper presented at the Education and Community Conference, Department of Educational Administration, Toronto.

May, P. J. (1997). Addressing natural hazards: challenges and lessons for public policy. *The Australian Journal of Emergency Management, 11,* 30–37.

McChargue, D. E., Gulliver, S. B., & Hitsman, B. (2003). Applying a stepped-care reduction approach to smokers with schizophrenia. *Psychiatric Times, 20,* 78.

McClure, J., Allen, M., & Walkey, F. (2001). Countering fatalism: Causal information in news reports affects judgements about earthquake damage. *Basic and Applied Social Psychology, 23,* 109–121.

McMurray, K., & Ronan, K.R. (2004). *Childhood anxiety treatment: A power and meta-analysis.* Manuscript submitted for publication.

McCrae, R. R. (1984). Situational determinants of coping responses - loss, threat, and challenge. *Journal of Personality and Social Psychology, 46,* 919–928.

MCDEM (New Zealand Ministry of Civil Defence and Emergency Management) (2002). *Public education resource survey 2002.* Online at *http://www.civildefence.govt.nz/memwebsite.NSF/*

wpg_URL/The-Emergency-Sector-Public-Education-And-Information-Strategic-Plans?Open-Document: Ministry of Civil Defence and Emergency Management, New Zealand.

Meichenbaum, D. (1997). *Treating Post-traumatic Stress Disorder: A handbook and practice manual for therapy.* New York: Wiley.

Mileti, D. (1999). *Disasters by design: a reassessment of natural hazards in the United States.* Washington, D.C.: Joseph Henry Press.

Mileti, D. S., & Darlington, J. D. (1997). The role of searching in shaping reactions to earthquake risk information. *Social Problems, 44,* 89–103.

Mileti, D. S., & Darlington, J. D. (1995). Societal response to revised earthquake probabilities in the San Francisco Bay area. *International Journal of Mass Emergencies and Disasters, 13,* 119–145.

Mileti, D. S., Drabek, T. E., & Haas, J. E. (1975). *Human systems in extreme environments.* Boulder, CO: University of Colorado, Institute of Behavioral Science, Program on Environment and Behavior.

Mileti, D. D., Drabek, T. E., & Haas, J. E. (1975). The analytic use of case study materials. *Sociological Inquiry 45,* 70–75.

Mileti, D. S., & Fitzpatrick, C. (1992). The causal sequence of risk communication in the Parkfield earthquake prediction experiment. *Risk Analysis, 12,* 393–400.

Mileti, D. S., & Fitzpatrick, C. (1993). *The Great Earthquake Experiment: Risk communication and public action.* Westview Press, Boulder, Colorado.

Mileti, D. S., & O'Brien, P. (1992). Warnings during disaster: Normalizing communicated risk. *Social Problems, 39,* 40–57.

Mileti, D. S., O'Brien, P. W. (1993). *Public response to aftershock warnings.* U.S. Geological Survey Professional Paper 1553–B: B31–B42.

Mileti, D. S., & Peek, L. (2000). The social psychology of public response to warnings of a nuclear power plant accident. *Journal of Hazardous Materials, 75,* 181–194.

Mileti, D. S., & Sorensen, J. H. (1990). *Communication of emergency public warnings: a social science perspective and state-of-the-art assessment.* Oak Ridge Laboratory ORNL-6609.

Miller, M. W. (2003). Personality and the etiology and expression of PTSD: A three-factor model perspective. *Clinical Psychology: Science & Practice, 10,* 373–393.

Miller, W. R., & Rollnick, S. (2002). *Motivational interviewing: Preparing people for change.* New York: Guilford Press.

Mitchell, J. T. (1983). When disaster strikes: The critical incident stress debriefing process. *Journal of Emergency Medical Services, 8,* 36–39.

Mitchell, J. T. (2003). Major misconceptions in crisis intervention. *International Journal of Emergency Mental Health, 5,* 185–197.

Mitchell, J. T. (2004). A response to the Devilly and Cotton article, "psychological debriefing and the workplace . . . " *Australian Psychologist, 39,* 24–28.

Mitchell, J. T., & Everly, G.S. (1993). *Critical incident stress debriefing: An operations manual for the prevention of trauma among emergency service and disaster workers.* Baltimore, MD: Chevron Publishing.

Mitchell, J. T., & Thomas D. S. K. (2001). Trends in disaster losses. In S. L. Cutter (ed.) *American hazardscapes: the regionalization of hazards and disasters.* Washington D.C.: Joseph Henry Press.

Moore, H. E. (1964). *. . . And the winds blew.* Austin: University of Texas Press.

Mulilis, J. P., & Duval, T. S. (1995). Negative threat appeals and earthquake preparedness: A Person-relative-to-Event (PrE) model of coping with threat. *Journal of Applied Social Psychology, 25,* 1319–1339.

Mulilis, J. P., & Lippa, R. (1990). Behavioral-change in earthquake preparedness due to negative threat appeals - a test of protection motivation theory. *Journal of Applied Social Psychology, 20,* 619–638.

Myers, J. R., Henderson-King, D. H., & Henderson-King, E. I. (1997). Facing technological risks: The importance of individual differences. *Journal of Research in Personality, 31,* 1–20.

Nader, K. (1996). Assessing trauma in children. In J. Wilson & T. M. Keane (Eds.), *Assessing psychological trauma and PTSD*. New York: Guilford.

National Institute of Mental Health. (2002). *Mental health and mass Violence: Evidence-based early psychological intervention for victims/survivors of mass violence*. Washington, DC: Author.

National Research Council (1994). *Mount Rainier Active Cascade Volcano*. Washington, D.C.: National Academy Press.

Newhall, C. G., & Punongbayan, R. S. (1996). The narrow margin of successful volcanic-risk mitigation. In R. Scarpa & I. Tilling Robert (Eds.), *Monitoring and mitigation of volcano hazards*. Berlin, Federal Republic of Germany: Springer-Verlag.

Nigg, J. M. (1997). *Emergency response following the 1994 Northridge earthquake: Inter-governmental coordination issues*. Newark, DE: University of Delaware Disaster Research Center. Preliminary Paper No. 250.

Norris, F. H. (1992). Epidemiology of trauma: Frequency and impact of different potentially traumatic events on different demographic groups. *Journal of Consulting and Clinical Psychology, 60,* 409–418.

Norris, F. H., Friedman, M. J., & Watson, P. J. (2002). 60,000 disaster victims speak: Part II. Summary and implications of the disaster mental health research. *Psychiatry, 65,* 240–260.

Norris, F. H., Friedman, M. J., Watson, P. J., Byrne, C. M., Diaz, E., & Kaniasty, K. (2002). 60,000 Disaster victims speak: Part I. An empirical review of the empirical literature, 1981–2001. *Psychiatry, 65,* 207–260.

Norris, F. H., Friedman, M. J., Watson, P. J., Byrne, C. M., Diaz, E., North, C., & Spitznagel, E., & Smith, E. (2001). A prospective study of coping after exposure to a mass murder episode. *Annals of Clinical Psychiatry, 13,* 1696–1702.

North, C., Spitznagel, E., & Smith, E. (2001). A prospective study of coping after exposure to a mass murder episode. *Annals of Clinical Psychiatry, 13,* 1696–1702.

Ollendick, T. H. (1983). Reliability and validity of the revised fear survey schedule for children (Fssc-R). *Behaviour Research and Therapy, 21,* 685–692.

Palm, R., & Hodgson, M. E. (1992). *After a California earthquake: Attitude and behaviour change*. Chicago: University of Chicago Press.

Palm, R., Hodgson, M., Blanchard, R. D., & Lyons, D. (1990). *Earthquake insurance in California*. Boulder, CO: Westview.

Paton D. (1996). Disaster relief work: an assessment of effectiveness. *Journal of Traumatic Stress, 7,* 275–288.

Paton, D. (2000). Emergency planning: Integrating community development, community resilience and hazard mitigation. *Journal of the American Society of Professional Emergency Managers, 7,* 109–118.

Paton, D. (2003). Disaster preparedness: A social-cognitive perspective. *Disaster Prevention and Management, 12,* 210–216.

Paton, D., & Johnston, D. (2001). Disasters and communities: vulnerability, resilience and preparedness. *Disaster Prevention and Management, 10,* 270–277.

Paton, D., Johnston, D., Houghton, Flin, R., Ronan, K., & Scott, B. (1999). Managing natural hazard consequences: planning for information management and decision making. *Journal of the American Society of Professional Emergency Planners, 6,* 37–48.

Paton, D., Johnston, D., Houghton, B., & Smith, L. (1998). Managing the effects of a volcanic eruption: Psychological perspectives on integrated emergency management. *Journal of the American Society of Professional Emergency Planners, 5,* 59–69.

Paton, D., Smith, L., Johnston, D. M., Johnson, M., & Ronan, K. R. (2003). *Developing a model to predict the adoption of natural hazard risk reduction and preparatory adjustments*. Wellington (NZ): Earthquake Commission Research Project Number 01–479.

Paton, D., Smith, L. M., & Johnston, D. (2000). Volcanic hazards: Risk perception and preparedness. *New Zealand Journal of Psychology, 29,* 84–88.

Paton, D., Violanti, J. M., & Smith, L. M. (Eds.) (2003). *Promoting capabilities to manage posttraumatic stress: Perspectives on resilience.* Springfield, IL: Charles C. Thomas Publisher, Ltd.

Peek, L. A., & Mileti, D. S. (2002). The history and future of disaster research. In R. B. Bechtel & A. Churchman (Eds.), *Handbook of environmental psychology.* New York, NY: John Wiley & Sons, Inc.

Perry, R. W. (1985). *Comprehensive emergency management: Evacuating threatened populations.* Greenwich, CT: JAI Press.

Perry, R. W., & Greene, M. R. (1983). *Citizen response to volcanic eruptions: The case of Mt. St. Helens.* New York: Irvington Publishers.

Perry, R. W., & Lindell, M. K. (1990). *Living with Mount St. Helens: human adjustment to volcano hazards.* Pullman, Washington: Washington University Press.

Perry, R. W., & Lindell, M. K. (2003). Understanding citizen response to disasters with implications for terrorism. *Journal of Contingencies and Crisis Management, 11,* 49–60.

Petak, W. J., & Atkisson, A. A. (1982). *Natural hazard risk assessment and public policy: anticipating the unexpected.* New York: Springer-Verlag.

Peterson, C., Maier, S. F., & Seligman, M. E. P. (1993). *Learned helplessness: A theory for the age of personal control.* New York: Oxford University Press.

Pinsker, L. M. (2004). Paths of destruction: the hidden threat at Mount Rainier. *Geotimes (April),* 18–23.

Prince, S. H. (1920). *Catastrophe and social change; based upon a sociological study of the halifax disaster.* Unpublished Doctoral Thesis, Columbia University, New York.

Prochaska, J. O., DiClemente, C. C., Norcross, J. C. (1992). In search of how people change: Applications to addictive behaviours. *American Psychologist, 47,* 1102–1114.

Quarantelli, E. L. (1982). General and particular observations on sheltering and housing in American disasters. *Disasters, 6,* 227–281.

Quarantelli, E. L. (1983). *Delivery of emergency medical services in disasters.* New York: Irvington.

Quarantelli, E. L. (1985). What is disaster? The need for clarification in definitiaon and conceptualization in research. In B. J. Sowder (Ed.) *Disasters and mental health: Selected contemporary perspectives.* Rockville MD: National Institute of Mental Health.

Quarantelli, E. L. (1988). Assessing disaster preparedness planning. *Regional Development Dialogue, 9,* 48–69.

Quarantelli, E. L. (1993). Converting disaster scholarship into effective disaster planning and managing: Possibilities and limitations. *International Journal of Mass Emergencies and Disasters, 11,* 15–39.

Quarantelli, E. L. (1995). What is a disaster? *International Journal of Mass Emergencies and Disasters, 13*(3), 221–229.

Quarantelli, E. L. (1998). *What is a disaster?* New York: Routledge.

Raphael, B., & Wilson, J. P. (2000). *Psychological debriefing: Theory, practice and evidence.* Cambridge, England: Cambridge University Press.

Rip, A. (1988). Should social amplification of risk be counteracted? *Risk Analysis, 8,* 193–197.

Ronan, K. R. (1997a). The effects of a series of volcanic eruptions on children with asthma. *New Zealand Medical Journal, 110,* 11–13.

Ronan, K. R. (1997b). The effects of a "benign" disaster: Symptoms of post-traumatic stress in children following a series of volcanic eruptions. *Australasian Journal of Disaster and Trauma Studies* (1) (http://www.massey.ac.nz/~trauma/).

Ronan, K. R., & Deane, F. P. (1998). Anxiety disorders. In P. Graham (Ed.), *Cognitive behaviour therapy for children and families.* Cambridge, UK: Cambridge University Press.

Ronan, K. R., Finnis, K., & Johnston, D. (2005). Interventions with youth and families: A prevention model. In G. Reyes & G. Jacobs (Eds.), *International handbook of disaster psychology.* In press.

Ronan, K. R., & Johnston, D. (1999). Behaviourally-based interventions for children following volcanic eruptions: an evaluation of effectiveness. *Disaster Prevention and Management, 8,* 169–176.

Ronan, K. R., & Johnston, D. (2001). School children's risk perceptions and preparedness: A hazards education survey. *Australasian Journal of Disaster and Trauma Studies*, 4 (http://www.massey.ac.nz/~trauma/).

Ronan, K. R., & Johnston, D. M. (1997). *Auckland school children's risk perceptions and preparedness: Hazards education survey*. Technical report prepared for Auckland Regional Council/Auckland City Council: Authors.

Ronan, K. R., & Johnston, D. M. (2001). Correlates of hazard education programs for youth. *Risk Analysis, 21*, 1055–1063.

Ronan, K. R., & Johnston, D. M. (2003). Hazards education for youth: A quasi-experimental investigation. *Risk Analysis, 23*, 1009–1020.

Ronan, K. R., Johnston, D. M., Daly, M., & Fairley, R. (2001). School children's risk perceptions and preparedness: A hazards education survey. *Australasian Journal of Disaster and Trauma Studies, 1 (on-line journal URL http://massey.ac.nz/~trauma/)*.

Ronan, K. R., Johnston, D. M., & Hull, A. (1998). *A community's understanding of earthquake risk in the Manawatu*. Technical report prepared for the New Zealand Earthquake Commission: Authors.

Ronan, K. R., Johnston, D. M., & Paton, D. (2001). Communities' understanding of earthquake risk in the Hawkes Bay and Manawatu-Wanganui Regions, New Zealand. In *Proceedings of NZ Society for Earthquake Engineering 2001 Conference, New Zealand, 1.03.01*, 1–9.

Ronan, K. R., Paton, D., Johnston, D. M., & Houghton, B. F. (2000). Managing societal uncertainty in volcanic hazards: A multidisciplinary approach. *Disaster Prevention and Research, 9*, 339–348.

Rose, S., Bisson, J., & Wessely, S. (2001). Psychological debriefing for preventing post traumatic stress disorder (PTSD) (Cochrane Review). In *The Cochrane Library*, Issue 3. Chichester, UK: John Wiley & Sons, Ltd.

Rubonis, A. V., & Bickman, L. (1991). Psychological impairment in the wake of disaster - the disaster psychopathology relationship. *Psychological Bulletin, 109*, 384–399.

Russell, L. A., Goltz, J. D., & Bourque, L. B. (1995). Preparedness and hazard mitigation actions before and after two earthquakes. *Environment and Behavior, 27*, 744–770.

Rüstelmi, A., & Karanci, A. N. (1999). Correlates of earthquake cognitions and preparedness behaviour in a victimized population. *The Journal of Social Psychology, 139*, 91–101.

Saarinen, T. F., & Sell, J. L. (1985). *Warnings and response to the Mount St helens eruption*. Albany: State University of New York Press.

Salmon, T. S. (1919). War neuroses and their lesson. *New York Medical Journal, 108*, 993–994.

Saltzman, W., Pynoos, R. S., Layne, C., Steinberg, A., & Steinberg, E. (1999). *School-based trauma-grief focused psychotherapy program for youth exposed to community violence*. Unpublished manuscript.

Salzer, M. S., Bickman, L., & Lambert, W. (1999). Dose-effect relationship in children's psychotherapy services. *Journal of Consulting and Clinical Psychology, 67*, 228–238.

Sanders, M. G. (2001). The role of "community" in comprehensive school, family, and community partnership programs. *The Elementary School Journal, 102*, 19–34.

Saylor, C. F. (1993). *Children and disasters*. New York: Plenum Press.

Saylor, C., & DeRoma, V. (2002). Assessment of children and adolescents exposed to disasters. In A. LaGreca, W. Silverman, E. Vernberg, & M. Roberts (Eds), *Helping children cope with disasters and terrorism*. Washington DC: American Psychological Association.

Scott, W., & Vallance, J. (1995). *Debris flow, debris avalanche, and flood hazards at and downstream from Mount Rainier, Washington*. US Geological Survey Atlas HA–729.

Seligman, M. E. P., & Pawelski, J. O. (2003). Positive psychology: FAQs. *Psychological Inquiry, 14*, 159–163.

Shaw, R., Shiwaku, K., Kobayashi, H., & Kobayashi, M. (2003). Linking experience, education, perception, and earthquake preparedness. *Disaster Prevention and Management, 13*, 39–49.

Showalter, P. S. (1993). Prognostication of doom: an earthquake prediction's effect on four small communities. *International Journal of Mass Emergencies and Disasters, 11*, 279–292.

Siqueland, L., Kendall, P. C., & Steinberg, L. (1996). Anxiety in children: Perceived family environments and observed family interaction. *Journal of Clinical Child Psychology, 25,* 225–237.

Sjoberg, L. (2000). Factors in risk perception. *Risk Analysis, 20,* 1–11.

Slovic, P. (1993). Perceived risk, trust and democracty. *Risk Analysis, 13,* 675–682.

Slovic, P. Fischhoff, B., & Lichtenstein, S. (1981). Perceived risk: psychological factors and social implications. In *Proceedings of the Royal Society of London, A376,* 17–34.

Smith, R. C., Lein, C., Collins, C., Lyles, J. S., Given, B., Dwamena, F. C., Coffey, J., Hodges, A. M., Gardiner, J. C., Goddeeris, J., & Given, C. W. (2003). Treating patients with medically unexplained symptoms in primary care. *JGIM: Journal of General Internal Medicine, 18,* 478–489.

Smith, M., & Smith, R. L. (2003). *Citizens of vulnerable community respond to Mt. Rainier lahar threat.* Paper presented at the Cities on Volcanoes 3, Hilo, Hawaii, July.

Sorensen, J. (2000). Hazard warning systems: review of 20 years of progress. *Natural Hazards Review, May,* 119–125.

Sorensen, J. H., Mileti D., & Copenhaver, E. (1985). *Evacuation: An assessment of planning research.* Washington, DC: Federal Emergency Management Agency.

Sprang, G. (2000). Coping strategies and traumatic stress symptomotology following the Oklahoma City bombing. *Social Work and Social Sciences Review, 8,* 207–218.

Stuart, N., & Ronan, K. R. (2005). *Biopsychosocial risk and protection for distress in youth: Test of a structural model.* Manuscript in preparation.

Sullivan, R., Mustart, D. A., & Galehouse, J. S. (1977). Living in earthquake country. *California Geology, 30,* 3–8.

Tedeschi, R. G., & Calhoun, L. G. (2003). Posttraumatic growth: Conceptual foundations and empirical evidence. *Psychological Inquiry, 15,* 1–18.

Tierney, K. (2004). Deciding what's safe: making choices about earthquake safety. *Natural Hazards Review, 5,* 61–63.

Tierney, K. J., Lindell, M. K., & Perry, R. W. (2001). *Facing the unexpected: Disaster response in the United States.* Washington, D.C.: Joseph Henry Press.

Turner, R. H., Nigg, J. M., & Heller-Paz. (1986). *Waiting for disaster: Earthquake watch in California.* Berkeley: University of California Press.

U.S. Geodynamics Committee, & National Research Council. (1994). *Mount Rainier: Active Cascade Volcano: Research strategies for mitigating risk from a high, snow-clad volcano in a populous region.* Washington, D.C.: National Academy Press.

United Nations News (2004). *UN: Population to double in flood prone areas.* (*http:// www.unmideast .com/*), June 15.

van Emmerik, A. A. P., Kamphuis, J. H., Hulsbosch, A. M., & Emmelkamp, P. M. G. (2002). Single session debriefing after psychological trauma: a meta-analysis. *Lancet, 360,* 766–771.

Vernberg, E. M., La Greca, A. M., Silverman, W. K., & Prinstein, M. J. (1996). Prediction of posttraumatic stress symptoms in children after Hurricane Andrew. *Journal of Abnormal Psychology, 105,* 237–248.

Vernberg, E. M., & Vogel, J. M. (1993). Interventions with children after disasters. *Journal of Clinical Child Psychology, 22,* 485–498.

Vogt, B. M., & Sorensen, J. H. (1994). *Risk communications and the chemical stockpile emergency-planning program.* Oak Ridge National Laboratory ORNL-6824.

Voight, B. (1990). The 1985 Nevado del Ruiz volcano catastrophe: anatomy and retrospection. *Journal of Volcanology and Geothermal Research, 42,* 151–188.

Voight, B. (1996). The management of volcano emergencies: Nevado del Ruiz. In R. Scarpa & Tilling R. I. (Eds.), *Monitoring and Mitigation of Volcanic Hazards* (pp. 719–769). New York: Springer-Verlag.

Walsh, J., Caruthers, C. G., Heinitz, A. C., Myers, E. P., Bapista, A. C., Erdakos, G. B., & Kamphaus, R. A. (2000). *Tsunami hazard Map of the Southern Washington coast: Modeled tsunami inunda-*

tion from a Cascadia Subduction Zone earthquake. Washington Division of Geology and Earth Resources Geological Map GM-9.

Ward, P. L., & Mileti, D. S. (1993). Public education and communication for disaster mitigation. In *Proceedings of the Workshop on Volcanic Disaster Prevention: the first meeting of the Panel on Volcanic Disaster Prevention under Japan-US Science and Technology Agreement*, 226–227.

Warrick, R. A., Anderson, J., Downing, T., Lyons, J., Ressler, J., Warrick, M., & Warrick, T. (1981). *Four communities under ash - after Mt St Helens.* Program on Technology, Environment and Man, Monograph 34, Institute of Behavioral Science, University of Colorado.

Watson, P. J., Friedman, M. J., Gibson, L. E., Ruzek, J. I., Norris, F. H., & Ritchie, E. C. (2003). Early intervention for trauma-related problems. In R.J. Ursano & A. E. Norwood, (Eds), *Trauma and disaster: responses and management.* Washington, DC: American Psychiatric Publishing.

Weinstein, N. D. (1989). Effects of personal experience on self-protective behaviour. *Psychology Bulletin, 105,* 31–50.

Weinstein, N. D., Lyon, J. E., Rothman, A. J., & Cuite, C. L. (2000). Preoccupation and affect as predictors of protective action following natural disaster. *British Journal of Health Psychology, 5,* 351–363.

Weisz, J. R., & Weiss, B. (1989). Assessing the effects of clinic based psychotherapy with children and adolescents. *Journal of Consulting and Clinical Psychology, 57,* 741–746.

Wenger, D. (1988). *Volcanic disaster prevention, warning, evacuation, and rescue.* Texas A&M: Hazard Reduction and Recovery Center.

White, G. F., & Haas, J. E. (1975). *Assessment of research on natural hazards.* Cambridge, MA: MIT Press.

Whitney, D. J., & Lindell, M. K. (2000). Member commitment and participation in local emergency planning committees. *Policy Studies Journal, 28,* 467–484.

Wilson, G. T., Vitousek, K. M., & Loeb, K. L. (2000). Stepped care treatment for eating disorders. *Journal of Consulting and Clinical Psychology, 68,* 564–572.

Wilson, J. P., Friedman, M. J., & Lindy, J. D. (2001). *Treating psychological trauma and PTSD.* New York: Guilford Press.

Wortmann, C. B., Loftus, E. B., & Weaver, C. A. (1999). *Psychology* (5th edition). New York: McGraw Hill.

Wrathall, J. E. (1992). Natural hazard reporting in the UK press. *Disaster, 12,* 177–182.

Yerkes, R. M., & Dodson, J. B. (1908). The relation of strength of stimulus to rapidity of habit formation. *Journal of Comparative Neurology and Psychology, 18,* 459–482.

Yule, W. (2001). Post-traumatic stress disorder in children and adolescents. *International Review of Psychiatry, 13,* 194–200.

Index

Lightning Source UK Ltd.
Milton Keynes UK
UKOW01f0054190117

292375UK00001B/141/P